A People's History of Modern Europe

A People's History of Modern Europe

William A. Pelz

PlutoPress
www.plutobooks.com

First published 2016 by Pluto Press
345 Archway Road, London N6 5AA

www.plutobooks.com

British Library Cataloguing in Publication Data
A catalogue record for this book is available from the British Library

ISBN   978 0 7453 3246 8   Hardback
ISBN   978 0 7453 3245 1   Paperback
ISBN   978 1 7837 1767 5   PDF eBook
ISBN   978 1 7837 1769 9   Kindle eBook
ISBN   978 1 7837 1768 2   EPUB eBook

This book is printed on paper suitable for recycling and made from fully managed
and sustained forest sources. Logging, pulping and manufacturing processes are
expected to conform to the environmental standards of the country of origin.

Typeset by Stanford DTP Services, Northampton, England

Simultaneously printed in the European Union and United States of America

Contents

Acknowledgements

First, I must praise David Castle, my editor at Pluto Press, who treated my manuscript with a level of skill, care, understanding and sophistication so sadly lacking in most modern editors. The book is only as good as it is because of David's expertise and dedication. As authors often note, there are countless people who contribute to any book whether directly or indirectly. As is so often the case there are more than can be credited. *So, I'd like to thank everyone whom I don't name for their contribution to the writing of this book.* Katie Stollenwerk, Secretary of the Institute of Working Class History (Chicago), was invaluable in correcting my often odd English (the author grew up in the working-class Englewood district of Chicago). If this book has sentences that contain verbs, much of the credit goes to Katie.

Embarrassing factual mistakes were discovered by Ian Birchall (London) and Boris Kagarlitsky (Moscow) when reviewing a draft of the book. These have been corrected but as they say "to err is human, to forgive divine." I have gained information, have had insights sharpened, and new approaches suggested by countless talks with generous and committed colleagues. Among these are Ottokar Luban (Berlin), Francis King (East Anglia), Eric Schuster (Chicago), Ralf Hoffrogge (Berlin), Raquel Varela (Lisbon), Marcel van der Linden (Amsterdam), Sobhanlal Datta Gupta (India), Sjaak van der Velden (Amsterdam), Mark Lause (Cincinnati), Bruno Drweski (Paris), Axel Fair-Schulz (Potsdam), Steven McGiffen (Paris), Roger Johansson (Malmo), Kasper Braskén (Finland), Norman LaPorte (Wales), John Barzman (LeHavre) and Mario Kessler (New York/Berlin).

I owe the greatest debt to Adrienne L. Butler, my wife, who endured seemingly endless months of piles of papers piled upon stacks of books. There was a mess everywhere in the house. Yet, never once did she resort to physical violence against her obsessed husband. Last, and never least, is the cat, Sputnik, who took time out of his busy schedule of naps to hop onto my papers and rearrange them in a manner more to his liking. Sometimes, he was right. Needless to say, any mistakes of fact, interpretation or imagination are solely Sputnik's fault, not mine.

William A. Pelz

Introduction

Imagine kings ruling without subjects, generals waging war without soldiers, or businesspeople making profits without workers. It's hard to take seriously any such silly situations, right? Yet, history is often written as if rulers, war leaders and moneymakers are the only people in society or, at least, the only people who matter. The current author dissents from this idea. It will be argued in this book that the common people matter and that their history matters. That is to say, the commoners' role in history is an integral, yet lacking, part of the story of modern Europe, that has too often been passed over. History allows us to see how societies develop and change while it points to various possible futures. It is the story of people struggling, often in dark times.

This book provides an alternative reading of European history starting with the Middle Ages. Instead of focusing on only the traditional themes and concerns that emphasize the rulers, this title highlights the dissidents, rebels and radicals who helped make Europe what it is. Most books focus on a rather conventional narrative with, more recently, a section on women or peasants included to add diversity. The average reader is in no doubt however as to who and what is important. That is, the rich and powerful are not only the most important subjects of serious study—they are typically the *only* worthwhile subjects of study.

A People's History of Modern Europe offers a concise, readable alternative to mainstream textbooks and surveys while suggesting a different understanding of the development and trajectory of European history. That is, history is presented as moving through conflicts between contending groups rather than as the result of brilliant insights by upper-class rulers and thinkers. To be sure, there are a number of specialized volumes that attempt this but typically they have a rather limited focus. The main problem is that these books often remain accessible solely to the scholar or the academic, as opposed to the general reader or student.

Starting with the decay and collapse of West European feudalism, this book traces in broad outline the contributions made by common people, rebels, dissenters and non-conformists. This book will give greater prominence to those individuals and events that are glossed over or ignored by other texts. For example, the reader here will have a more in-depth look at the role of John Hus during the Reformation and the Paris Commune in the nineteenth century. In addition to highlighting those lesser known individuals and events, this text will highlight alternative viewpoints to commonly understood events. World War I soldiers are shown rejecting the patriotism spread by their governments and at times even killing their own "superiors" if they thought them cruel. After the war, revolutions break out and reaction strives to crush them.

At the end of the 1920s, the winds of economic crisis hit the common people. Fascism develops, murders and tortures millions, but is fiercely resisted by countless average Europeans. Later, we see social movements crushed, distorted and subverted. Spies, clandestine operations, massive bribery and brutal military dictatorships are among only a few of the tactics employed to preserve the status quo and leave the ruling classes' power unchanged. Yet, the common people return to movement, protest and resistance, again and yet again ... and despite overwhelming odds, they often win ... at least partial victories. It is these victories that allow us to live in a world with more rights and autonomy than our medieval precursors could dream of.

The guiding spirit of the book is informed by the view expressed in Brecht's famous "A worker reads history" quoted below. In other words, this text will continually encourage the reader to ask "and what about the common people?" How did they regard this development? What were their thoughts? How did they feel? Above all, the reader will be prodded to question the mainstream narratives that they have been taught. One must understand history or we will never be mentioned in it, let alone make it. Unless you are the direct descendent of blood-thirsty feudal lords or a member of the top .01 percent, this book is about your people. After all, most humans are neither rich nor famous, but working people. Their story needs to be told.

The first step is to supply students and readers with some tools so that this history can be fairly examined. Regardless of intellectual influences or political viewpoints, there remain a number of methodological problems that need be discussed in regards to the study of history. What follows is far from a complete list, but will give some idea of the pitfalls the historian must avoid if they are to arrive at conclusions that may be deemed fair, if not completely scientific. After all, history, it can be argued, may be a science but it is not an exact science in the same way as physics or chemistry.

When exploring problems of history, we are not so concerned with the most obvious bias discussed in the media. That is, history being consciously abused to serve a contemporary personal or political end.[1] Nonetheless, there are real problems that plague all those who venture into a study of the past with any degree of honesty, such as the problem of *survival*. Simply put, not all historical evidence makes it into the present (no matter when the present is). Often, documents or other facts are destroyed so as to hide crimes, eliminate alternative opinions or simply to make a group or personage look better to society. One famous example is the riots by fanatical Christians in AD 391 that destroyed countless irreplaceable books in Alexandria's fabled library. The works that survived were largely destroyed in AD 641 by an equally fanatical Islamic ruler. The modern-day shredder may protect privacy but also complicates the historian's task. In other cases, fire, war, or the ravages of time cause evidence to disappear.

An apparently contradictory problem concerns the bias of *selection*. The book you are holding is an example of this in as much as any history of modern Europe could easily run into dozens of volumes and tens of thousands of pages without exhausting the subject. So, the historian must pick and choose which topics to investigate and which to ignore, which facts are relevant and which are not. Further, the inherent human limitation of any historian adds to this problem. The current author knows not a word of Finnish, Portuguese, Icelandic, medieval Latin, or Greek among others and only a tiny number of words in, for example, Dutch, Italian, or Polish. This book depends too heavily on English, German and French sources—most obviously the former. Also, scholars tend to be drawn towards accounts and evidence that fit with their pre-existing thoughts on a subject.[2] Of course, sometimes the selection bias may be motivated by not wanting to deal with the potentially controversial, leaving the historian to opt for the vacuous instead. As Tristram Hunt comments, "How much information about Anne Boleyn can modern Britain really cope with?"[3]

That this is a widespread problem is confirmed by a famous experiment conducted in 1999. Participants were shown a video presenting two teams of three persons each, one team in black and the other in white, as they moved around and passed basketballs to each other. The viewers were asked to count the number of passes made by the team dressed in white. During the video, a person in a gorilla suit walked across the screen pounding her chest for 5 seconds. In test after test, around 50 percent did not notice the gorilla. In fact, many participants insisted that there had been no gorilla even when told and shown the video a second time.[4] For our purposes in this historical investigation, the common people are the "gorilla" that scholars and students often fail to see. After all, in any society at any given time, there is a generally dominant narrative that marginalizes all other views, relegating them to at best wrong and at worst, heresy. As Napoleon rather cynically commented, "What is the truth of history? A fable agreed upon."[5]

Another problem, that this book hopes to address, is *class* bias. As noted before, most history has been written as if only kings, queens, generals and later big businessmen—in brief, the rich and powerful—are the only fit subjects for history. This book sides with Bertolt Brecht who wryly noted in his poem, "A Worker Reads History,"[6]

Who built the seven gates of Thebes?
The books are filled with names of kings.
Was it the kings who hauled the craggy blocks of stone?

The point isn't that rulers aren't important but rather that so are the common people ... and it is the average woman and man who are so often forgotten or ignored when history is written—forgotten because there are more written sources on the upper class, ignored because historians often did not consider them very important, unimportant or often even dangerous, as when the American Alexander Hamilton referred to the people as a "great beast"[7] ... and he did not mean it in a favorable way.

If the common people are ignored in general, it is fair to say that *sexist* bias causes women to be dismissed or trivialized in particular. This is not because there is any body of evidence to support the thesis that women are unimportant,[8] but rather because it suits the ruling-class males who dominate the status quo. Sure, there have been discussions of Queen Elizabeth I or Margaret Thatcher, but these exceptions merely serve to prove the rule. If one looks at it dispassionately, it seems rather silly to think that half of the world's population is not a worthy subject for the historian. In common with the class bias, this anti-woman prejudice has a long, and not very honorable, history. As Sheila Rowbotham demonstrated almost half a century ago, women's oppression, and thus their exclusion from history, is part of the same ideology that holds that only the ruling class of any time or territory is important.[9] It might be argued that this is no longer true and that feminism is now part of the mainstream in our best of all possible worlds in the West.[10] The reality remains that, for all the growth of women's studies programs and the like, "even within the field of woman's history, feminism has an insecure and eroding foothold."[11]

The unholy trinity[12] of class and sexist prejudice is completed with *racism* or ethnic prejudice. Historians will talk about the conquest of the Western Hemisphere with only passing mention of the humans who lived there before conquest, while African slavery, when discussed in any detail, becomes merely a tragedy ... not part of a larger problem that, for example, saw John Locke, often praised as an Anglo-Saxon philosopher of liberty, investing heavily as a charter member of a British slave trading company.[13] In his novel, *The Great Gatsby*, F. Scott Fitzgerald gives a fictional example of this racial view of history. He has a rich male argue, "It's up to us, who are the dominant race, to watch out or these other races will control things … [as Nordics] we've produced all the things that go to make civilisation— oh, science and art, and all that."[14] Few would publicly be quite so crude about it these days but the attitude continues. Take, for example, Niall Ferguson's *Civilization: The West and Rest*[15] that argues it is no accident that the Westerners are ahead of the "Resterners," but warns this may not last. In a glowing review, one US newspaper summed up the message of Ferguson's book as "they're gaining on us."[16] So, instead of world history being moved by class struggle[17] or gender conflict,[18] we are told that humans are divided into distinct and warring subgroups based on the arbitrary and artificial category of race. We do well to remember race is a social concept, not a scientific one.[19]

There is an even trickier problem living historians must avoid since they, by definition, live in the present. Even with the best will in the world, as if such a thing could be, historians often think of the past in terms of the present. This bias of *present-mindedness* means at worst we see people who lived before us as exactly like us albeit having the habit of wearing funny clothes. At best, it subtlety warps the way we look at the past. An extreme, if rather obvious, example is the cartoon series/films "The Flintstones." In this great creation of US culture in the late twentieth century, people from the Stone Age live like we do: they drive cars, have music systems, telephones and so on. If this was an isolated example, it would not matter but the media and Hollywood are infamous for this, and even respected historians often fail to place things in an accurate historical context.[20]

This brings to mind the obvious but often forgotten fact that historians are people who study people and there is a *problem with people*. Geologists are also people but they examine rocks. The convenient thing about rocks is that they are rather predictable. Diamonds always cut glass, regardless of whether the geologist had a rough night or is in a bad mood. The point is that people are very much unlike rocks. They are unpredictable, contradictory and quite capable not only of lying to others but also to themselves. It is common for people, even historians, to confuse their own petty personal situations with the flow of history. As the British scholar A.J.P. Taylor once noted, all sorts of talk about the decline of civilization really "means that university professors used to have domestic servants and now do their own washing-up."[21] One wonders what similar trauma has led to Professor

Ferguson's doom and gloom. It would be fair to note that it is not just university professors who have such tendencies.

People also have belief systems, that is, *religions* and *ideologies*. Even those who think they have neither religious nor ideological convictions continue to organize their life around some set of guiding ideas. None of this is wrong, particularly since some ideas *are* more valid than others.[22] Still, what beliefs one holds will tend to influence one's view of the historical past. Whereas a Marxist like George Rudé[23] would find evidence of reason in the behavior of crowds, a reactionary Catholic like Roland Mousnier[24] would suspect the influence of original sin within peasant revolts.[25] Harvard historian Niall Ferguson apparently thinks belated protests notwithstanding, gays and people who are childless don't care about the future and somehow contribute to the decline of civilization.[26] Since it is impossible to completely escape having ideas, it may well be best to acknowledge them so what impact they may have is more transparent.[27]

One area where the reader often fails to realize the need for a skeptical rationalism is the problem of *translation*. Most of the evidence for history, outside your own nation-state, may well be in a language you do not understand. Whether reading the Bible or the latest European Union directives, one often finds oneself at the mercy of translators. Being human, translators sometimes make mistakes. Or they may tend to read their own views into what they are rendering from one language to another. More than we imagine, they may be under pressure to come up with a certain spin or tone. So, it was with the King James Bible, a political project unleashed in 1611 by James Stuart, who was motivated by the increasing circulation of unauthorized English translations from Calvin or Luther's versions.[28] It was a project that it would be fair to say was not completely without bias or political purpose.

One final problem to be mentioned is that historians must be aware of *disinformation*. Besides honest mistakes or subtle bias, there are sometimes conscious efforts to fabricate history. One of the most notorious is the invention of the *Protocols of the Elders of Zion*[29] by the Russian czar's secret police in the late nineteenth century. This book claims to be a Jewish blueprint for world conquest. Although repeatedly shown to be a fake, numerous groups, from Hitler and the Nazis to various anti-Semites today, have promoted the *Protocols* as a true document. Henry Ford reprinted the book by the hundreds of thousands and publicly vouched for its accuracy.[30] Sadly, this is not an isolated example, as the rich and powerful and their governments regularly churn out propaganda for their own purposes. During World War I, the British government even had the creator of

Sherlock Holmes, Sir Arthur Conan Doyle, in their stable of tame authors producing books for the war effort … with little regard for truth or accuracy.[31]

So with all these pitfalls awaiting the historian, what is to be done? Above all else, be careful. As they used to say to starting journalists, "if your mother says she loves you, check it out." Try to verify evidence and lines of argument from multiple sources. Also, ask yourself does this make any sense in this historical context? Figure out who gains from this version of history. Determine who pays for this type of history. (For example, would a biography of Stalin printed in the USSR in the 1940s likely be unbiased?) Remember the words of Christopher Hill, "Historians, like Humpty Dumpty, can make words mean anything they like."[32] Above all, we should think for ourselves.

"The King's in His Castle ... All's Right with the World": The Collapse of the Middle Ages

For about a thousand years after the collapse of the Roman Empire[1] (the artificial date usually given is AD 476), Western Europe became decentralized and chaotic, struggling to reclaim some organizational structure in a more localized manner under what we may call the feudal system.[2] This period is commonly referred to as the Middle Ages. Unlike the Roman governments before, this was a time when Europe had little centralized political authority. Laws, customs, even interpretations of Christianity might vary from place to place. Everywhere, the feudal period was a confusing socioeconomic soup made up from three main ingredients: Roman traditions, Christian beliefs and the customs of the Germanic tribal immigrants (barbarian invaders, if you must) who had settled in Western Europe.

The relative weight of each ingredient differed widely (and often wildly) from place to place. Still, there were some markedly regional tendencies. The Roman traditions were strongest in Italy, while those parts of Europe only lightly touched by the Romans were more prey to non-Roman, Germanic traditions. In places that had never been part of the Roman world, like Scandinavia, both Roman traditions and the veneer of Christianity could be spread rather thin. The Roman Catholic Church was formally accepted throughout Western Europe but, in practice, the clergy's actual influence depended on the local strength of bishops and how much attention the region received from the Papal establishment in Rome.

Unlike the Roman Empire with its centralized government, feudal Europe was a decentralized world where local rulers were lords, in fact as well as in name. Particularly in the early Middle Ages, the will of the local barons was primary and the power of kings nominal outside their immediate holdings. It was a society crudely divided into three estates: those who fought (the warrior nobility), those who prayed (the churchmen),[3] and those who worked (the vast majority of the population—mainly serfs who were tied to the land and a minority of free peasants.) This was a world quite different from the days of the Roman Empire. There were few cities and most were small, weak places in the early centuries. Once-mighty Rome, which during the third century boasted a population of over a million, fell during the Dark Ages. Its permanent population dwindled to around 50,000, and this persisted until around the eleventh century. At the same time, Paris was little more than a collection of shacks by the side of the River Seine.

Science, medicine and literacy were markedly less common, at least during the so-called "Dark Ages," or about the first five hundred years of the feudal period, than during Roman rule. While concrete had been an accepted building material in the Roman Empire, the formula was lost and not rediscovered until the Renaissance. Book production during the length of the fifteenth century had reached 4,999,161 for Western Europe, while in the entire seventh century the area produced only 10,639 volumes with none recorded for Central Europe, Bohemia, Germany, Austria—almost half were from Italy.[4] Of course, things were not necessarily "dark" for the common people of the time. Most continued to be born, live, love, farm and die more or less as their ancestors had. If their life was very hard, so had it been for their ancestors. Most historians no longer like to use the term "Dark Ages" with its judgmental connotations. This early period of feudalism was given this label because it suffered, in scholar's minds at least, in comparison to the glories of Rome. Moreover, historians who are so wedded to written sources find it frustrating that at least until the ninth century AD there was little written documentation to work with. As one prominent French historian has proclaimed in frustration, "We are victims of our sources!"[5] He went on to argue that if "a century is mute, as was the case from the fifth century to the eighth century and also of the tenth century, it has a bad reputation and we call it 'black'—the Dark Ages, as the English say."[6]

Before turning to the focus of this work—the common people—a look at the two dominant classes of nobles and church officials is useful. The nobility was a warrior class who enjoyed a military monopoly of force. They may have claimed God's blessing but the bottom line was they had the best land, with most of it protected by professional killers (knights). These knights possessed armor, swords, lances, trained war horses and so on. A peasant farmer with a club or sharp knife was seldom a match for one of these professionals. While the local baron provided the peasantry with protection in the event of invasion, it was in reality more often protection against the very knights sworn to protect them. Try to imagine a society with little effective central government, where power and wealth went to those who had the arms and the will to seize and keep the land.

The warrior elite was made up of those who had once been little better than local thugs. Over time, however, they began to develop rituals and ideology (known as "chivalry") that allowed them to see themselves as part of a God-ordained aristocracy. Still, their status was based on naked force. When not at war, they trained for war. When not training directly for warfare, they relaxed by engaging in sports. To the nobles, most sports meant killing something ... hunting deer or boar, using trained birds of prey to kill other birds. They sometimes entertained themselves and even the commoners by torturing bears, chaining them to a fixed place and then setting dogs on the luckless creature. It is important to remember that the nobles thought little more, sometimes less, of the peasantry than the animals they hunted.

Even should an average European have thought to resist this secular oppression, and as time went on more and more did just that, they would face another obstacle: the Church. By the Middle Ages, Christianity had already become institutionalized as the tool of power and the powerful.[7] Anyone who dared rebel against the status quo risked death not just in this world but also a sentence to hell in the next; any revolt against secular lords was condemned as an attack on Christ himself. The common people were told constantly that there was but one path to Paradise ... and that was through complete, unquestioning obedience to God's instrument on earth—Holy Mother Church.

This is far from saying that the Church was an entirely religious or spiritual organization. The Church helped organize countless aspects of society and the economy that in more recent times have become the province of government or corporations. This included caring for those of the population who were lepers, organizing popular fairs and entertainments, acting as a diplomatic service between feuding warlords, providing what education there was and preserving ancient knowledge, as monks copied manuscripts by hand in their monasteries. In more populated urban enclaves, the Church, while fiercely condemning prostitution, took responsibility for organizing the female sex workers into houses (frequently Church-owned); when advancing age reduced the women's market value, it was the Church who found them a retirement position in a religious community or as a clerical house servant.[8] Of course, if, as was often the case, the male clients of these houses felt compelled to atone for their sins by donating to the Church, so much the better.

Despite the official imposition of celibacy on the clergy, priests and other male clerics often entered into relations equated by the Church with fornication. As one recent study noted, "long-term stable sexual relationships between clerics and women remained common across Europe during the Middle Ages."[9] Many unmarried women were forced to turn to domestic work and "the servants of priests could easily have found themselves coerced into sexual relations."[10] Still, the relation between clerics and the women they slept with remains complex. Laywomen typically depended on their lovers for food and shelter while nuns retained "their own social networks and living situations within their religious houses during the relationships."[11] Even if the evidence suggests there were seldom truly happy endings for women involved with male clerics, their experiences were much more diverse than scholars may have thought.[12] Given the common practice of priests taking women as partners, sanctioned or not, it is hardly surprising that Reformation leader Martin Luther would so quickly decide to allow his clergy to marry.[13]

Of course, we can never know how much the common people believed what the Church preached to them, although the amount of sincere belief no doubt varied greatly from one time to another. Yet we know that long before the Reformation, there were people interpreting Christianity in a manner far different than Rome's. The Catholic Church had a name for these dissenting believers: heretics. A heretic was one who challenged the practices and the dogma of the Church, and were thought to be a danger to Christian unity and the power of the high clergy. The institution dedicated to dealing with these heretics was called the Inquisition. The first medieval Inquisition began in 1184 and was directed against a group known as the Cathars who were predominantly situated in southern France.[14] While members of this group regarded themselves as good Christians, the Church most decidedly did not. At first, the Pope's emphasis was on peaceful conversion, but this was a failure in all but a few isolated cases.

Having tired of persuasion, the Papal establishment ordered a full-scale crusade against the said-to-be spiritually wayward Cathars. For over two decades at the beginning of the thirteenth century, armed forces under the direction of the papal appointed representative waged unrelenting and cruel war against the so-called "heretics." The fighting that took place inevitably included unspeakable massacres where little effort was made to distinguish between Cathar and faithful Catholic. Asked how to tell heretic from loyal child of the Church, the papal legate is reported to have said, "Kill them all, the Lord will recognize his own."[15] Along with mass slaughter running into the tens of thousands, many taken prisoner were blinded or otherwise mutilated. It may have taken decades, but the organized Cathar heresy was finally destroyed, at least on the surface. It lingered on for a century and some of their views would reappear in changed form in future protests against Rome. The Cathars were a case study in how difficult it was for even the most powerful institutions to rid themselves of firmly held beliefs among the average Europeans.

There is evidence, however, that Cathars may not have been so much advocates of some toxic theology but were, rather, radical Catholics who demanded more reform than the Roman Catholic Church was interested in undertaking. Charges of falling into eastern dualistic error were leveled at the heretics as needed, a handy excuse and a doctrinal error outlined in the theology textbooks used at the great school of Paris[16] How much more convenient it was to charge political opponents demanding radical reform of Church institutions with spiritual crimes, than to actually confront their political critique of the powers that be.[17] Brutal, fierce, savage physical force proved more useful in defeating critics than reasoned debate.

However, the Cathars' treatment at the hands of the Church did not prevent other heresies from arising out of popular opposition to the Church and the feudal order. Sometimes these were massive movements, that prefigured the Reformation. But often, the Inquisition hunted down isolated groups and individuals who were thought to have strayed from the one path to salvation. In truth, the Inquisition may be seen as a tool to target those who thought differently or were viewed as a threat to the feudal lords. In many cases, such as that of Joan of Arc who was tried and executed by her English enemies, the charge of heresy was convenient politically. At times, inquisitors enriched themselves with the confiscated property of those they condemned.

Enriching themselves was something beyond most ordinary Europeans. What was life like for the common people? By occupation, they were artisans, blacksmiths, merchants, musicians, but most of all, they were peasants. Members of the farming class and ignorant of nearly everything but agriculture, something like 75 percent of the peasants were serfs bound to the land. Not slaves but not quite free either, the serf was bound by an elaborate set of obligations to the lord and master. The lord owned the land and for his generosity rarely demanded more than three days a week unpaid labor, and as much as 25 percent in other taxes, along with periodical forced donations for, or participation in, wars.[18] Of course, the Church demanded its dime as well (10 percent). Even the few more fortunate city dwellers had little influence or security. As economist Adam Smith commented in the eighteenth century, during "the barbarous times of feudal anarchy, merchants, like all the other inhabitants of burghs, were considered so little better than emancipated bondsmen, whose persons were despised, and whose gains were envied."[19]

The life of the common people was not only harsh, it might appear even shocking to contemporary eyes. As many as one woman in ten died in childbirth[20] while 25–30 percent of babies arrived stillborn.[21] Even children born healthy spent the first five years of life prey to serious and often deadly diseases. While it is difficult to calculate the survival rate of children, the fact that in Europe's cemeteries a fifth of those interned seem to have been under the age of seven suggests a fearful toll.[22] There is also the often-ignored issue of sexual exploitation. One need not agree with Laura Betzig, who argues that of every 100,000 people living today over 99,000 carry genes from ancient rulers,[23] to admit to widespread sexual predation on the common people. In the feudal period, peasants were subject to *jus primae noctis*, or the right of the lord of the manor to have intercourse with a peasant bride on her wedding night. How often or widespread this right of the first night was practiced is a matter of considerable debate, as *jus primae noctis* could be waived for a cash payment. What remains clear is that this custom was symbolic of the feudal lord's power over his serfs.[24]

The medieval diet was clearly determined by social class. For the peasants, i.e. the vast majority of the population, grains like wheat, rye, oats, or barley made up most of their meals. Although relatively healthy by modern standards, fluctuations in food supply and poor harvests frequently caused bleak times of malnourishment.[25] The common diet left much to be desired, as it was based heavily on carbohydrates that accounted for up to 80 percent of daily calorie intake; people typically ingested up to 2 kilos of bread daily.[26] Despite the image sometimes projected by Hollywood movies, ordinary Europeans ate little meat. As one study found, the bulk of their diet was

> … made up of cereals. Boiled pottage on the basis of grain or pulses, supplemented with vegetables, was a ubiquitous dish. Although meat was available to peasants and labourers, it was consumed in much smaller quantities and probably less quality cuts than by the elites.[27]

The reason for the lack of meat in an environment that would appear to offer so many edible mammals was neither religious nor ethical. While everything was consumed, even dogs, many protein sources, like deer and fish, were often officially off limits to the commoners. As one author noted, the average people of this time "could not fish in the village brook or kill the deer that devoured his crops. Poaching was regarded as one of the most heinous crimes ... ."[28]

There is certainly truth in the popular idea that the nobles prosecuted poachers in order to keep the game and fish for themselves and their households. However, there was another darker/political purpose. By making poaching a serious, even capital, offense, the feudal lords had a lever of social control. At one time, they might turn a blind eye to the never really eliminated peasant poaching, while at another they could use the crime as an excuse to lawfully teach their "inferiors" a lesson. There is evidence for this theory in the fact that Sweden, where there was more than enough game to satisfy both lord and commoner, had anti-poaching laws as rigorous as other areas of Europe. Hunting, for the nobles, was not just about sport and food; it was about displaying authority and power.[29]

This was a system that endured for centuries and imposed its will on generations of Europeans. How did it begin to come apart? First, remember how it came into being during the chaos and invasions of the late Roman Empire in the West. If oppression was the price one paid to be protected from invaders, what justified the same system of political, social and economic suppression when the external threat receded? Once external invasions became rare, the warrior elite often turned on their own common people. The peasantry found themselves pawns in various petty local conflicts between rival lords. The only good thing to come out of this situation was a modest revival in trade, if only in weapons and food for soldiers on campaign. This modest upturn in trade helped merchants and bankers, but few others.

It might be useful to remember at this point that, as befits a system so decentralized, the actual end of feudalism varied greatly from place to place, both in terms of timing and method. The biggest gap was between Western and Eastern Europe. The eastern portion of what had been the Roman Empire had never experienced the number of invasions that plagued the West. Eastern Europe retained more of the old traditions of the Greco-Roman world. In contrast, absolutism in the West led to an "increase in the general rights of private property."[30] The end result was a series of very different outcomes. Many monarchies in the West, most notably the English (1640s) and French (1780s), were overthrown by bourgeois revolutions from below, as Italy (1860s) and Germany (1870s) were transformed by bourgeois revolutions from above. Meanwhile, to the east, the mighty Russian Empire was able to limp into the twentieth century and not be overthrown until the revolutions of 1917.[31]

Space will not allow a full discussion of the differences between Western and Eastern Europe, but one historical difference is each region's relationship to the nearly two hundred years of on again/off again assaults on Islamic rule in the Near East or Holy land, known as the Crusades. As the invasions declined in number in the West, the Eastern Roman Empire (now known as the Byzantine Empire) came under attack by a newly insurgent religion: Islam. Islam had arisen from the margins of the known Christian world, the Arabian Desert, to become a major force in the area. The followers of the Prophet Mohammed battered the Christian areas of North Africa and West Asia. This was no mere military conquest on the part of Islam, as Christians freely converted en masse to a religion that appeared to lack the corrupt, parasitic priesthood and strange theological doctrines that merely confused the average believer. For example, the Prophet Mohammed said there was only one God, not a three-in-one trinity. Moreover, this God was the same one that the Christians had worshipped. While Christianity confounded the commoner with obscure theological formations, Islam offered clarity in its belief system.

Although Jerusalem and the Holy Land had been under the control of Islam for over four centuries, on November 27, 1095 Pope Urban II proclaimed a holy crusade[32] against the Islamic peoples in the Holy Land.[33] Labeling the Muslims a despised and base race that worships demons, the Pope urged everyone, including robbers, to join in the fight against the "pagans." All who died fighting Islam were promised forgiveness of their sins and thus a place in heaven. Pope Urban II said that this was not merely the will of the Church but that Christ himself commanded it.[34] The Church's motivations were multiple. As clearly stated, one goal was to help the beleaguered Byzantine Empire as part of a diplomatic offense to re-unite Roman Catholic and Greek Christians under the authority of the Papacy. At the same time, Urban II thought that by propping up the Eastern Christians, Western Europe would be spared from further assault by an expanding Islam. Yet Rome had other reasons for organizing an invasion of the Near East. The Church had long tired of the seemingly endless, petty and pointless fighting between various barons over what the nobles said were affairs of honor, which were at heart really attempts to expand their land holdings.

If the Crusades were intended to put Jerusalem and the Holy Land under Christian control for eternity, they were a failure. While unsuccessful in either this regard or fundamentally helping the Byzantines, the almost two hundred years of on again/off again invasions had a profound effect within the Roman Catholic world. The Crusades, as the popes had hoped, caused the most troublesome and warlike Europeans to "take the cross," with the result that many were killed in their battle with Islam. At worst, these destabilizing warriors were kept out of Europe for a number of years. This facilitated the rise of strong central monarchies, particularly in France and England, which imposed something resembling order on the territories under their (previously nominal) control. Many feudal lords became bankrupt from their ruinous assault on the Holy Land. This situation stimulated the growth of businessmen, those whom some call the "bourgeoisie," others call "middle class"—mainly merchants and moneylenders—who gained from the loans and sale of supplies to the heaven-bent crusaders. Some serfs were released from their feudal obligations in return for participation in a crusade, while others were able to renegotiate the terms of their servitude as cash-strapped warriors left their manors to surrogates, often wives or brothers, and trotted off towards the Near East. Of course, it would be a mistake to think only of men when discussing the Crusades or the Middle Ages. Recent scholarship has shown that women had far more influence than traditionally noted by historians.[35] This is a theme that will reappear throughout this book.

Another impact came from those tens of thousands of Europeans who managed to survive participation in a crusade and return home. Those who returned typically returned changed. In the East, they had come in contact with a more advanced society. Islamic society had superior medical and scientific knowledge, and had even preserved much from the ancient Greco-Roman world. For people who had previously seldom left their village or at most traveled a few days' walk from their homes, being on a crusade, no matter how militarily disastrous it may have been, was a transformative experience. The things they experienced, witnessed and brought back would spread by word of mouth among all the people of Western Europe. The claim of various popes that Christ would guarantee the recovery of the Holy Land increasingly sounded hollow, as the brief Christian victory in the First Crusade was followed by failure upon failure. By overselling the certainty of victory over Islam, the popes had inadvertently undermined the Church's claims to infallibility.

The papacy's desire to reunite Christianity and strengthen the Byzantine Empire was not only unsuccessful, but the Crusades, most notably the Fourth Crusade, made matters worse. The insular crusaders had taken a strong dislike to the Greek-speaking Christians of the East from the time of the First Crusade. In 1204, the Fourth Crusade, originally sent to attack Jerusalem, sacked Constantinople, capital of the Byzantine Empire. As one historian tells the story, for three days, the crusaders

... murdered, raped, looted and destroyed on a scale which even the ancient Vandals and Goths would have found unbelievable ... [they] destroyed indiscriminately, halting to refresh themselves with wine, violation of nuns and murder of Orthodox clerics.[36]

This appalling carnage solidified, rather than overcame, the schism in Christianity, just as it weakened, rather than strengthened, the Byzantine Empire.

Still, the seeds of change that the Crusades planted were not, in and of themselves, enough to transform feudal Europe. The system still survived on the basis of the nobles' control of agriculture, a military monopoly for the warrior elite, as well as their own belief in themselves[37] and, of course, the intellectual/spiritual power of the Roman Catholic Church. Both feudal lord and Pope would take a further battering in the fourteenth century as the overlapping impact of the Hundred Years War and the Black Death shook medieval society to its core.

The so-called "Hundred Years War" was fought mainly between France and England from 1337 until 1453 (obviously more than a hundred years in length, it should be noted that this war was actually a series of conflicts interspersed with periods of uneasy peace). This series of wars was witness to the end of the feudal ruling classes' complete military monopoly. Heavily armored knights mounted on specially trained warhorses proved to be less than invincible to peasants using the longbow. Cannons saw general use during this period and even in their early crude incarnation, respected neither the knight's armor nor the lord's castle walls. By the end of the conflict, it was clear that there was little long-term military future for the highly trained knight, while the nobility would see their political power increasingly eroded.[38] As noted previously, one can only imagine the despair and self-doubt that the success of Joan of Arc must have engendered among the feudal lords.[39] Joan was a peasant woman who claimed to have divine orders to save France. Thousands of the common people seem to have believed her. The defeats of the French feudal lords at the hands of the English were such that many thought she had been sent by God. This caused the would-be French king to deploy her, in the hope of inspiring his troops and rallying the common people. She proved to be difficult to control, so there was some relief among the French ruling class when Joan was taken into English custody. After all, neither women nor commoners were meant to be great generals. The English, when they captured Joan, had her condemned as a witch and burned, since only the powers of the devil could explain her successes against their male noble-led army.

Nor should we think that armed conflicts were limited to the French and English armies. In various parts of France, knights and their assortment of military adventurers were often to be found attacking their own rural population. With little effective royal control, soldiers, who often were left without food or pay, found that raiding their own peasants provided a respite from their hunger. If the need for food failed to provide sufficient motivation, many knights were pushed into fratricide by simple greed. Neither livestock nor people were free from capture by those traditionally painted as the protector of the common people. For many French commoners, the knights and castles of the nobility became as hated as the English invaders. In response, the people sometimes turned to banditry, on occasion rose up in rebellion and even were known to destroy local defense installations. A class war raged throughout the better-studied national war.[40]

In the fall of 1347, plague was brought to Italy by the Genoese, from Crimea, after an epidemic erupted there. This disease would become known then and ever since as the Black Death. Historians have argued over exactly what disease or diseases made up the Plague. No matter what the infectious agent might have been, it allied with periodic famine and civil strife to produce a catastrophe seldom seen in modern history.[41] Some estimate the plague may have killed as much as two-thirds of Western Europe's population by 1420. No matter if this estimate is exaggerated; all scholars agree that the percentages were shockingly high. Although everyone in society was impacted, the common people, often undernourished and living in unhealthy environments, were most susceptible.

The rapid decline of the population fundamentally altered the economic situation. Those commoners who survived found themselves in a much stronger bargaining position, as feudal lords found themselves competing for peasants with offers of wages and freedoms. Craftworkers were able to earn far more as well. The introduction of a more competitive market for labor is often suggested to be one of the steps that ultimately led to capitalism. The rulers were so fearful of these changes that they attempted, with little success, to enforce wage controls that would keep the common people in the same economic misery they had been in before the Plague.[42] This was a doomed attempt, as there was now more fertile land available for peasants, while workers could leave their current situation knowing that they could easily find another. Cheaper land prices, a higher level of consumption and a significant increase in average income can all be traced back to the effects of the Black Death.

If the Plague shifted the balance of power in secular affairs, its impact was, if anything, greater within the Roman Catholic Church. Although much was unknown about the causes of the epidemic, it was clear that avoiding areas where the plague was flourishing greatly increased one's chances for survival. Since the Church had long held that the dying required a "last rites" from a priest in order to increase the chance of eternal salvation, dedicated clergy sought out the plague sufferers to give comfort and administer this potentially soul-saving ritual. This resulted in the most faithful members of the clergy dying in disproportionate numbers, while those who had joined the priesthood in a desire for ease or status were more likely to go into hiding. The end result was that the Church was left with not only fewer priests but also the least honest or devout. As the labor shortage hit the Church along with all other sectors of the feudal economy, there was an influx of barely trained, inexperienced clergy whose dubious activities led to a further decline in the popular perception of Rome.

Without losing ourselves in the maze of academic debates on the subject of feudal decline, it is important to rescue average Europeans from the common stereotype that portrays them as passive subjects waiting hat in hand for their "betters" to decide the great issues of the day. The reality is far more complex, as the common people repeatedly and forcefully asserted themselves into the flow of medieval history. There were not only the often recognized revolts of the Middle Ages—such as Ciompi (1378), the Jacquerie (1358) and the English peasant revolt (1381)—but also countless popular resistances little noted in most histories. One historian who did study the commoners, found in Italy, France and Flanders "1600 descriptions of popular movements, which amounted to 1,112 separate incidents."[43]

Moreover, these revolts were not irrational outbursts occasioned by drought, famine or other external hardships. Overwhelmingly, the people who rebelled appear motivated by a desire for political rights.[44] This was not the special pleading of people who saw their status threatened and therefore demanded a return to past privilege. The rebellious commoners in both Northern and Southern Europe increasingly showed "an implicit sense of equality."[45] Although there is the problem of not having enough first-hand sources, it could well be that manifestations of popular discontent took place long before the latter period of feudalism. For example, in ninth-century Saxony, a group of lower-class pagans fought against oppressive feudal obligations.[46]

Let us turn to the famous English Peasants Revolt of 1381 for a useful example. As noted before, the Black Death had weakened both state and

Church in Europe. In not so jolly old England, a law was passed in 1351 to control rising real wages and prop up the old order. This so-called "Statute of Laborers" demanded that common people work for the same price as before the Plague's onset, and allowed landowners to insist on payment in the form of labor instead of money. As prices rose, many were squeezed by stagnant income and an ever higher cost of living. This situation continued for a generation, with various minor but significant scrimmages between lords and serfs, rich and poor. In 1377, the burden of England's military campaigns in France caused the government to introduce a head tax. Payable by all adult males in cash not produce, this new tax was seen as a real hardship by many commoners. Within a few years, men often hid from the tax collectors, leading to a decline in revenue. In spring 1381, the Royal Council, worried by the drop in income, ordered a new round of tax collections with collectors charged to obtain the full amount due.

People, particularly those who had already paid the tax previously, were furious at the thought of paying what had become a hated tax again. In Essex and then in Kent, peasants resisted and soon rose in up revolt. These radicals appear to have taken inspiration from the rebel priest John Ball, who is often credited with the saying: "When Adam delved and Eve span, who then was the gentleman?"[47] Many of Ball's sermons seemed to promote a type of Christian communism that would later appear in Europe during the Reformation. Not surprisingly, Ball's activities came to the attention of the Archbishop of Canterbury who had Ball imprisoned. In June 1381, rebellious peasants from Kent captured Maidstone Castle where Ball was confined and set him free. By mid-June, rebel armies that formed in Essex and Kent had separately reached London, the capital.

As is normal in such situations, the estimates about the size of the rebel forces varies wildly but, even if they did not reach the six figures often attributed to them, there were certainly tens of thousands. With few troops on hand to protect him, the king, Richard II, agreed to meet the angry peasants. Led by a man named Wat Tyler, the demands included: 1) abolition of the poll tax, 2) pardons for all involved in the rebellion, 3) written charters outlining the rights of the peasants, 4) reduction of land rents, and 5) execution of all traitors (e.g. people who the commoners especially felt oppressed by.) The king agreed to all their demands with the qualification that the royal court alone could judge cases of treason. Reasonably enough, many peasants considered that they had won a great victory and began to leave London.

Others in the rebel army, including Wat Tyler, insisted on another meeting with the king to press for even more concessions. Although the king agreed, his acquiescence was a trap. At the arranged meeting, Tyler was assassinated. Before the confused peasants knew what was happening, the king boldly shouted that all demands were granted and that everyone should follow him out of London so that written charters could be given out. As many deceived or confused peasants began to wander towards their homes, troops summoned by the monarch hunted down and slaughtered all those thought to be involved. Ironically, any peasant who actually received a written charter of rights was assured death as well; the charter served as proof of participation in the revolt if it was found on their person. On July 15, 1381, John Ball, whose preaching was seen as such an influence on the peasantry, was hung, drawn and quartered in public, so as to comfort the rich and intimidate the common people.

Thus far, the events described are, more or less, generally accepted by most historians. It turns out, however, that a number of key details have escaped the attention of most scholars. The fateful events of 1381 have traditionally been related as if they were an all-male affair. If women were seen as playing a role, it was as unimportant camp followers. Court records, examined and translated from Latin by historian Sylvia Federico, tell a different story.[48] The primary sources indicate that women were as militant (and violent) in defense of their rights as men. For example, the leader of the rebel band that dragged Lord Chancellor Simon of Sudbury from the Tower of London and beheaded him was a woman named Johanna Ferrour. This was no isolated incident, as the court records show women were often at the very heart of the revolt. Since the events of 1381 are recounted mainly through the eyes of the male elite, women have been systematically written out of this example of popular resistance.

Further, despite the vicious repression of dissent, the ruling feudal lords were profoundly shaken. They would never again try to impose the discredited head tax. Parliament gave up any immediate attempt to control wage demands, while the nobles grew more wary of making excessive demands of their common people. In England, 1381 would prove to be more dirt on the grave of feudalism. It may well be argued that social revolts were, in the final analysis, an expression of the contradictions inherent in the feudal economy of medieval Europe.[49] It would be strange if the common people fighting their way onto the stage of history had no impact. Given that the economy, wealth and power of the feudal lords depended on their non-titled subjects, it would be a particularly socially tone-deaf noble who did not realize the potential power of his subjects. The commoners' power was reinforced by ever more frequent revolts, as feudalism went into decline. With the growth of cities, protest and rebellion spread to urban areas.[50] No system is completely closed in and of itself. As noted before, feudal Europe was greatly impacted by the Islamic world from an early time. In the late fifteenth century, the conquest of the Western Hemisphere would transform Europe in a number of diverse ways. Silver from the Americas would allow the European nobility to pay for imported silk and spices from Asia, while new plants like the tomato and the potato transformed European agriculture and diet. Ultimately, the intercourse between the two hemispheres would undermine the feudal system itself.[51]

For a social and economic system to decay is one thing; for a new class to rise up is quite another. So far, we have discussed only the problems inherent in the socioeconomic system that developed out of the demise of the Western Roman Empire. Even before the decline of feudalism was evident, a new class had begun to rise, in fits and starts, to ever-greater importance. This class is often called the "bourgeoisie" or "capitalists." This is, simply put, a class whose power is based on wealth as opposed to hereditary right. As the French origin of the name "bourgeois" suggests, capitalists are often most closely identified with the growth of urban areas. Those that ran feudal society based themselves on the control of agriculture and fought to expand their holdings. The capitalists, in contrast, based themselves on money and the control of trade and production.

The classic French historian of feudalism, Marc Bloch, commented:

> ... the evolution of the economy involved a genuine revision of social values. There had always been artisans and merchants ... [but] from the end of the eleventh century the artisan class and the merchant class, having become much more numerous and much more indispensable to the life of the community, made themselves felt more and more vigorously in the urban settings. This applies especially to the merchant class, for the medieval economy, after the great revival of these decisive years, was always dominated, not by the producer, by the trade.[52]

The rise of cities went hand-in-hand with the rise of merchant capitalists. Cities would grow not only in population but also would become protected by walls and even on occasion by moats. A city's fortifications could even be superior to that of the local feudal lord. Within the city, the local "patricians" or rich often ruled with a fair degree of autonomy, if they had been able to purchase a charter from their feudal overlord granting urban self-governance. There were conflicts with the feudal lords but the latter was restrained by the need for the loans and taxes that these new cities produced.

Although this growth of the bourgeois urban area was most apparent by late feudalism, it actually had begun as soon as the reasons that gave rise to the medieval system began to disappear. Invasions and constant disorder had laid the foundation for the feudal system. When by the eleventh century, the cycle of invasions ended and later the Crusades drained Europe of some of her most riotous inhabitants, society began to change. The decline of warfare led to the enormous growth of population that "favoured the revival of towns, the artisan class, and trade."[53] By the fifteenth century, this tendency had been greatly enhanced partially due to the effects of the Black Death, as noted before. Money, as a medium of exchange in the form of coins made from precious metals, regained an importance not seen since the heads of Caesars adorned Roman silver cash. It resumed its role as a generally accepted medium of exchange and formerly independent lords were impelled to turn to the urban moneylender. The insertion of money into feudal society undermined the status quo in ways that people of the time could hardly imagine.

With the changing economy pointing increasingly towards the feudal nobles' need for money, the rulers became obsessed with a lust for gold. The Portuguese raided the African coastal areas for gold, while their Spanish neighbors crossed the formidable Atlantic Ocean in search of the precious metal. Although this frantic scramble was conducted by feudal powers, the new emphasis on money was incompatible with a system that had arisen on the non-monetary foundation of land, bound labor and obligation. The cycle of petty, if not pointless, wars that had always plagued Europe in the Middle Ages seemed more and more outdated. If warfare was an important part of the feudal ethic and the rubric by which lord and knight proved their worth, to most of the common people it seemed a brutal and pointless exercise in destruction. Alongside those brief moments when the peasants and other commoners pushed themselves onto the historical stage, from which they were typically excluded, other more common forms of resistance must be acknowledged including "everyday forms of indirect resistance, such as passive non-cooperation or sabotage."[54] Less dramatic than revolts, or even riots, these day-to-day modes of resistance should not be forgotten, even when looking at better-documented and forceful forms of protest.

While neither merchant nor peasant had the power to put an end to the repetitive cycle of slaughter, they had an unlikely ally in any number of power-hungry monarchs. Kings, and the occasional queen, increasingly saw the petty quarrels of the nobility and their ongoing resistance to royal authority as limitations and threats to their rule. Monarchies found themselves trying to run nations that, at times, seemed to be in a permanent state of lordly rebellion. In this confusion of war and riot, the monarchs often found themselves in a de facto alliance with the common people, notably the bourgeoisie whose loans they might depend on. A king or queen faced with rebellious nobles might well ask the common people for money and to be soldiers for their army. In return, the monarch would grant further rights to repay their non-noble supporters.

As the feudal nobility became economically less important, kings created their own armies, relying on recruited or hired troops as opposed to being dependent on their unreliable vassals within the feudal nobility. By the end of the Middle Ages, many knights contracted themselves and their foot soldiers into mercenary service, with the result that feudal obligation and honor were replaced by a naked desire for cash.[55] The end of feudalism in Europe was less a single event than a process[56] that would include that permanent fracturing of Christianity known to history as the Reformation.

CHAPTER TWO

"The Other Reformation": Martin Luther, Religious Dogma and the Common People

Before the official Reformation that we read about in textbooks, there was Jan Hus of Bohemia, a precursor to all the changes of the sixteenth century. Hus became active in the fifteenth century. As a professor at Prague University, Hus made a critique of the Catholic Church that was in many ways deeper and more biting than that of Luther a century later. Despite widespread support, Hus made the fatal mistake of believing the clerical establishment would honor the immunity granted him to attend a Church council. Instead of the theological debate he had been expecting, Hus was tried for heresy, condemned and burned at the stake in the summer of 1415. Far from ending the matter, the Roman Catholic Church thereby unwittingly unleashed a wave of rebellion that lasted into the 1430s and spread from Bohemia into Poland.

The Hussite movement, as it is generally called, ranged from moderates who would have been comfortable as Lutheran reformers in a later century (Luther had not yet been born) to the radical Taborites (named after the Bohemian town of Tábor). The latter can be seen as Christian communists who sought to establish a Christian community where all goods would be shared in common. A Bohemian translation of the Bible had existed since 1630; this translation allowed radical clerics and educated laity to see for themselves contradictions between the original teachings of Christ and established Church practice. As one nineteenth-century critic suggested:

> As soon as the populace could read the Bible in their own language (the Roman Catholic priesthood understood well why they wished to make the knowledge of this book their own privilege), they did not draw from the New Testament its lessons of humility and self-denial, but those of hatred to the rich.[1]

After the murder of Hus, those called Taborites proceeded to set up their ideal society. Their rules included:

> ... there shall be no king, ruler or subject on the earth, and all imposts and taxes shall cease; no one shall force another to do anything, for all shall be equal brothers and sisters ... there is no mine or thine, but all is held in common to all, and no one own anything for himself alone. Whoever does so commits a deadly sin.[2]

Even an enemy of these radicals admitted the importance they placed on education, including the training of women. The hostile witness additionally conceded that among the Taborites "you will find hardly one young woman who is not versed in both the Old and New Testaments."[3] It has also been said that a great many of these radicals were wool-weavers, rather than there being only peasants taking part.[4] It is important to note that these rebels were not unwilling to fight. They, like radicals after them, looked to Christ's words: "Do not think that I came to bring peace on earth. I did not come to bring peace but a sword,"[5] and found legitimation in their right to use physical force—that is, legitimation of physical force for, at the very least, self-defense.

In any event, most agree that there was little in the way of long-term prospects for these radicals. The movement was effectively crushed on May 30, 1434 when an army led by nobles slaughtered 13,000 out of 18,000 armed Taborite soldiers. Defeat in one manner or the other was most likely inevitable. Well over a century ago, Karl Kautsky argued that the "needs of the poor engendered the struggle for communism, those of production demanded the existence of private proprietorship. Hence communism could never become the universal form of society in those days."[6] This may be a bit dogmatic but it may well be largely true.

A more commonly told story of the Reformation is the tale of pious individuals reacting to the misguided if not venial practices of the Roman Catholic Church. Pride of place is often given to a German monk, Martin Luther, who ignited the movement by nailing 95 theses onto a Wittenberg church door in 1517. In and of itself, this was not necessarily a grave matter as this was the accepted manner to call for a theological debate. Luther did not, however, ask for a debate over mere details of the faith. He wished to strike at the heart of Church practice, most notably the selling of indulgences that allowed the common people to pay a fee to Rome in return for the forgiveness of sin, which would reduce the time that their souls would spend in purgatory. Since everyone was said to have sinned, even the most clean-living person could expect thousands of years in purgatory where the soul would be painfully purified. To many people, indulgences appeared a good deal.

Martin Luther did not think it was a good deal at all. He quickly began to promote the idea that not only indulgences but also any such practices or beliefs not found in the Bible were useless in the quest for salvation. The former monk who had become a professor of theology argued for *sola scriptura*: that only the Bible was a guide to Christian faith and practice. No longer would papal pronouncements or the decisions of Church councils matter. As his oppositional ideas began to come together into a new theology, Martin Luther came to insist that salvation could come only through Christ and faith in his grace.[7] He was not quibbling about the finer nuances of theology; Luther was interrogating the established faith of Western Europe.

Another Protestant leader, John Calvin, believed the Holy Spirit draws people towards Christ. Originally from France, Calvin established a theocracy in Geneva, Switzerland. Believing that Church and State should be one, the establishment of theocratic government was completely consistent with his thoughts.[8] Not to be forgotten was Huldreich Zwingli who, like Martin Luther, vigorously fought against the sale of indulgences as early as 1518. And then there was Henry VIII of England, who Protestants sometimes argue did the right thing for the wrong reason. Unable to convince the pope to allow him to set aside his wife and take another in hopes of fathering a legitimate male heir, Henry broke from Rome in 1533. The list of prominent figures in the Reformation could go on for some time but our main points lie elsewhere.

Entire forests have been leveled to produce the paper needed to recount the story above, in vast and often bewildering detail. What these mountains of books, articles and essays often overlook is that the Reformation was a process, not an event. Most importantly, it was far more than an argument over who got to drink wine at Sunday mass or other aspects of Christian praxis/practice and liturgy. Many issues, even interpretations of history, were in dispute.[9] Long before Luther nailed to that church door what would prove to be, unknown to Luther at the time, a declaration of war against papal authority, there were others who challenged medieval Christian practices and dogma. In the fourteenth century, John Wycliffe attacked Rome in terms highly suggestive of the later Martin Luther. Wycliffe railed against Church corruption, which included the sale of indulgences and the veneration of saints, not to mention the appalling ignorance and low moral standards of the clergy. Likewise, Jan Hus fought along the same line of thought as Wycliffe and even translated the latter's writings into the tongue of his native Bohemia. As we know, the Roman Catholic Church burnt Hus in 1415 for the trouble he incited. In this he followed in a long line of Church suppression, as witnessed in the case of the Cathars.

The point is that, while theologians may have seen their opposition to the Roman Catholic Church establishment mainly as matters of faith, the common people often interpreted religious dissent as a call to reject the established order—both lay and clerical. Any call to resist papal exploitation, such as church taxes, quickly led people to question secular oppression. If the Church had strayed from the teachings of Christ, should not Christians live as the Son of God in the same manner his disciples had? If, as Jesus said, "It is easier for a camel to go through the eye of a needle than for a rich man to enter the kingdom of God,"[10] how should we think of the nobility? And, if Christ is the model, why not share everything as had been the practice of Jesus and the early believers. When commoners learned from readings from Acts of the Apostles the manner of Christian life in past times, some found inspiration to reject the feudal order. Imagine a European peasant hearing for the first time that Christians had held "all things in common,"[11] and any surplus was "distributed to each as anyone had need."[12] Since Christianity pervaded European language and culture at that time, the rebellion, too, would be phrased in Biblical tones even if, for some, the motivation may have been a bit more secular. At this time, commoners were shielded from the texts both as a deliberate move by Rome, which stated only clergy could interpret and dispense this knowledge, coupled with illiteracy and lack of access to books.

An important difference between Jan Hus's time and Luther's was the development of the printing press and the increase in literacy. One estimate suggests that male literacy was less than 10 percent at the start of the sixteenth century but rose to around 50 percent by the century's end.[13] Regardless of the actual literacy rate (a subject open to debate and inter-pretation), it is certain that there was an explosive spread of knowledge and ideas following the development of printing in Western Europe. This new information technology doubtlessly spurred on the Reformation. With it, Martin Luther became a best-selling author who sold over 300,000 copies of his works in the three years following 1517. Even in the media-saturated world of the twenty-first century, that is impressive. No wonder Luther proclaimed the printing press as an example of God's grace.[14] It was the printing press, as much as brilliant theology, which made the Reformation popular among much of the population. As the dissemination of books and information became more common and affordable, people learned of new scriptures and doctrines. Numerous attacks on established Christianity took place in various parts of Western Europe throughout feudalism. Despite the viciousness of the Church assault on heresy, is it reasonable to assume a total victory of the entrenched clerical order over the dissenters? One scholar who has studied this issue at length noted: "It is rather hard to believe that heresies, which had secretly lived on in certain towns and villages for one or two hundred years should suddenly have died out by 1500."[15] In fact, there exists overwhelming documentation to support the idea that various heresies survived until the Reformation and beyond.[16]

It may well be that profound discontent with rulers, both lay and clerical, was widespread in at least some parts of Europe before the Reformation per se began. Common people were often less than satisfied with their lot in feudal society, yet revolts and rebellions were but the most dramatic manifestation. Unlike Jan Hus and those who followed his teachings, Luther, Calvin and many others were successful in breaking from Rome largely because they had gained the protection of local rulers and regional elites. In rejecting the Roman Catholic Church, they did not necessarily denounce the idea of a hierarchical society. Some even quipped that Lutheranism was Roman Catholicism without the Pope, but with a handful of tweaks to traditional practice. While this is too simplistic a judgment, it is true the religious reform largely stopped at the castle gates. That is, religious reform was on the European agenda in the sixteenth century, social revolution was not: nor, even, was serious reform. Whether founded by Luther, the man the Pope famously called "that little drunken monk," or Henry VIII of England, the new Churches were to be as supportive of secular authority as the Roman Church had ever been.

Perhaps, the most dramatic, and bloody, confrontation between the conservative and radical theories of the Reformation took place in central Europe ... in the German states.[17] It is known to history as the German Peasant War of 1525. According to most estimates, this popular rebellion was the largest and most widespread until at least the English Revolution of the 1640s, if not the French Revolution of 1789. Although Engels's early work on the Peasant War[18] has led the topic to be a favorite of Marxist historians, key points like the doctrine of the community of goods and the life of the common people have now been acknowledged by non-Marxist historians as well.[19] If the name of Martin Luther is tied forever to the Reformation, Thomas Müntzer[20] was the spiritual leader of those who rejected not only papal exploitation but secular oppression as well.

Müntzer[21] was a highly educated priest, who was attracted to the ideas of Luther in 1518. By the following year, he was preaching against the

Church's veneration of saints and the papal hierarchy. Serving as a pastor at Zwickau, Saxony, which was well-known as a town where clear conflict existed between miners and the upper class. Müntzer quickly sided with miners against the upper class. As time went on, he became convinced not only of his opposition to the Roman Catholic hierarchy but to Luther's reformist program. Chased from Zwickau in 1521, he traveled to Bohemia to gain the support of the remaining Taborites who had been inspired by Jan Hus. By the following year, he recognized his total opposition to Luther and his followers. His theology took on an increasingly revolutionary tone as he came to believe that the common people were the true instruments of God. Müntzer turned on Luther, who he referred to as "Dr. Liar." He was convinced that Luther was the mouthpiece for the rich and powerful. As Müntzer wrote in his *Sermon to the Princes*: "It is thanks to the German nobility whose snouts you have petted and given honey, that you stood before the Holy Roman Empire at Worms ... the devil should devour you ... Your flesh is like that of an ass, and you would have to be cooked slowly."[22]

As time went on, the theological emphasis of Müntzers' work appears to have taken a back seat to his more secular demands. In any case, the peasants put forth demands that were certainly not obscure discussions on the nature of salvation. In March 1525, a collection of German-speaking commoners agreed upon Twelve Articles, which had a press run of over 25,000 copies within two months.[23] These demands included the redirection of the higher than 10 percent tithe for public purposes, allowing only a reasonable subtraction for a pastor's living. Among the other demands were the abolition of serfdom, restoration of fishing and hunting rights, and restrictions on taxes, rents and forced labor, as well as an end to all arbitrary justice and administration.[24]

Whether this rebellion was religiously motivated or caused by economic oppression has been a matter of intense debate. It is probably fair to argue it was the latter dressed up in the theological clothes of the former. Of course, for the average sixteenth-century German, the idea of some separation between religion and everyday life might well have seemed puzzling. This was a popular, if ultimately failed, revolution that included the participation of women.[25] The established powers took great alarm at a movement that may have involved as many as 300,000 people; the anti-peasant response was brutal repression. The commoners lacked artillery and cavalry, not to mention military experience. Many rebels were pacifists in their belief and unwilling to fight. As Conrad Grebel wrote to Thomas Müntzer in 1524, many followers would not "use worldly sword or war, since all killing has ceased with them."[26] Further, the democratic nature of the movement may have been ill-suited to the demands for all-out class war.

This did not prevent Martin Luther from urging on the peasants' assassins to ever greater violence. Rather than searching for a negotiated settlement that would spare the blood of the commoners, Luther egged on the upper-class military forces to show no mercy whatsoever. His words are as vile and as much an incitement to murder as those he wrote against his Jewish neighbors.[27] Even Christian peasants, who sought to change the secular world, were beyond any hope of mercy in Luther's mind. So Luther urged the knights to "Stab, smite, slay whoever can. If you die in doing it, well for you! A more blessed death can never be yours … [as this killing] pleases God; this I know."[28] By the time the military had finished their task of restoring order on behalf of the rulers, there were an estimated 100,000 German commoners slain.[29] Proportionate to the population of Germany today, this would equate to over a million victims; it was a holocaust of the German peasantry if you will.

Nor did matters end there. It is important to understand the price paid by the German peasants for their failed rebellion not only in terms of lives lost, but also the economic impact on the survivors. The rulers, who ultimately suppressed the uprising, had been desperate to raise huge sums to pay the needed mercenary armies. Lacking sufficient cash reserves, short-term loans were asked or demanded to cover the immediate cost of the anti-peasant war. Loans were slow in coming and the contribution extracted by force from various urban Jewish communities was not enough to fund the slaughter.[30] Later, to cover the cost of these loans, reparations payments were demanded from those areas that had risen in revolt.[31] Ultimately, the pressure applied to the peasantry resulted in the collection of approximately twice the actual cost of the war.[32] As one author commented, "The costs of the campaign of suppression were borne largely by the rebels themselves … The struggle which had begun with the call for recognition of the social, political, and economic rights of the peasants ended in their deeper subjection."[33]

With this massive repression, the rulers were able to suppress the radical or left wing of the Reformation, that is, those who wished to change secular society and rulers not just the people's relationship with the Church. An unknown number of Europeans continued to insist on changes more drastic than those allowed by Luther. History has lumped all these dissenters under the label "Anabaptist." This, like all strict descriptions of early Protestantism, suffers from oversimplification.[34] It is also important to note that those given the title Anabaptist seldom, if ever, accepted the label. They normally preferred to simply call themselves Christians.[35] Luther's hostility towards them is well known and documented, but that of John Calvin is often overlooked.

Calvin, an urban (or bourgeois) Frenchman, possessed the worldview of the rising so-called "middle classes." A former theology student at the University of Paris who later dabbled in the study of law, John Calvin provided a justification for the increasing independence of the new developing urban business class from their feudal rulers. Unsurprisingly, Calvin's theology, with its limited tolerance for feudal political authority and an emphasis on the work ethic, fit nicely with the needs and desires of the untitled well-off and other city dwellers. Calvin's thought provided a religious argument against those radical Protestant ideas that might justify discontent, or even revolt, among the masses. If there is any doubt about his anti-populist attitudes, it is only necessary to consult Calvin's published works. He wrote bitterly against Müntzer and all who followed radical teachings, whom he lumped together as Anabaptists.[36]

Why such vigor in attacking the Anabaptists when the Roman Catholic Church remained the most powerful religious organization in Europe? Of course, that fundamental differences in theology played a part is clear, but far from the whole story. Correctly or not, those they called Anabaptists were seen as the seed of the 1525 German Peasant Revolt and as such, a threat to established order—be it Catholic, Lutheran, or Calvinist. Luther and Calvin were both in the process of carving out zones of power and influence outside the writ of the Roman Catholic Church. This took place with the blessing of many local nobles and the wealthy—neither man was anxious to bite the hand that fed them by appearing to be soft on those seen as rebels against property and position. The Anabaptists were perceived as a potential enemy to the ordered world as envisioned, albeit in different ways by the Pope, Luther, and Calvin alike.[37] In some cases, theological concerns appear to have taken second place to economic distress.

In 1515, Pope Leo X sent a papal legate to Scandinavia to collect money to pay for work on St. Peter's Church in Rome. His mission was quite fruitful, as he raised more than a million florins from Sweden and Denmark. It is held by many that this planted the idea of the Reformation in many northern European minds. After a series of bloody repressions supported by papal authority, Gustavas Vasa, son of a murdered Swedish senator, raised an army of commoners and defeated the pro-papal forces led by King Christian II of Denmark. Vasa became king of Sweden in 1523 and Christian II lost his throne in Denmark. King Vasa had become a supporter of Lutheran beliefs and systematically worked to destroy papal power in northern Europe. Whatever sincere conflicts of conscience the Swedish monarchy had with the Roman Catholic Church, there was also the reality of the Church as a massive property holder. For reasons that may have mixed together nationalism against a distant power (Rome) and perhaps simple lust for wealth and power, Church power and property was targeted in Sweden. As the Church had more wealth within its kingdom than did the monarch and other nobles combined, Vasa proceeded to tax ecclesiastical property, and as many as 20,000 estates, houses and farms were seized and given to lay ownership.[38] It is widely considered that the Reformation in Sweden was consolidated by 1529. Denmark was to remain outside the circle of Lutheranism, but had forever broken from Rome by 1547.

As stressed before, women played a vital role in the Reformation.[39] This does not, however, mean that the Reformation was always and everywhere an advance for women's rights. In a careful examination of the Norwegian Reformation, the traditional view is that the situation of women may have actually deteriorated. Women's rights and participation in these movements specifically varied considerably across location and time, and class concerns were an aspect of commonality. Men like Luther and Calvin were successful because of their message—protection of the powerful—but also because many commoners saw them as attacking systems of privilege that had long exploited the people. In short, where the people were unhappy about their position in society they tended to back Protestants whereas those areas where the Church was seen more as an employer, provider of welfare to the poor and sick, and promoter of trade typically remained loyal to Rome.

Even Henry VIII would have been loath to move so boldly against the Roman Church if it had had massive popular support in England. Yet, the impulses that led to attack on the Roman Church were strong throughout most of Western Europe. Consider that these impulses were evident even in places little mentioned as areas of Reformation support such as Hungary,[40] Poland[41] and even Spain.[42] Of course, the long-term significance of some of these movements can certainly be questioned, as the Church was able to weather the popular storms by rallying their supporters.

Meanwhile in England, under the Tudor monarchs, there unfolded a type of Reformation from above. The story of Henry VIII breaking from Rome in his desire to secure a divorce from Catherine of Aragon in the hope of fathering a legitimate male heir with another woman is well known. Therefore, we need not recount the details here. Of more interest is the fact that Henry was positively hostile when Luther first raised the banner of rebellion against the papacy. His attack on Lutheranism was so fierce that Pope Leo X was moved to award the English king with the title

"Defender of the Faith."[43] Even after the break from the Roman Catholic Church, Henry and later his daughter Queen Elizabeth I always maintained that they remained Catholics and rejected, by and large, the teachings of Luther, Calvin and other Protestant theologians. Many historians argue that Henry VIII's break from centuries of religious obedience was at base political not theological. The king was quite careful about not falling into what he considered heresy. Henry steered a middle way between Rome and Luther or Calvin and the Pope.

So, what did the average person make of Henry and the break from Rome, the dissolution of the religious houses and the (minor) changes in Christian ritual? Although this question, like so much about the Tudors, remains a subject of much debate, it appears that overall, commoners saw little to complain about. Many, perhaps most, had seen the Church as corrupt and they resented the mandatory payments for sacraments and arbitrary clerical authority, and envied the vast land holdings of the religious orders. When the Crown confiscated Church wealth, most people were indifferent, if not supportive.[44] Soon, there arose a new class of men who would directly profit by purchasing Church holdings from King Henry. By participating in what Rome called "the rape of Mother Church," these people would tie themselves to the fortunes of the Tudor project. A later restoration of papal authority threatened not merely religious reform but the new landowners' very economic wealth.[45] After Henry, Christianity in England would be based on neither papal nor biblical authority—instead, power would lay with the will of the sovereign.[46]

The upheaval caused by the Reformation led to increased possibilities, or what might even be considered freedoms, for common Europeans. At the same time, the shock waves of social change threatened those of the established order who often looked for a scapegoat. The most frequent victims of what has become known as the "Burning Times" of the sixteenth century were Jews, Muslims and largely women accused of being witches. With the former two groups, the element of racial and religious bigotry is pretty apparent.[47] The situation as regards witches needs further investigation. Witches, the vast majority of whom were independent women, were executed in huge numbers.[48] Rather than a local or minor problem, evidence suggests that this was a type of "gender cleansing" of free-spirited women in Reformation Europe.[49] The most notable text used by Catholic authorities (not to suggest that Protestants did not equally engage in witch-hunts) was *Malleus Maleficarum* (*The Hammer of Witches*) published by the Catholic Inquisition in 1485–86. Finding that women were inclined by their very nature toward Satan, much like Jews and Muslims, this book provided the moral and theological justification "for a horrible, endless march of suffering, torture, and human disgrace inflicted on thousands of women."[50]

Despite the fact that witch-hunts took place from the fourteenth through seventeenth century, it is important to note that the period between 1570 and 1630 was the most significant, intense and vicious phase. During these sixty years, around 80 percent of the accused were female. Most usually, the arrested were not only women but also poor, elderly, unmarried, widows and, what one scholar termed, the "vagabonds of the rural or urban working class."[51] There were social considerations as well, since the unrest sweeping Europe had allowed some women to achieve a level of independence that frightened male authorities. This all took place in the context of crisis: feudalism was in decline; the Roman Catholic Church was traumatized by the Reformation, and strong states and monarchies had emerged, as well as an ever more powerful bourgeoisie.

A profusion of crises came about, particularly after the Reformation, to establish a cultural climate of fear. In this atmosphere, witch-hunts flourished since "the devil could be blamed for these woes, it remained merely to identify his human agents … 'cunning women,' midwives and healers became easy targets."[52] Interestingly, these assaults on the common people, and women in particular, were not the exclusive domain of Rome, the Pope, or the Holy Inquisition. While the Catholic authorities arrested, condemned and burned Protestants as witches, Protestants eagerly returned the favor and did the same to Catholics. Meanwhile, both were happy to kill members of their own faith if the "evidence" demanded it. Lutherans joined Calvinists in persecuting the Anabaptists and everyone scapegoated the Jews and Muslims. The connection between the witch paranoia and the Reformation has been established. The brunt of the repression, as so often was the case, fell heavily on women, especially those who refused conventional female roles.[53]

Though often portrayed by historians as passive or even hapless, women were neither. Evidence suggests that assertive women were not isolated exceptions. When women gathered as a social group or community, they posed a perceived threat to the authorities. This was particularly true when these female communities were based in guidance and support for one another on personal and domestic matters. According to records of the Inquisition, Spanish women "shared information about sexual practices among themselves and relied on each other for advice and guidance in intimate matters."[54] In England, many men and not a few women were executed for allegedly committing acts of sodomy.[55] Notably, sexuality, particularly homosexuality, became linked to heresy and ultimately witchcraft.[56] After all, such charges were easy to put forth and difficult to defend against, making them a useful form of social control over women and the lower classes. In other words, those rebels who may have failed to keep their heads down often found themselves executed for crimes, real or invented, other than those that drew the attention of the authorities.

It can be argued that the same social and economic forces that facilitated the Reformation helped give rise to witch-hunts. If the printing press and strong states willing to defy the papacy made the Reformation a success, they also intensified attacks against the commoners. By 1550, the ruling classes

> ... possessed the technological and administrative means of Christian-izing the European peasantry. Carrying uniformly printed Bibles and catechisms and backed by the armed might of centralized principalities, post-Reformation clergy everywhere set out to suppress all unorthodox belief and behaviour.[57]

Therefore, although the Reformation may have freed a portion of Europeans from the exploitation of Rome, it suppressed any attempt to move beyond the limits decreed by Luther, Calvin, or their sponsors. Those who sought to expand the freedom from Rome to a society of justice and equality were crushed without a trace of Christian mercy. The vision of a world where all would be bound by ties of solidarity and freedom was everywhere drowned in blood. Whether Christian communists inspired by Hus or Müntzer, or "cunning" women branded as witches, or simply people who worshipped differently such as Jews and Muslims, the rulers proposed but one choice: submit or perish. The victims came from varying backgrounds, and may have had even conflicting beliefs and practices from one another, but in the end they all posed a threat to Rome and endured much of the same persecution and punishment.

"The World Turned Upside Down": The Crisis of the Seventeenth Century and the English Revolution, 1640–49

Even conservative historians have had to acknowledge that Europe in the middle of the seventeenth century was in a period of revolutionary upheaval. Most famous is the English Revolution that may be said to have run from 1640 till 1660. But other crises marked the period as well. France saw a series of revolts known as the *Frondes*, there was revolution in the Netherlands, an unsuccessful revolt in Catalonia and a victorious rebellion in Portugal. Add to these upheaval in Naples, Bohemia, Ireland and some of the German states and it would seem that European society was in general crisis.[1] For some Marxist historians, this "general crisis" was "the last phase of the general transition from a feudal to a capitalist economy."[2] That is, an economy that had been based on a land-owning nobility was shifting into one run by a capital-owning business class. Wealth increasingly mattered over and above title or nobility, as the old feudal lords lost control over the economy and struggled to maintain their traditional political power. None of these changes took place without disruption, struggle and even violence. The very economic changes that society witnessed caused crisis within portions of society. Though there was rapid industrial development in Switzerland, Sweden and England, production was not uniformly progressing across the continent, and more generally, there was a commercial crisis.[3] In fact, there is even evidence that the average height of Europeans declined during this period due to malnutrition.[4]

For the common people, the seventeenth century was a time of social revolt. To the examples listed above may be added the Swiss peasant war of 1653, the Ukrainian revolution of 1648–54 and various peasant uprisings in Hungary, Russia and Brittany. While there were many causes, like the oft-cited effects of the Thirty Years War (1618–48), a major factor was that the economic expansion of the fifteenth and sixteenth centuries created its own crisis, as "feudal businessmen" struggled to overcome the results of their enrichment.[5] All the different economic aspects of the crisis may be summed up as "economic expansion took place within a social framework which it was not yet strong enough to burst, and in ways adapted to it rather than to the world of modern capitalism."[6]

The seventeenth century saw considerable concentration of economic power, suggesting that the old feudal structure had already been greatly weakened, as witnessed by the inability to revert to an economy of small local producers.[7] Of course, had the English Revolution failed, these economic developments may have been retarded. The rise to Empire accomplished by Britain, it is interesting to note, was done *against* the free trade policy of the Dutch. In fact, the British upheld "protectionist policies backed by aggressive wars for markets."[8] It may come as a slight surprise that this general view of the crisis of the seventeenth century was widely unpopular with many, particularly more conservative, historians. While the details of the various disputes are best left for a scholarly study of historiography, it is notable that half a century later the basic tenets would be supported by fresh research.[9]

Let us now turn to a specific case study of how rebellion developed in the Netherlands. In the late fifteenth and early sixteenth centuries, feudal relations were weakening as capitalist businesses had successfully been established in such diverse economic spheres as textiles, brewing and shipbuilding, while trade became re-organized along non-feudal lines. In the countryside, very profitable dairy farming combined with an increase in other forms of commercial agriculture. By 1600, there were more towns in the Netherlands with over ten thousand inhabitants than in Britain and more than a quarter of the Dutch population lived in one of these urban areas.[10] These shifts all pointed towards future capitalist development. They faced, however, a serious obstacle in the form of Spanish absolutism that did not favor this, or most other forms of socioeconomic change. As the Roman Catholic Church was the most visible supporter of Spanish feudal domination, the more critical or radical elements of Dutch society gravitated towards the Protestant ideas of John Calvin, which by the 1560s had clearly replaced the Anabaptists as the main opposition. The latter had made a credible bid to be the alternative to Catholicism earlier in the century, but that soon diminished with the brutal suppression of the German Peasants Revolt of 1525.[11]

The hand of Spain on the Netherlands grew heavier under the reign of Philip II, who ascended the throne in 1556. His policies limited Dutch economic development, resulting in a decline in the common people's standard of living. By the 1560s, this helped increase the support for

Calvinism which in turn led Spanish officials to order the arrest and execution of heretics. That is to say: Protestants. In August 1566, an uprising broke out in Flanders and spread quickly across all the Netherlands. The revolt heavily targeted Catholic institutions, with thousands of monasteries and churches attacked and looted. By the following summer of 1567, Spanish troops had arrived in some force and carried out what was seen by the residents as a reign of terror. Over ten thousand citizens were charged and many executed. Fierce resistance from the Dutch was aided by German Protestant princes, but the movement was suppressed. A mere four years later, in 1571, Spain introduced a tax that crippled the commercial sectors of the Netherlands, resulting in shop closures, bankruptcies and unemployment. Under the banner of Calvinism, a broad struggle against Spain and, implicitly, feudalism, broke out. The Netherlands was increasingly a commercial society based on trade and led by businessmen, placing them at odds with the agrarian nobility of Spain. A truce was later signed on November 8, 1576, that established peace between the Calvinist northern and Catholic southern provinces.

After years of conflict, both covert and open, the Protestant north inflicted a series of defeats on Spain. In 1609, Spain accepted the de facto independence of the United Provinces of the Netherlands. By 1648, this new Dutch Republic was given international recognition in the Treaty of Westphalia. Although it was the common people who did the majority of the fighting, dying and suffering during these decades of struggle, the fruits of victory fell to the big commercial capitalists who dominated the Netherlands. This was not the end of matters. The masses of common people would continue to struggle against their domination by commercial elites in variegated ways.

The Dutch uprisings illustrate the importance of popular self-activity. Thus, rising food prices were behind a dozen riots and eighteen demonstrations in the seventy years before 1760. Meanwhile tax riots were more common and more violent, with thirty-eight riots and seventy lesser protests largely in the period 1600–1750.[12] Dutch women were active in these as well as other political riots.[13] To cite only a few examples, in 1624 a tax riot saw a woman shouting: "Instead of introducing new taxes on butter, my children should [be fed]."[14] Later in 1672 in Brill, fishwives surrounded the mayor and lifted their skirts, causing him no little discomfort. There are many "cases in which men were humiliated by women, which made their humiliation even more shameful. During riots women ruled, and men were forced to obey."[15] This is all taking place in the context of a Netherlands that was the dominant financial power in Europe and the core of the world economy in the seventeenth century.[16]

Popular unrest was far from limited to the Low Countries during the seventeenth century. In Central Europe, the end of the Thirty Years War[17] led to the revival of the southern German economy. This in turn caused economic distress among the Swiss, notably among the peasantry. The decline in exports and a devastation of the currency conspired with growing hostility towards the concentration of urban power to produce the Swiss peasants' war in 1653. From the rural population, armies were created, and a representative assembly gathered on February 10, 1653. The idea of having representative gatherings was far from unknown during the medieval period. Mainly, they served as window dressing for the actual power brokers, who remained the nobility. The 1653 assembly differed in that it was an institution thrown up by the common people themselves. It was decided to suspend all tax payments until the authorities agreed to a reduction in financial demands. The Swiss peasants were particularly upset by taxes on cattle, salt and horse trades. At first, negotiations between the elite and commoners seemed promising, but an impasse was soon reached. The authorities thought the revolt could be crushed, while peasant rebels were attempting to organize new support in hitherto unaffected rural areas.

In April 1653, the Huttwil League was formed on the part of the peasants. It is significant, in the context of the times, that the new organization united Catholics and Protestants across the land, in a movement based upon class rather than confessional considerations. The urban-based elite found itself in a dilemma, as they normally recruited their soldiers from the very same peasantry that was now in revolt. The Zürich urban elite hired an army of 8,000 soldiers from unaffected rural areas. When these troops marched on a peasant army that was 24,000 strong, they routed the more numerous rebels. One immediate result was the Huttwil League was ordered to be dissolved.

The victors promised the defeated peasants an amnesty for all but their most important leaders. These proved to be empty words, as a vast purge reached well beyond anyone who could be considered a leader. The rural population was disarmed and, in some regions, forced to pay for the cost of suppressing the rebellion. The peasant losers in this class war were first defeated and then required to bear the cost of their enemies' expenses. Although the peasant revolt apparently failed, from a historical point of view, it is interesting that it was a national and class, rather than a local or religiously, based movement. In the long run, the revolt was not completely without success for the rural insurgents. Rulers, fearing another revolt in the future, quietly granted many of the peasants' original economic demands.[18]

Another incident of profound unrest, this one in Naples, deserves a brief mention. By 1650, Naples had a population of much more than 250,000 and was well known for both its wealth and instability. In 1646, Spain sent the Duke of Arcos to Naples to rapidly collect huge sums in the hope of propping up the finances of the cash-strapped Hapsburg Empire. When a tax was raised on fruit, the duke all but guaranteed mass discontent. The son of a fisherman, named Masaniello, led a demonstration of young, unemployed workers and a riot soon broke out. The duke's armed defenders, dispatched to the scene to restore order, were pelted with fruit by the youths who were often referred to in the historical literature as "street urchins." The defenders' assault failed in the face of determined resistance.

Masaniello led a thousand-strong crowd that seized arms depots and freed those in prison. It was quickly apparent that Masaniello and his supporters were in control of Naples. To placate the angry citizens, the government gave him honors and proclaimed Masaniello to be captain-general of the people. Of course, the old powers were far from accepting the situation passively. To regain power, they had their newly minted "captain-general" assassinated and repealed the hated fruit tax. When order still could not be restored, the rulers appealed to Spain for help. The Hapsburgs finally regained power in April 1648 by using Spanish troops. Unrest and crisis, as noted previously, was widespread throughout seventeenth-century Europe up to and including the Ottoman Empire.[19]

Few serious historians would doubt the widespread unease amongst the common people at various times during the 1600s.[20] While social tensions between the people and those who controlled the commanding heights of society were present throughout seventeenth-century Europe, it was to be England where a successful revolution would have lasting, historical consequences.[21] Although what is sometimes called reductively the "English Civil War" is often thought to be about religion, there is evidence that class relations were primary and theology was a secondary means of whipping up popular emotions. Numerous contemporaries understood matters in this way, including Oliver Cromwell,[22] who was to become the leader of the New Model Army and ultimately dictator of a (brief-lived) non-monarchical England. The New Model Army was original in that it was a national army rather than a federation of regional armies, as was the case with King Charles's forces. It operated under a merit promotion system within the ranks that allowed for the rapid promotion of those who showed talent and courage; likewise, rapid demotion threatened those wanting in the necessary martial skills and attitudes. High birth did not assure, nor did low birth preclude, important appointments.

To understand the massive outpouring of opposition to King Charles I in London and elsewhere, it is important to look at the populace's economic situation. While Europe in the seventeenth century was notable for its lack of equalitarian societies, the gulf between rich and poor was especially glaring in England. A population explosion in the 150 years before 1640 resulted in an almost 300 percent increase in the number of stomachs that needed to be filled. Food production had not kept pace; as a result, food prices increased more rapidly than those of other commodities. The price of cheap grains, the mainstay of poorer English people, increased most of all.

Had the vast majority of the people still had access to at least some agricultural land, the impact would have been mitigated. Throughout the Tudor era, vast sections of the populace had been forced from the land and were ever more dependent on wage labor. Earlier, many of the poor had survived by access to the commons, that is, land that belonged to the community where the poor could hunt, gather firewood for heating or even plant modest-sized crops. More and more the wealthy had closed off or enclosed the commons and made it private rather than public property. One motivation for this was the growing need for land for raising sheep to supply the wool trade. Thus, as early as the reign of Henry VIII, Sir Thomas More could remark that England had become a land where sheep eat men. Having lost their land or access to the commons, many more than before were forced to buy food at market prices. Existing conflicts between rich and poor now saw growing tension, with merchants, nobles and rich farmers on one side and the bulk of the population on the other.[23] This would not have been sufficient cause for a revolution in and of itself as the long-suffering patience of average people is legendary, but it was an important precondition. In this context, it is little wonder that people often destroyed the enclosure fences that led to so much poverty.[24] As noted, these fences had prevented the rural poor from grazing their animals, collecting firewood, or trapping small animals on the common lands that had for centuries provided the thin margin that allowed many of the rural poor to survive.

Much has been made of the marriage of Charles I to Henrietta Maria, Catholic daughter of France's King Henri IV in June, 1625. No doubt this was a matter of no little concern for those who feared the kingdom's return to papal obedience would violate their conscience or cause the Church lands they had obtained from Henry VIII to be put at risk. In the secular sphere, Charles I undertook a series of actions that suggested he had little of the sensitivity to the common people that many of his predecessors had. Though the Tudor monarchs like Henry VII,[25] Henry VIII and his daughter Elizabeth I made more pretence than practice in advancing the well-being of their subjects, Charles I seemed completely tone-deaf to the feelings of those below him. For over a decade, Charles ruled England without the advice or consent of Parliament. While Parliament had limited power, it did have the power to raise taxes. It had two houses, the House of Lords, made up of wealthy titled men, and the House of Commons, made up of men without titles but with money. Elections for this house were limited to men and to a small minority of very wealthy men at that. Although the House of Commons was hardly a radical rabble, Charles managed to alienate the property owners with his tax policy, the lower classes due to their poverty and the religiously zealous Protestants with the reputed Catholic influence of the Queen. This king retreated from previous Tudor practice and returned to "the old politics of ruling without parliament and without patience for church reformers of any variety."[26]

When, in April 1640, Charles I summoned together Parliament to vote in taxes for his unpopular war with Scotland, this being the one real power the Houses had, he found the members disinclined to support his wishes unless he would be willing to grant a number of demands increasing the power of Parliament. The leaders of the House of Commons were more than willing to compromise. Yet, after a mere three weeks, the king dissolved Parliament and sought other fund sources. He went so far as to attempt to raise loans from Spain, France and the Pope. These and further efforts were all in vain. Having run out of alternatives, Charles I was forced to recall Parliament in November. The elections were brilliantly managed by Charles's enemies to ensure an anti-Court majority. It is little surprise that the Crown and Parliament clashed almost constantly. Parliament defied the king's authority and passed laws trimming the power of royal courts, establishing a regular meeting of the legislature and declaring all taxes passed without the consent of Parliament to be illegal. In a comic attempt to regain control, the king assembled a large crowd of swordsmen and led them into the House of Commons to arrest the radical leadership of that body. All, however, had fled in plenty of time.

In 1642, the king fled London and called on his feudal barons to rise up with armies to put down the impertinent commoners and their bourgeois leaders. This started the Civil War that would ravish England. Although one would assume the Royal forces would have overwhelming military superiority, this was not the case. The king's men were not as formidable as they might have been in an earlier age. The Parliamentary forces led by the extremely able Oliver Cromwell were innovative, utilizing the newest European military knowledge. Moreover, Cromwell created a national army bound together by at least some sense of purpose. As discussed prior, in Cromwell's New Model Army, ability often counted more than birth in terms of promotion whereas the Royalist army was mired in the dead weight of tradition.

Space does not allow a full recounting of the military campaigns fought until Cromwell's popular forces defeated the royal military at Naseby in June, 1645. Soon thereafter, the victors began to disagree over what should be done next. Much of Parliament was content to consolidate the anti-Royalist gains of the first years of rebellion, most of all the greatly enhanced power of the wealthy commoners' representatives in the House of Commons. Beyond this, there existed a large number of radicals in the New Model Army. These radicals, whatever divisions existed between them, were united in the idea that things could and should change much more fundamentally than the moderates in the House of Commons wished. At first, Cromwell was willing to listen to these new ideas but as the agitators moved beyond disobeying Parliament to discussing far more revolutionary democratic ideas, the army leadership parted company with them.

Charles I learned little from his defeat. He continued to believe that he was God's chosen ruler and plotted a return to absolute divine right rule. He was also not the cleverest of men: he wove plots and conspiracies by writing to those he hoped would support him, communications the agents of Parliament easily and systematically intercepted. He had, from the radical view, committed treason as well as broken his word. Some wished to quietly dispose of him, a fate that has befallen so many monarchs throughout the ages. The argument won out within Cromwell's leaders that he should be given a trial. Charles I was tried, found guilty and executed in public. Kings have often been murdered but to legally execute the sovereign ... this had not been done before. This set the precedent that no one, not even the monarch, was above the law or the nation.

As he had driven conservatives from Parliament, Cromwell now threw radicals into prison. He distracted the army from radical ideas with a vicious and successful war against the Catholic Irish. He settled his soldiers on Irish land expropriated from its Irish owners. Growing intolerant of criticism even from the rump of Parliament, Cromwell issued a new constitution with power given to him as "Lord Protector." Like George Washington 150 years later, Cromwell was offered the Crown. And, just like Washington, he rejected it. But unlike his later colonial counterpart,

Cromwell died in 1658 before a clear political order could be organized. On his death, Cromwell's son Richard became Lord Protector but the Army's revolutionary energy was soon exhausted. Thus, a new Parliament restored the Stuarts, Charles I's royal family, by giving the Crown to Charles II on conditions that protected the newly ascendant bourgeoisie's property interests and religious leanings.

The most widespread democratic ideas that Cromwell felt bound to suppress were those of radicals called the "Levellers." Named because of their supposed desire to make all equal or to level society, these radicals were mostly from London and notably non-religious.[27] This group, which rejected the name given to them, were less radical than alleged, as they wanted the vote only for men with property and excluded women, servants and the homeless. They wanted the right to work their own land and to have some real say over their lives. In seventeenth-century England, they represented something new and, to the wealthy, subversive. In our day, the New Model Army rebels have been seen by one British radical author

> ... as workers struggling to maintain control over their own labour by organizing themselves into a military soviet ... [struggling to see whether the English Revolution] ... would be the bourgeois revolution of a new capitalist ruling class, or a democratic revolution of small producers."[28]

Even more radical, if far less significant, is the group called the "Diggers," led by Gerrard Winstanley. In various published tracts, he argued for a community based on the abolition of individual possessions and even money. Abolishing and redistributing private property would benefit all of England, Winstanley argued, as he wrote what we might call the outline of a utopian socialist theory.[29]

The Diggers movement never amounted to anything approaching the significance of the Levellers. Diggers' occupations of untilled soil were short-lived and posed little difficulty for authorities when it was determined that they were a public nuisance. At the same time, the Diggers movement, so weak in practice, was to become a beacon of inspiration to later generations of radicals. Winstanley began as a Christian dreamer and after years of conflict with the authorities, evolved into a secular thinker.[30] His message that "there shall be no buying and selling of the earth nor of the fruits thereof"[31] remains a powerful vision.

With the execution of Charles as a traitor to the nation on January 30, 1649, divine right was crushed forever in England. When conservative reaction to popular radicalism led Parliament to invite Charles II to return home and be king, it was to be monarch, not by God's will but by assent of an elected legislature. It would be easy to see the English Revolution as a failure or even, as is often said, a short period of disorder in the otherwise peaceful, gradual evolution of society. The reality is that a fundamental transformation had taken place. Divine right monarchy had been superseded by a monarchy that ruled not by the grace of God, but by the grace of Parliament. Now, the king could lead, but all the basic policies of the realm had to have Parliament's approval. The capitalist classes gained more security for their investments and freedom from arbitrary royal taxation. The rising bourgeoisie, in both town and countryside, no longer had to fear the old nobility. A century of bitter arguments over religion were largely laid to rest. The revolution made England a capitalist nation ready to embark into industrialization in the next century without the dead weight of the old aristocracy. The new moneyed class had eclipsed the nobles economically, while the increased importance of the House of Commons, elected by men of property not noble birth, now limited the nobility's political influence. The half-century after the English Revolution saw wages rise significantly above other European nations.[32] Moreover, this was reflected physically, as the British appear to have become, by at least the eighteenth century if not earlier, the tallest Europeans, with the Dutch very close in height. Meanwhile, the French and Spanish were significantly shorter, often explained by the nutritional deprivation suffered by so many under the feudal system.[33] Economic data further indicates that northern Europe's relative prosperity was due, not to cheap labor, but high productivity,[34] which can be argued, was a result of the bourgeois revolutions.

Now, it was wealth based on trade, banking and soon, industrial innovation, that mattered. Tradition was still paid lip service but what really mattered was production and results that could be recorded on the market. The old nobles were still in office in the House of Lords and a king sat on the throne. These men still had the trappings of power, but not real power itself. That resided with the new class who everywhere in the nation grew richer, bolder and more prominent.

CHAPTER FOUR

The Rise of the Third Estate:
The French People Revolt

Legend has it that Chinese Premier Zhou Enlai was once asked his opinion of the French Revolution. He is reported to have responded, "It is too soon to say."[1] For better or worse, few have followed this example of withholding judgment. Within the English-speaking world, the image implanted upon millions of minds is one of crazed French revolutionaries running amok, as depicted in the famous Charles Dickens work, *A Tale of Two Cities*.[2] Not only has this book sold hundreds of millions of copies,[3] there have been four silent films and at least three sound movies not to mention comic books, television and radio adaptations. A revenge-crazed woman actually knits to the rhythm of the guillotine's blade lopping off the heads of condemned counter-revolutionaries. This chapter will attempt to show that Dickens, among many others, was promoting an anti-French, anti-revolutionary bias and did not allow facts to complicate his opinions.

This bias is not limited to Dickens or nineteenth-century Britain. In the United States, it is far from difficult to run across the same type of narrative. Films have often shown the French revolutionaries as mobs of crazed rabble with an irrational blood lust.[4] This is significant, since films so often create impressions in the viewer that resist even the most documented historical refutation. One example is the American film, *Marie Antoinette*, made in 2006. Devoting itself to ignoring everything of historical importance, this movie, in the words of a *San Francisco Chronicle* critic, "is an extended brief extolling the all-embracing exuberance and sterling humanity of rich girls who like to shop."[5] The unstated message of *Marie Antoinette*, at least to many better-off English speakers who have already read *A Tale of Two Cities* in high school, may well be: why would those evil commoners kill such a cool girl?

All of this is to argue that we should try to approach the revolt of the common people in France without accepting the dominant narrative with which most of us have been raised. Few events have changed the course of history the way the French Revolution did. Nor as noted before, have most events suffered such a sustained history of libel. What contemporaries saw as a brilliant, if at times confused, movement towards freedom, democracy and human solidarity[6] has been reduced to a caricature. This negative image is often tinged with anti-female and ethnic biases. In 1790, conservative author Edmund Burke intellectually assassinated the revolution,[7] while US slave owners were terrified by the revolution's abolition of slavery.[8] Once former slaves established a government in the French colony now known as Haiti, President Jefferson did all he could to convince the French to crush the blacks, even offering American assistance.[9] Even in France today, rejection of the revolution is part of the neo-fascist movements' credo. As one member of the far-right National Front stated, "France died in 1789, and what we're left with now—it's disgusting."[10]

So if it was not mere bloodlust that motivated the French revolutionaries, what did? Why was there a revolution in eighteenth-century France? It was certainly not that France was a poor or backward country compared with her European neighbors. On the contrary, France was one of the great powers of the Western world. In the 1780s, she had just humiliated Britain, the world's greatest naval power, by intervening in North America to make possible a successful war of independence for thirteen of Britain's North American colonies. Still, however advanced France was in many ways, the country remained ruled by feudal elite of king, nobility and Church. With this unholy trinity in charge, the remainder of the French people were forced to pay heavy taxes for foreign wars, the luxury of the royal Court, the unrestrained living of the nobles and high Church officials. Peasants were subject to feudal regulation and forced labor, while all had to pay the hated dime (10 percent tax) to the Church.

As the nation had grown in wealth, urban areas had become more important as centers of unrest. A popular political culture developed in towns that sought to better the social, economic and political positions of the urban populace.[11] Moreover, among intellectuals within the bourgeoisie, the ideas that formed the foundations of the old order were being subverted by the ideas of the Enlightenment. Thinkers influenced by the Enlightenment believed in reason and change, while the old order was based on belief and tradition. Naturally, different thinkers advocated various, often conflicting, theories but two commonalities among almost all were an attack in one way or another upon tradition and an openness to some type of popular rule. For many businessmen, such theories only added an intellectual gloss onto the resentment they felt watching their class counterparts across the English Channel ruling through Parliament with the British king an important, but not all-powerful chief executive. That tens of thousands of French soldiers had served in North America during the anti-British revolution meant that many had become influenced by radical ideas of self-government.

Despite all these developments, feudal France may well have limped onward for a time had it not been for a conjuncture of circumstances. First, the decadence of the French ruling classes had reached the point where few understood that things had to change if they were to remain largely the same. One notable exception to this was Lafayette, a liberal noble and aid to George Washington. At the apex of the noble pyramid, sat King Louis XVI, a particularly inept, if not downright stupid monarch. Added to this politically lethal cocktail was his insensitive and self-absorbed foreign wife, Marie Antoinette. While she most likely never actually told starving French who had no bread that they should eat cake instead, it is just the sort of thing she might have said. The fact that the queen was Austrian played into the growing nationalism of sections of France's population. Through her weak husband, the king, it was thought she ruled France with scant regard for the French people.

Yet, there were more concrete reasons behind the revolutionary upsurge. There was, in fact, a material basis to the discontent that pushed the French common people to throw off centuries of tradition and revolt. This can be seen if we compare the plight of Paris, the heart of the revolution, with other European cities. By combining real wages with the cost of living, economic historians have devised a welfare index. Using this tool, it is possible to see real differences between Paris and other bourgeois urban areas within Western Europe. A score of "1" on the index means a barely acceptable standard of living. Above "1" would mean that certain personal luxury items might be purchased, while below "1" suggests a family would be unable to have what was then considered a decent life.[12]

In the period 1750–99, building craftsmen had a ratio of 1.20 in Paris, above the level of bare survival but far below London (2.21) and Amsterdam (1.83). For the less skilled in Paris, the data suggest an even harder life. While laborers in the French capital had a score of only 0.74, their London counterparts were at 1.42, with Amsterdam close behind at 1.41.[13] Put another way, Parisian laborers lived a life of desperation as members of the working poor. By contrast, those in the same occupational category in London and Amsterdam had enough left over to save or buy new consumer luxuries like sugar or tobacco. Why were the people of Paris so much poorer? There are many theories but at the time revolutionaries attributed this to the corruption and exploitation of the French feudal rulers. Note that these numbers, like all statistics, should be approached with great care. They are indicative but far from definitive in their description of past realities. Nonetheless, such huge differences suggests that Parisian workers lived only half as well as workers in London or Amsterdam. Fairly, one might ask did the revolution made any significant changes? Taking the period 1800–49, that is after the achievements of the revolution were largely safeguarded, the numbers show important improvements for both craftsmen (1.20 to 1.72) and laborers (0.74 to 1.08). By contrast, during the exact same years, London and Amsterdam largely showed decline or stagnation.[14]

So having insensitive and incompetent rulers, as noted above, is never good for a regime even in the best of times. As the statistics just discussed indicate, France in the 1780s was not experiencing the best of times. Rather, it was marked by food shortages, unemployment and poverty combined with a low standard of living, while the government was saddled with a huge public debt that reduced the king's room for granting concessions. This debt had not been helped by the great amount of resources spent to help the American rebels defeat the British Empire, and reached crisis point when the privileged feudal lords refused to aid the national treasury. In desperation, Louis XVI called together a long-dormant type of feudal parliament, the Estates-General, in the hope of solving the crisis. The Estates-General was divided into three houses or estates: clergy, nobility, and everyone else. Each house had a single vote, which meant that the Third Estate, despite representing well over 90 percent of the population, could always be outvoted by the nobles and high Church officials. Not assembled since 1614, the Estates-General met on May 5, 1789.

It soon became apparent that most representatives of the Third Estate refused to play their assigned part in this elaborate farce. They had instead arrived with long lists of complaints, demands and a thirst for fundamental reform. The elected representatives of the Third Estate quickly insisted on a voting system that would be one member, one vote, rather than each Estate having a vote. Some even argued that the Third Estate was the true representative of the people. After a feeble attempt to disband them, the Third Estate declared itself the National Assembly and swore to meet until a just constitution had been obtained. Of course, factions soon developed in the Assembly, one of the most notable being the Jacobin political club that would play a major role in the events of 1793–94. Uncertain, maybe even confused, Louis XVI legalized the National Assembly on June 27. A few weeks later, a crowd mobilized on July 14 and stormed the infamous Bastille Prison. This took on a symbolic importance far beyond the actual importance of seizing one jail. The Bastille was infamous as the place where the French kings sent political prisoners to suffer and often die. It was so much more than a penal institution: it was a symbol of much that was hated in the old order.

Many see this as the masses entering the stage of history—notably it is celebrated as France's National Day. The events of July 14, 1789 were, are and no doubt will remain clouded in controversy. The Left celebrates the storming of the Bastille as an act of liberation, while the Right sees only violence and disorder. This sort of division is inevitable. Commenting on two completely contradictory accounts of that day, one by a monarchist and the other by a radical, one historian notes "no matter how honest the two men may have been, the event described by one has quite different flavour from that described by the other."[15] It is true that only some hundreds of citizens were directly involved in the assault on the famous prison, but it has been argued by George Rudé, a scholar who helped pioneer looking at history from the bottom up, said that it was the business "of the people of Paris as a whole," with a minimum of 250,000 citizens armed in defense of the revolution by that time.[16] As for the violence unleashed in the taking of the Bastille, it has been argued that it is surprising how few, maybe seven, defenders were actually killed given the violence previously visited upon the radicals.[17] Further, rather than being criminals or the so-called dregs of society, the people who threw themselves against the prison were more representative of Paris's population than we might suspect. A careful study of the crowd finds that besides soldiers, "about two-thirds [were] small workshop masters, craftsmen, and journeymen ... the remainder [were] engaged in manufacture, distribution, building, the professions and general trades."[18]

Yet, why were the common people of Paris so outraged? Had they, as critics of the revolution have charged, been manipulated by power-hungry ideologues? Actually, there was a much more clear reason for the Parisian anger: bread. It is well to remember that bread was the basic article of food consumption in eighteenth-century France. Earlier in the century, the wage earner spent around half their income on bread. But, during the economic crisis of 1788–89, the portion of income spent on bread "rose to an average of 58 per cent; in the months of famine and top-level prices of 1789, it soared to the fantastic figure of 88 per cent."[19] It is likely more than mere coincidence that the Bastille fell on the day that grain prices hit their cyclical peak.[20] In fact, there is evidence that high prices and scarcity of bread acted as the main stimulant to the popular movements of 1789.[21] Nor was this a problem only in Paris; a study of Bordeaux noted that "subsistence at any level among the peasantry and industrial proletariat of eighteen century France was largely dependent on bread."[22] People may not live on bread alone but, at least in eighteenth-century France, without enough they went hungry. If there was no bread at all, they might even die of starvation.

Pressure from the common people led the National Assembly to officially abolish feudalism in France in August 1789. This meant that all the old rights and privileges of the feudal lords were gone. For example, they now had to pay taxes like anyone else and could be brought before courts for suspected wrongdoing, just like everyone else. By the end of the month, the famous "Rights of Man and the Citizen" was proclaimed. In a sign that woman would henceforth play an important role in France's affairs, a crowd of female citizens marched on the Royal Palace at Versailles in October. With a boldness that belies claims of female passivity, the women forced Louis XVI and his family to return to Paris. During the struggle that this demand precipitated, the women even killed a number of the royals' elite Swiss guards. This is often noted. That many of these same women had perhaps watched their children suffer from hunger is absent from most textbooks. Returning the monarch, whom the crowd of women called "the baker," to the heart of the French capital was far more than symbolic. Many believed that with the Bourbon king and queen back in the urban heartland, it would be easier to intimidate the royals by demonstrations and protests so they would be pressured into solving the people's needs.

Besides the power of the Bourbon monarchy, the people had to contend with the might of the Roman Catholic Church, one of, if not the, largest landowners in France. To undercut their power, in November 1789, the Church's property was expropriated by the National Assembly, which spoke in the name of the majority of France, the Third Estate. This singular strike crippled one of the most powerful pillars of the old order—a lesson in dealing with faith-based organizations that England's Henry VIII had learned more than two centuries earlier. This was followed by legislation that still embitters the far Right: the removal, in the early months of 1790, of all restrictions on France's Jews, who could now work in the civil service, openly practice their religion and enjoy the full rights of citizenship. By halfway through 1790, religious orders were suppressed and the nobility's rights and titles abolished. Of course, the Pope responded by excommunicating the French.

These measures indicate a clear rejection of centuries of feudalism and social tradition. Naturally, the new laws and customs were unpopular in certain parts of the population who could not imagine a France without the leadership of Crown and Cross. Interestingly, some lower clergy had been swept into the revolutionary reflection. Jean Meslier had been a poor country priest in the Champagne region who criticized the powerful for abusing the peasants. Before his death only a few decades before the revolution, Meslier had concluded, "All religions are nothing but error, illusion and imposture."[23]

What was taking place was an ever more radical bourgeois government being put under pressure from an even more radical popular movement, at least in Paris. In reality, there had always been a clear division between what the Assembly members wanted and the goals of the radical commoners. While the better-off lawyers and professionals who made up the government agreed about abolishing the privileges of the feudal lords and the Church, they were also committed to laissez-faire economics and representative government, as opposed to any type of more direct democracy. While radical Paris agreed about political equality, they also wanted social and economic equality. If the bourgeoisie wanted a government like Britain's or the United States', radicals demanded something more democratic. If the former sought free markets, the latter wanted bread and the free market could be damned. The famous, if lightly documented, story of a radical leader abruptly leaving a group of friends at a café is indicative. Seeing a crowd march past, the man jumped up and said, "I must follow them because I am their leader." When in 1791, the black citizens of French colonies were given equal rights, a gulf larger than the Atlantic opened between France and the United States. American slave owners were not impressed with all these rights-of-man arguments applying to those of African descent. Meanwhile in France, the common people appear to have been mainly satisfied with their own situation as the price of essential goods such as bread, wine and so on remained favorable until fall 1791.[24]

Throughout the revolution, women became more interested in and involved in politics. This even carried over into the private sphere, where women sometimes acted in a way that had political undertones.[25] Women in the revolution often only appear in the popular mind as maladjusted criminals à la the characters of Dickens's imagination. In reality, despite overwhelming male prejudice that ultimately marginalized female voices, women were important actors in the events under discussion. As early as November 1789, the National Assembly received feminist proposals, crafted by educated women in part but largely the effort of working women in Paris, "that attacked the economic subordination of women and the evils of convent life."[26] Although the male politicians took no serious action in response to this and other petitions, women failed to remain passive. In 1791, for example, a feminist declaration circulated throughout the Paris region. Following closely on the outlines of the famous "rights of man," the text declared "all women are born free and remain equal to men in rights

... the aim of all political associations is the presentation of the natural and inalienable rights of women and men."[27] In the final analysis, revolutionary feminism no doubt made mistakes and was unable to achieve broad popularity. Yet, it was the inability of men to comprehend it and break free of century-old prejudices that helped to defeat it.[28]

Not all conflicts originated within the republican camp. When in 1791, Louis XVI attempted to flee Paris with his family, he was doubtlessly hoping to remove himself from the eye of the revolutionary storm. Under pressure from reactionary nobles and his wife, the king desired to be free to organize counter-revolutionary activities with an eye to the restoration of a divine right monarchy. When forcefully returned in disgrace to the French capital, the anti-revolutionary faction of the old ruling class maintained their confidence that the old order could still be restored. Less than a month later, a radical crowd illustrated that many commoners had different ideas. The protesters clashed with the National Guard, still under the king's command, as they pressed their opposition to the king's restoration to executive power. In the chaos of the confrontation, the Marquis de Lafayette, former aide to and life-long friend of George Washington, ordered his troops to open fire, resulting in the massacre of many of the assembled French citizens. Although he always remained a favorite of America's rulers, Lafayette was now hopelessly compromised in the eyes of popular Paris. When he fled his native France the following year, it was notable that he chose to go to arch-reactionary, monarchical Austria rather than more moderate Britain or America.[29]

This utilization of murderous force dispersed *that* particularly popular mobilization, but the violence of the old order failed to stop the revolution. Being convinced that the order to shoot protesters had come from the king, many no longer could support the idea of even a constitutional monarchy. In 1792, war broke out with the French queen's native land of Austria. By summer, the Duke of Brunswick, a German-speaking feudal lord, was calling for foreign intervention against the French people. In August, radical crowds of commoners, many supporters of the Jacobin political club, stormed the palace, arrested and imprisoned the Bourbon royal family. In mainstream narratives, the fact that the radicals were forced to kill well-paid, Swiss mercenaries to get at the royals is highlighted. On the other hand, the fact that the king and queen had committed—and continued to commit—treason against their country and its people is often not worthy of mention. For what else could one call conspiring with foreign powers to militarily invade their own country if not treason?

In September, a general mobilization of (male) citizens gives birth to a massive army sent to the front to repel foreign invaders. Later that same month, the elected government abolishes the monarchy and France becomes a republic. Then, on December 11, 1792, what had been unthinkable only a few years before happens. Louis XVI, King of France by Grace of God, is put on trial like a common criminal. Having been convicted, Louis XVI goes to his execution proclaiming: "I die innocent." This represents a remarkable historical shift. As one author commented:

> At first, Louis XVI was not revered as a man, but as the embodiment of divinely sanctioned monarchy ... [after his attempted flight from Paris] ... He was discredited as a traitor in popular consciousness. On the day he "kissed Madame Guillotine" in January 1793, the idea of monarchy died with him."[30]

In response to foreign aggression, the next month France officially declared war on Britain and Holland. In April 1793, elected representatives established a Committee of Public Safety. Their hope was that a small group with concentrated power might be able to save France from the ruinous foreign assaults and unending royalist plots within. One of the committee's first actions was to fix a maximum price for bread, so that the masses would not go hungry. Bakers were forbidden to produce cakes for the rich as all meager grain reserves had to be used to make the "people's bread." This early example of war rationing took place in what may rightly be called a Jacobin dictatorship, as the leaders of that political club wielded almost all effective power. Jacobinism was a radical but clearly bourgeois movement. The common people of Paris—the "sans-culottes" as they are often referred to because they could not afford the expensive pants or culottes of the rich—continued to affirm the idea of direct democracy. They did so in the face of the hostility from the national government as represented by the Committee of Public Safety. To the committee, the unruly democracy of the neighborhood meetings was undermining their control and, by extension, the revolution. Much contended was the matter of whether the revolution would result in only formal political equality or genuine social equality.[31] The fear whispered through the common slums was that the revolution would create new institutions, but leave them dominated by the rich. This provoked radicals such as Jean-Paul Marat to demand a radical state that would place power firmly in the hands of the people.[32]

Meanwhile, women had not only political demands but also more immediate economic concerns. The revolution caused great economic upheaval and among other results was the collapse of the luxury goods trade. This brought about extreme hardship for the many women working in that industry. In response, the National Assembly created spinning workshops. Those female workers fortunate enough to gain a place—there were always more applicants than jobs—spun thread for both private and government use. During the crisis years of 1793–94, these workshops became "centers of war production and produced almost exclusively for the war effort."[33] The period 1793–94 was not an easy one for revolutionary France. The economy was in chaos and foreign armies threatened the revolution's very existence. Paris seemed awash with traitors, both real and imagined. Many doubted that the revolution could survive.

The Reign of Terror was a period of repression that remains forever linked to the name Robespierre. A leading member of the Assembly and the Jacobin Club, Maximilien Robespierre was a supporter of democracy and considered himself a friend of the poor. Still, he felt there must be limits and opposed the idea of the De-Christianization of France. During the Reign of Terror, he did not hesitate to execute those who demanded a more egalitarian society or launched assaults against property rights. The Reign of Terror was actually an operation designed to put a brake "on the legitimate violence of the people and [give] a public and institutional form to vengeance. Terror as justice was thus a desperate and despairing attempt to constrain both political crime and the legitimate popular vengeance."[34] In other words, the Terror was a tool against counter-revolution but, at the same time, an attempt to channel popular anger into forms acceptable to the bourgeois, albeit radical, governmental apparatus. The Committee of Public Safety was troubled not just by royalist plots but also by movements of the people demanding more equality and a more radical form of democracy. The response to critics from the Left was just as deadly as to monarchical conspiracies. When Robespierre and the committee were challenged by radicals who decried the drift towards dictatorship and opposed non-noble privilege as they had rejected aristocratic rights, the response was swift and deadly, as the dissenters were send to the guillotine.[35]

Although the radical grouping's actual numbers are difficult to calculate, it is clear that there existed within the revolution those who sought a socialist solution to the problems facing Republican France. That is, they wanted a France of social equals, not a nation of rich and poor. For all their radical rhetoric, Robespierre and his allies in the government, whether Jacobin or not, were far from socialists or proponents of social equality. As one historian summed up, "the leading parties had more in common with each other and feared each other less than an incipient proletarian group."[36]

Robespierre increasingly attacked critics as often as serious counter-revolutionaries; his position grew untenable as he became unpopular with both radical commoners demanding more social equality as well as moderate bourgeois who wanted stability. While his fall has been extensively documented and commented upon, the role of the average French citizen has not. Accounts always, with reason, point to the crisis caused by war and counter-revolution. What is often left unsaid is the passionate involvement of men and women determined to make their own history. When they thought of democracy, they thought it meant the people should forcefully involve themselves in the affairs of France.[37]

After the end of the Terror, a more moderate republicanism came to dominate the government. While wars continued, the new government, known as the Directory (*Directoire*), ended the previous policy of subsidizing basic necessities such as bread. Establishing a more stable currency and more moderate policies did not prevent corruption from becoming a major problem for the Directory.[38] By 1795, the rightward drift of the government resulted in the end of the workshop experiment, of such importance to many, especially women. Rather than exhibiting only passivity, women and some male radicals demonstrated against the termination of this form of female public employment. In the end, the forces of governmental order prevailed. The point should be made, however, that in spite of ultimate defeat, these activities "illustrate how the women workers, could and did participate in the revolutionary process."[39] Even with their limited political rights, French women fought for their interests. In the long run, the exclusion of women from the public sphere and the limitation of their rights show that male radicals set clear limits to the exercise of the universal rights they had proclaimed.[40]

Gathering support from alienated radicals and the urban poor, Francois "Gracchus" Babeuf, a man without any great political or social standing, put forth what may be the first socialist program in France. Reacting to the rightward drift of the revolution under the Directory, Babeuf organized a conspiracy to overthrow the government and establish a society of equals. While small in number, his supporters were still important enough for the government to crush them in 1795–96. Though they lost, their words survive in the *Manifesto of the Equals*. Among other things, it declared, "Let disappear, once for all, the revolting distinction of rich and poor, of great and small, of masters and valets, of governors and governed!"[41]

Under assault from critics from both left and right, this government paved the way for the "restoration of order" by Napoleon Bonaparte. In a *coup d'état* in November 1799, General Bonaparte established a military dictatorship, first dressing himself up as the "First Consul" and later "Emperor." Tired and fearful of the demands of the common citizens, the better-off longed for an end to radical experiments and for the establishment of measures that would promote the revival of trade and business. It was time, as they say, to cash in their chips. "General Bonaparte and his co-conspirators did not agree on everything," noted one historian, "but they all wished to depoliticize government and society."[42] And so, the revolution was over. Napoleon[43] played at being emperor from 1804 onwards. Still, he did not and could not return France to the days before 1789. Many of the most basic changes in French society would remain untouched, the Church's power remained curbed and the power of feudal lords never recovered. To the untrained eye, it might appear that the masses were quietly following their new leaders. Still, from within the working-class districts of Paris, Lyons and elsewhere, many still thought, "Long live the Revolution." They and their descendants would reappear in 1830, 1848, 1871, in the French resistance to fascism, the protests in May–June 1968 ... .

CHAPTER FIVE

Becoming an Appendage to the Machine: The Revolution in Production

The Revolution in Production, or the Industrial Revolution,[1] as it is more commonly known, is typically presented as a dull series of inventions by a cast of male, mainly British geniuses. So we have a parade of names and inventions presented without substantial discussion of the human costs. James Hargreave invents the "spinning jenny" to allow an increased amount of cotton to be produced by the one worker (1764). James Watt creates the steam engine (1769). Cartwright patents the power loom (1785). The first steam-powered textile factory is established in Nottingham, England (1790). And on the list goes. But what is more significant is that each new innovation destroyed the traditional artisan trades, which could no longer compete with cheaper machine-made goods.

In the typical version of history, these wonderful inventions may have caused some momentary discomfort as societies adjusted to the new systems, but they were part of the march of progress that made everyone's life better. This sounds like a dry run for later commercials that attempt to convince the viewer that world civilization has just changed because of a new type of cleaning product. Although these inventions and their creators are an important part of the story, they are far from the most important components. What caused this revolution, apart from the oft-mentioned geniuses, is left unanswered, as are the results.

What this chapter will highlight is how the Industrial Revolution changed people's relationship to craftsmanship, time, community and their own role in society as a whole. For one thing, people in the twenty-first century have grown up in a world shaped by industrial capitalism, meaning it is difficult for most to imagine another type of world. People had fundamentally produced goods in the same manner for thousands of years. That is, they made products by using human labor with perhaps the assistance of animal muscle or running water. Of course, there was from time to time this or that noteworthy innovation in agricultural production: crop rotation, new methods of irrigation, and so on. And no doubt, the eighteenth-century shoemaker created a different style of footwear than the cobbler of ancient Rome. Yet in all, the basics were the same. Products of nature were raised and then made into products by human beings (living labor). Thus, an early modern shoemaker would easily have recognized the technique of someone making footwear centuries before the birth of Christ or Mohammed.

All of this changes with the rise of the machine: tools would no longer serve people, but rather people would serve machines. One noted historian argues that industrialism is on the same level as the change to settled agriculture and the domestication of animals. He contends that the Industrial Revolution is "one of those rare occasions in world history when the human species altered its framework of existence."[2] One way to look at this transformation of European society is that the products of human labor (dead labor) became as important as actual people (living labor). That is to say that the machines (dead labor) created by human labor were quickly overwhelming actual living human beings. As more and more improved machines were created, dead labor grew in importance at the expense of living labor. Put differently, the human became an appendage to the machine. Or, the person was put in bondage within the industrial system. Whereas in pre-industrial Europe, individuals used tools to create things, under industrial capitalism the machines used (and still use) people to make products. What did this mean to the average person? First, the revolution in production ultimately reinvented society by increasing life spans and providing a greater quantity and variety of articles of consumption even for the average person. Still, without in any way denigrating the uplifting cultural importance of shopping malls, one might still ask, "What was the price? What was lost?"

Life in pre-industrial Europe was horrible in many ways. There was disease, hunger, poverty, oppression, ignorance, and the list could go on. It would be foolish to try and present the times before the machines as some type of golden age for the common folk. Still, there were things that made life bearable for most Europeans. Commoners, for examples, had a high degree of autonomy in their daily lives. They had little political say in the affairs of their country, were exploited by the powerful, deluded by the Church and often lived in poverty. All the same, they were left alone on most days that did not include church attendance, tax payment, or war. Feudal lords had far more interesting things to occupy their time than checking up on their serfs regularly. The ruling class saw no advantage in making a great effort to monitor the work habits of commoners. As long as the masses appeared appropriately subservient, followed the rules and did as they were told, they were left alone on a day-to-day basis. A woman in a seventeenth-century village might go for weeks or months without anyone other than relatives and neighbors seeing her go about her labors.

Along with the loss of their independence, normal Europeans lost control of time itself. Before the establishment of industrial capitalism, people had mainly been subject to task-work discipline. Like many college students today, they could do what they wanted when they wanted, so long as a given task was completed by a certain date. Take the case of the shoemaker: a person comes and orders a pair of shoes on Monday. The customer and the artisan agree on a style, price, leather type and that delivery will be on Friday. The shoemaker can set to work on the footwear the moment the customer leaves or the new order may sit unattended till late on Thursday. The person who ordered the shoes cares nothing for any of that as long as the promised product is completed by the agreed-upon time on Friday. When the shoe (or boot) factory comes into being, the competition will most likely drive the shoemaker out of business. It is run on quite different lines than the previous artisan producer. The shoe worker must appear at a certain hour and can neither take a break nor have a meal nor leave until the hour set by the factory management. If the owners want the factory run 16 hours a day with an hour for lunch, so be it. The factory owner is not purchasing the product of the workers' labor but the laborers' time. The industrial system ushers in the age of time-work discipline.[3]

This was not an easy transition for either craft worker or peasant entering the new industrial world. Rather than being master of their own time and working conditions, the industrial worker was left at the mercy of the factory owners. The workers now had to work at the pace set by the machines. They were now under the constant supervision of overseers, who badgered, threatened and on occasion even hit workers who appeared to be falling behind in their service to the machines. Raised in or with family memories of a different world, these first generations of newly industrial-ized workers were forced into a situation they held to be inhumane. In 1806, a commission of the British Parliament looked into the state of working conditions. They found one worker who testified that it was extremely difficult to get accustomed to being under time-work discipline. The workers hated having regular hours. They resented the fact that "they could not go in and out as they pleased, and have what holidays they pleased, and go on just as they had been used to do."[4] It has been said that breaking in workers new to industrialism was difficult and often required physical force whereas those accustomed to the factory system were much easier to manage.

Not only did the common people of Europe lose control of their time, they no longer had any say over their working conditions. Whether a workshop or factory was cold or hot was a matter over which the workers had little influence or control. Many pre-industrial Europeans may have enjoyed singing while working but the new industrial workers, or proletarians as they are sometimes called, would be told whether or not they could even talk with their colleagues during working hours. Before the turn to industry, peasants and craft workers sometimes drank beer or wine during the working day. Now, this liberty was in the hands of the bourgeois owner. On the other hand, the worker who rejected all drink on religious grounds might have the misfortune to be employed in a place where the owner decided to pay part of the wages in alcoholic beverages. Some mine owners, for example, believed that large amounts of rum or gin distributed at lunchtime would encourage more initiative on the part of the miners they hired.

Moreover, the average people lost the protection that their skills had previously afforded them. That is to say, the years of training that might have made it difficult to replace a skilled worker was eliminated as the machines required service by humans with relatively minimal training. With each new wave of technological advance, another group of people would find themselves as if naked before the Capital, as their old skills became irrelevant. The handloom worker was rendered unskilled by the power loom just as later on bookkeepers, who would add long columns of numbers, have been rendered obsolete by computer software. In fact, taken as a whole, the Industrial Revolution destroyed old social relations and people's very way of existence. Although this certainly had positive aspects in breaking down centuries-old prejudices, it also eliminated centuries-old communities. As this happened, people felt more and more alienated from both their work and their fellow humans. When thinking about the impact of the Industrial Revolution, the historian certainly needs to examine data concerning wages, health and living conditions. Still, there are many losses that are less likely to appear on the ledger sheets. As British historian Eric Hobsbawm reminds us, it is vital to remember "that men do not live by bread alone."[5]

Of course, some observers, like the economist Adam Smith, found the resulting developments of the Industrial Revolution as "natural." The point is, however, the vast majority of workers at that moment in history did not. They felt the new industrial system was unnatural and even against the teachings of the Bible. Often the commandment, "Thou shall not steal" was used as an insult to the new capitalist owners. Likewise, supporters of industrial capitalism talked about how these new developments had created so much freedom. Now, people were *free* to sell their labor, *free* to move in search of work, *free* to choose their employers, *free* to make contracts and, of course, *free* to work hard and get ahead. To make sure they were free, the government at the behest of the capitalists ended any welfare measures or social safety net. According to a Report of the Poor Law Commissioners, any social assistance was

> ...a check to industry, a reward for improvident marriages, a stimulant to population, and a blind to its effects on wages; a national institution for discountenancing the industrious and honest, and for protecting the idle, the improvident and the vicious; the destroyer [of the bonds of family life]; a system for preventing the accumulation of capital, for destroying that which exists, and for reducing the rate-payer to pauperism; and a premium for illegitimate children in the provision of aliment.[6]

In reply, many average people said this freedom was an illusion, as the economic power of the bourgeoisie backed by the political power of supportive governments enabled employers to keep workers poorly paid and without any real power over their own lives. As Adam Smith himself noted:

> ... workmen desire to get as much, the masters to give as little as possible ... it is not, however, difficult to see which of the two parties have the advantage in the dispute. The masters, being fewer in number can combine much more easily [and neither government actions nor laws prevent this] while it prohibits those of the workmen.[7]

All the same, defenders of the system chirped on that industry almost immediately raised the common people to a higher standard of living. This line of thinking is widely debated and often disputed by historians.[8] Without becoming too distracted by this seemingly endless debate, it is worthwhile to look at some facts about the generations caught up in the industrial juggernaut of the nineteenth century.

Those who have focused exclusively on wages as indicative of an increased standard of living often overlook important nuances that other facts reveal. How could so many contemporary observers bemoan the housing that workers lived in if those same workers were making more in wages? Those who once lived in rural poverty amid fresh air, clean water and within a village community were now pushed into polluted cities with inferior housing stock. This could be because even with rising wages, "rents rose substantially relative to other costs during the industrial revolution ... housing quality appears to have declined from 1760 to 1860."[9] Most are at least somewhat familiar with the horrors associated with child labor during the early part of the industrialization process. Those children old and able enough to perform factory work were horribly exploited and brutally treated in many cases. Their young siblings were, if anything, more in harm's way. A working-class mother thrown into public employment by economic necessity often had no choice but to leave these infants without quality care. The young children were frequently rendered manageable by narcotic-laced patent medicines with such grand names as "Atkins Patent Infant Preservative." Under such desperate circumstances, the infant mortality rate may have been close to 70 percent.[10]

When discussing living standards during the Industrial Revolution, defenders of the system are wont to point to the drunkenness of many workers. The argument made is that wages were not too low but that the common people chose to drink rather than make better use of their income. The solution to the poverty of the masses in industrial society was, therefore, to convince workers not to waste their resources on drink. Thus, the temperance movement developed, intertwined with religion and a firm moralistic belief in the individual's responsibility to take care of themselves. John Wesley, the founder of Methodism, preached: "You see the wine when it sparkles in the cup, and are going to drink of it. I tell you there is poison in it! And, therefore, beg you to throw it away."[11]

This individualistic ethos flew in the face of centuries of community-oriented tradition. Of course, it is quite true that money spent on drink impacted negatively on living standards. Moreover, the taxes imposed on alcohol meant that drinking workers paid a greater part of their income to the state than non-drinkers.[12] It may be fair to say drinking posed a threat to the well-being of much of the industrial working class. The question that needs to be asked is, why did workers often drink excessively?

Nor was it just alcohol consumption that cut into the funds of the impoverished worker. A habit that was more morally acceptable but nonetheless had a high cost was the purchase of caffeinated drinks. That is, tea and coffee. The creation of a global market that took place before and continued during the period of industrialization targeted workers as consumers of tea or coffee. While arguably less problematic than gin or beer, tea and coffee became socially defined necessities and thereby another drain of proletarian resources.[13] Over time, caffeine became the world's most popular drug.[14] This was no small matter when workers' already low wages limited the number of calories they could afford to consume. The lack of sufficient calorie intake often reduced physical productivity and also caused depressed "learning skills, increasing diseases and absenteeism, inducing lethargy and low mental performance."[15] During the early stages of industrialization, calorie consumption often declined and made the problem of poverty more acute.[16]

A detailed case study of Antwerp illustrates the decline in food consumption by the common people. Up until 1830, every resident ate an average of 40 to 50 kilograms of meat yearly. By the 1850s, this had dropped over 20 percent to barely 38 kilograms.[17] It would be a mistake to assume these numbers meant that the good people of Antwerp were turning instead to the products of the sea for their dining pleasure. With regard to fish, per capita annual consumption fell from 8 kilograms early in the nineteenth century to 4.3 by the middle. In the same period, grain consumption also declined albeit not as dramatically.[18] The authors of this study conclude that this reduced consumption resulted in, "the absolute pauperization of large sectors of the Belgian population ... [and] the explanation must be sought in the definite breakthrough of the capitalist mode of production, causing widespread social dislocation."[19]

Within factories, workers were subject to hitherto little-known ailments like silicosis, a disease that poisons and ultimately destroys the lymphatic system. This disease not only killed many miners but also other workers exposed to the dangerous by-products of industry.[20] All the varied changes associated with the Industrial Revolution put immense strain on family life. There is evidence that suggests an increase in family violence. A study of northern France found that before industrialization, murder had largely been an anonymous affair. As the pressures of the industrial system mounted, so too did violence among family members. By the 1870s, fatal violence "in intimate relationships increased to become the single most frequent type of murder."[21]

During the early period of industrialization, 1790–1850, the use of child labor increased greatly and in many cases the work of children as young as ten was essential for the growth of new industries. A particularly vulnerable demographic of children has often been overlooked by those historians examining the period through the lens of the family. That is, children without adult guardians would often find themselves thrown into factories at very young ages.[22] As one such person, a Robert Collyer, explained that when the local labor supply could not satisfy the demands of industry in Yorkshire, the industry owners scoured orphanages "where children were to be found in swarms [and] set them to work as apprentices who [were kept] until the girls were eighteen and the boys twenty-one."[23] Beside the lack of available adult labor, children as laborers appealed to owners because they were cheap; in addition to room and board such as these were, a young child would make perhaps 10–20 percent of an adult male's wage. One might ask, what would motivate these children, sometimes called "white slaves," to be productive factory workers? Both violence and discipline were important factors, but it appears that hunger was the prime motivation.[24]

The transfer of labor from kinship-based food production to the larger industrial society created a new need for family labor. After 1850, factories became more sophisticated and required workers with at least a minimum level of education. Now, we are not talking about courses in philosophy. Education in basic maths and literacy was needed, as adjusting machines and reading instructions became more important. The change from a peasant society to an industrial wage-labor one changed family structures and dynamics. Before, the family unit had been focused on food production, tasks to which children as young as five could make a contribution. In the new wage-labor economy, the family's

> ... primary function was to socialize and educate labourers for an industrial labour market ... [what put a special burden on the family was] the extension of childhood from age five or six to age fifteen or sixteen ... whereas previously children worked when they became old enough to do so, now their parents found themselves supporting adolescents.[25]

While few would argue against education for children, the result of this shift for the family was enormous. The family was now given the added burden of providing for their offspring for as long as an additional decade.

Another way to approach this whirlwind of arguments and counter-arguments is to examine directly the physical condition of proletarianized Europeans. At least in Britain, the first industrial nation, it would appear that the common people were worse off, if physical stature is any indication. One study found that both rural and urban laborers became shorter after 1780, that is, once the Industrial Revolution had begun. The evidence indicates that, "urban Englishmen were over 1.5 inches shorter in 1802 than cohorts born in the late 1770s."[26] As usual, if things were bad for men, they were worse for women. English women in this period saw their height fall even further than their male counterparts. This was not mere accident but rather part of the increasing pressure placed on women by the emerging industrial wage-labor system. Two scholars note the "fall in heights of English women relative to men is consistent with the increasing gender inequality in intra-household food allocation."[27] Aside from physical changes, the number of English females unable to read increased during this same period.[28] One should be clear, industrialization was a, maybe *the*, fundamental transformation within European society. The change from an agriculturally based society to one rooted in industrial production was certain to cause disruptions and extensive changes in community and family life, as well as in the situation of individuals.[29]

The question remaining is: what caused the Industrial Revolution to take place? Although we find their statues littering the Western world, we can set aside the typical and unsatisfying idea that industrialism was merely the result of the inspired genius of great men. Even if one were to grant that this or that individual had a good idea, the conditions must have been ripe for the idea to be realized. The ancient slave state of Athens had its fair share of original thinkers, but they produced relatively few technological breakthroughs that could compare with the inventions of the eighteenth and nineteenth centuries. The other contributing factors—aside from individual "genius"—that allowed industrialization to take hold and fundamentally alter the way of life was the convergence of new wealth and new forms of handling this Capital. One development that allowed Britain to become the first industrial nation was the shift from wood to coal as an energy source. In the two hundred years preceding industrialization, beginning in 1560, there was ever-increasing replacement of wood with coal. The latter is a great advance over the former as a fuel: Britain had an abundance of coal and a relative shortage of wood after many centuries of turning trees into charcoal. It can be argued that each "successive industry which acquired a coal base was free to expand to a degree previously impossible—salt, paper, glass, non-ferrous metals, brewing, brick-making, and iron to name only the most prominent."[30]

By way of contrast, Sweden's reluctance to replace wood with coal due to its abundant expanses of forests may explain why Sweden industrialized after Britain. Yet, this Scandinavian nation went from one of the very poorest places in Europe to one of the richest in the course of the nineteenth century. In Sweden, it was not abundant coal, although they did have tremendous wood resources, but a highly educated common people that made the difference. It was, one might say, not energy resources but human capital that transformed Sweden into a successful industrial society.[31] So, if Britain accumulated capital for industrialization by seizing the common land from the average citizen, profiting from the transatlantic slave trade and exploiting coal deposits, Swedish capitalism exploited the fact that their version of Lutheranism had produced a largely literate population. Still, Sweden would never become the industrial world leader that Britain was, partly because the country lacked overseas colonies and their markets, that is, raw material as well as the capital raised in Britain by its expropriation of domestic land and foreign bodies.

But these factors alone are insufficient to explain the genesis of the Capital that made industry successful. The evidence suggests that in every case, this wealth came from two sources, internal exploitation and overseas pillage. Internally, Capital came from cannibalizing the wealth of dying feudalism. In Britain, Church land was seized and sold by King Henry VIII. In Sweden, Lutheranism provided pretence for the confiscation of Roman Catholic Church property, while in France it was a popular revolution that seized church/feudal holdings. These massive seizures had two notable aspects. First, the tremendous shift of wealth (and power) from feudal institutions to people with money, be they merchants, bankers or well-off peasants, changed all those areas that underwent this transition to industrialism. Pushing rural people off small self-sufficient farms and establishing large estates for raising sheep for the wool trade released a huge amount of labor from their traditional obligations, forcing them to look for other work. These people were suddenly and unexpectedly free from centuries of bondage, oppression and exploitation. They were often, at least in the short run, out of a job. All of this made the new industrial enterprises more of a physical necessity rather than an attractive alternative. That is, the people may or may not have been happy with pre-industrial society, but it did not matter: they had to join the brave new world of industrial capitalism regardless of their feelings about the matter.

It is important to remember that the European common people were dispossessed, thus providing both capital and an abundant supply of landless and desperate potential workers. While the details are still being debated, the fact that peasants were forced from the land their families had farmed for centuries is not in dispute.[32] Many of the dispossessed would doubtlessly have agreed with E.P. Thompson when he argued that the enclosure movement was "a plain enough case of class robbery."[33]

Externally, Capital would flow into Western Europe as a result of the conquest and colonization of the Americas. The gold and silver looted from the once mighty Native American empires of the Aztec and Inca flowed into Europe from the sixteenth century onwards. With weak bourgeois classes, Spain and Portugal saw their wealth fly off to more developed centers of trade like London, Amsterdam and Paris. This historic influx of precious metal would have, in and of itself, been insufficient to finance the revolution in production. The European powers did not, however, simply loot the Western Hemisphere and leave. They set up colonies that served as sources of raw material on the one hand, and markets for finished goods on the other. There was, however, a significant obstacle to this model of exploitation. While the land mass conquered was extremely large, the amount of available labor was not.

Enslaved natives and colonists from Europe were too few in number to take full advantage of the territory conquered. The European elites sought to solve this problem by importing Africans to the new world. At first, some of these Africans were free but the transportation of these people quickly became the slave trade. As important as slavery was to the economic development of the Industrial Revolution, "it did not by itself cause the British industrial revolution."[34] Nonetheless, it is hard to envision a way the Industrial Revolution could have developed without the slave trade. This is because both the capital for industrial growth, markets for industrial production and raw materials for the new machines were bound up with slavery, where profit rates could reach 30 percent.[35] Of course, some scholars have disputed this figure, but the larger and more significant fact is that the slave trade made European colonies successful. Regardless of what profit rate came from the slave trade, the key point is that the American colonies were built by and dependent on slave labor.

Without the raw materials and markets the colonies provided, industrialism would have been hindered. It was the slave system that made exploitation of the new world such an economic success. The French government understood this when they gave a subsidy to French traders to provide African slave labor for their colonies. As one Nigerian scholar has concluded, "the expansion of the Atlantic system provided adequate opportunities for the launching of industrial capitalism in Britain from the late eighteenth century, thanks to the Atlantic slave trade and African slavery in the New World."[36] As profitable as the slave trade and colonialism were, it would be wrong to think that industrial capitalism was financed only from external plunder. It should be understood that this experience was in no way unique to Britain. In Sweden, the nineteenth century and industrial capitalism profoundly changed the common peoples' relation to the land. As agrarian capitalism grew, the Swedish people saw two important changes: "the creation of large farms and the emergence of a new landless working class."[37] It is also important to remember that most advances in industrialization were due to "helpful government intervention."[38] As a recent, detailed study of the rise of industrial capitalism found, "the fact that the artisan-led resistance to the conversion of British manufacturing to capitalism was only overcome through the direct application of state power demonstrates that the state played a very active and central role in the Industrial Revolution."[39]

The common person did not just accept all these changes without a murmur of dissent. Some fled across the Atlantic to where the promise, if not always the reality, of cheap land seemed to offer an alternative to being crushed by the ever-growing industrial machine. Some protested against the very idea of mechanization and hoped they could hold back technological change. To cite only one example from France, in the decade after the fall of Napoleon, hundreds of workers gathered in front of the Mayor of Vienne shouting, "Down with the shearing-machine! Down with all machines!"[40] Further, it is vital to point out that (all often repeated libels to the contrary), there was no connection between protest or even collective violence and crime or criminals.[41]

To show another more significant example of resistance, it is useful to look at the revolt of the Silesian weavers. These workers had been relatively well-off and had a fair amount of control over their lives because of the protection afforded by their skill. With the introduction of machinery, the weavers' skill was rendered unimportant. This rapidly drove those in the trade into poverty. In 1844, with their wages posed to dip below subsistence, masses of weavers in Silesia rose up, broke into factories and destroyed the equipment. At first glance, this would appear to be a mere repeat, albeit on a larger scale, of the so-called Luddite protests that had already seen machine breaking in Britain and France.

Karl Marx noted a major difference between the protests in an article appearing on August 10, 1844, in which he pointed out that this time

> ... [not] only were machines destroyed, those competitors of the workers, but also *account books*, the titles of ownership, and whereas all other movements had directed their attacks primarily at the visible enemy, namely the *industrialists*, the Silesian workers turned also against the hidden enemy, the bankers."[42] [emphasis in original]

This and other revolts have often been portrayed as mindless rebellion against technology and progress. The facts point in another direction. The weavers only decided to storm the mills after negotiation, mediation and appeal had each failed. Also, in the short term, the "tactic of 'collective bargaining by riot' had indeed paid off in the case of the Silesian weavers' revolt."[43] They were able to slow down the inevitable destruction of their craft. Of course, in the long run they were doomed. Still, one should neither assume that mass action is merely the result of a "mob" nor that mass action damages the interests of those resisting ... and in the nineteenth century there would be far more people resisting than just the weavers.

From the Revolutions of 1848–49 to the First People's Democracy: The Paris Commune

The Revolution in Production was far from the only upheaval to upset nine-teenth-century European society. With the end of the French Revolution and the later, final defeat of Napoleon at Waterloo, the forces of the old order appeared to consign the spirit of revolution to footnotes in historical tomes. In France, the fall of Napoleon allowed the so-called "holy alliance" of Britain, Russia, the Austrian Empire and reactionary Prussia to put a member of the Bourbon line back on the restored French throne in 1815. Exhausted by years of revolution, sacrifice and war, it was thought that the French people would accept this sad situation for generations to come. As it turned out, those that thought this way were dead wrong.

One of the most important dignitaries who misunderstood the mood of the population was King Charles X. Whether Charles actually thought God had chosen him to rule France or he merely had an unusually inept secret police, Charles was, one might say, clueless. By early 1830, Charles X had dissolved Parliament, suspended press freedom and called for new elections following his cleverly altered electoral system in which only one out of four former voters would still have the right to cast a ballot. The people responded with strikes and protests. At the end of July, after three days of street fighting, Charles X abandoned being "King by Grace of God" and opted more modestly for being alive by the grace of Britain and took flight across the Channel. This Bourbon ruler was quickly replaced by Louis-Phillipe, the liberal Duke of Orléans, who was said to have fought on the side of the Republic in 1792. This liberal, indeed bourgeois, monarch had the backing of businessmen who had deftly blocked attempts by other classes to establish a republic. Many bourgeois hoped this model of "consti-tutional monarchy" would spread. But Europe stayed, if not quiet, mostly subdued by the old regimes of order, as evident in the revolts within Italy and Germany that were quickly reduced to oblivion. One notable exception were the Poles, who rose up bravely against the Russian czar, only to be brutally crushed and to watch another part of Poland disappear into the vastness of the Russian Empire.

The story of the 1830 revolution is oft presented as if it was achieved by highly nuanced arguments articulated in upper-class salons. In reality, it was the Paris crowd that forced Charles to abandon his throne for rainy England. Were the concerns of these ordinary people the same as the better-educated and much better-funded businessmen? Hardly. One detailed study of the 1830 crowd in revolutionary Paris suggests workers in the capital had reasons to revolt that owed little to the disputes between the Crown and the rich. Put simply, those who worked for a living were less preoccupied with constitutional disputes than with "lack of work, low wages [and] the high price of bread."[1]

It is also worth reflecting on the fact that the crowd very closely resembled that of 1789. These were not the desperate and dispossessed of society, but neither were they members of the middle class.[2] The crowds were made up of a large number of skilled craftsmen, as indicated in French police records. Most were not extremely young, but still not old enough to have personal experience of the 1789 revolution.[3] By July, economic distress had become a vital motive behind the crowd protests. Beyond economic complaints, the most commonly voiced motive for the revolt was hatred of the Bourbons. In other words, the revolution came about because of traditional economic oppression and resentment towards the old regime, which fused into a radical cocktail backed by vague notions of liberty, equality and fraternity.[4] These slogans and beliefs had now circulated throughout popular France for generations. They gave a common language and clear goals to people motivated to revolt by a number of varied grievances.

Within a generation, these and other causes would lead to a broader European Revolution in 1848. Sometimes called the "spring time of the people," this revolution would once more start in Paris, but this time it would not end there. Massive popular demonstrations in Paris caused the abdication of King Louis Philippe, who was forced to flee to England in February 1848. The following month, large demonstrations in Vienna caused Prince von Metternich, architect of the post-Napoleonic European order, to resign and join the former French king in English exile. That same March of 1848 saw revolutionary crowds gather in Berlin where a startled king verbally accepted demands for elections, a constitution, freedom of the press and the unification of Prussia with other German states.

Throughout German-speaking lands that spring, rebels appeared to have the upper hand. An all-German National Assembly was elected and began deliberations on May 18, 1848. This assembly was largely made up of liberals, and is also often called the "professors' parliament," as so many members were academics. Unable to agree on a constitution or much of anything else, the assembly quickly degenerated into little more than a debating society. By late 1848, the nobles and generals in Berlin, Vienna and elsewhere had regained their nerve and began to reverse all the changes set in motion earlier in the year. When in April 1849, the National Assembly proposed to the Prussian king that he become German emperor, he refused. With neither an army nor broad popular support, the Frankfurt Assembly was dissolved on May 31, 1849.[5] Rebellion in Italy and elsewhere was largely crushed the same year.

While there were a wide range of motivations each reflecting the diverse interests of the rebels, as is always true in cases of social upheaval, the significance of the economic situation cannot be overstated. All too often, school textbooks mistakenly give the impression that the entire movement was wrapped up merely in histrionic debates regarding high ideals. But word on the streets, at the events themselves, was that the revolution had been sparked by economic want. Ideas like liberalism and nationalism helped to shape the events of 1848–49. Yet the urgency of the working people's uprisings was largely the result of economic misery and the fear of future economic pain. Across Europe, wherever there was economic crisis, popular revolt soon followed. This is not to say that lawyers, journalists, doctors, academics and a wide range of professionals from the middle class were not part of the revolutionary wave. These people were important— some might argue vital. The point remains that it was laboring people who gave the movement the "muscle" it needed to have any chance of success. As Eric Hobsbawm commented,

> ... those who made the revolution were unquestionably the labouring poor. It was they who died on the urban barricades: in Berlin, there were only about fifteen representatives of the educated classes, about thirty master craftsmen, among the three hundred victims of the March fighting; in Milan only twelve students, white-collar workers or landlords among the 350 dead of the insurrection."[6]

In theory, this mobilization of the working people was the great achievement of 1848, but proved to be an ideological challenge once realized. The appearance of common people on the stage of history became a problem for those who were accustomed to controlling the performance themselves. The republican-minded middle class may have been all for "the people" on some rhetorical plane, but feared them in real life. The self-activity of workers, and other such "uncultured types," was seen as little more than gate-crashing at the party that liberals wanted to attend exclusively. Middle-class republicans, who wanted to control the movement, now faced a clear choice: risk social revolution, or abandon liberal ideals by submitting to the old elites. The bulk of bourgeois reformers chose the latter out of fear of the former.

When assaulted with demands for representative government, a free press or, particularly in Italy and Germany, national unity, the old conservative ruling class had a powerful card to play. As soon as the fragile nature of the alliance between the bourgeois liberals and lower-class radicals became apparent, it was simply a matter of encouraging disunity among the opposition. There was a conscious policy of divide and conquer. The more perceptive representatives of the old order understood this well. As Count Cavour of Piedmont commented in 1846, when faced with the specter of social revolution, "the most enthusiastic republicans would be, we are convinced, the first to join the ranks of the conservative party."[7] In other words, formal equality is politically acceptable, actual economic equality is not.

There were other divisions and weaknesses within the opposition camp, notably the issue of women's roles. The male-dominated rebels appear to have made little effort to mobilize or incorporate women into the radical project.[8] Parisian women made up 40 percent of the manufacturing work force, often began strikes and in other ways asserted their own independence.[9] As the nineteenth century progressed, working-class women became more active, from the Chartists to the 1848 revolutionaries.[10] Women were increasingly forcing themselves into the public sphere.[11] Women were greatly influenced by and, at certain key junctures, influential in the events of 1848–49. Some scholars argue that, in Germany at least, 1848 marks the beginning of the modern women's movement.[12]

Additionally, the distorting effects of the apparently easy and early successes of 1848 bred complacency among some. With the noteworthy exception of Marx, Engels and a handful of hardened radicals, a vast number of people believed that fundamental change had been achieved when a period of calm followed the initial revolts. This allowed the forces of reaction to regroup. In France, the establishment of the Second Republic underwrote these popular illusions. In German-speaking lands, it appeared that the princes and the nobility were ready to surrender their hold on power. Street fighting in Berlin and Vienna drove back the traditional military to such an extent that many thought the people had won. These dreams of a popular victory by the people were soon dispelled.

A few words about Karl Marx[13] and Frederick Engels are in order. Both were born into well-off German-speaking families; Engels was actually the son of a factory owner. In addition, each man was influenced by the philosophy of the Young Hegelians in Berlin. For many, this would mark a youthful period of intellectual curiosity followed by a return to a conventional position in society. Neither Marx nor Engels would follow this pattern. In fact, they would do just the opposite, by leaving purely philosophical pursuits behind for the more daring path of political activism. The pair first met in 1842 and became increasing radicalized, drifting into a lifelong political collaboration. Marx was impressed with the first-hand research Engels had done on the English working class, while the latter had the deepest respect for the intellect of the slightly older Marx. They would remain friends for the rest of their lives while they turned out works like the *Communist Manifesto*, which was written jointly. Especially after the publication of Volume One of *Das Kapital*, Engels organized and edited Marx's writing.

Both radicals were active in the 1848–49 revolutions in their native Germany, and Engels even participated in some actual fighting in 1849. Later, they would provide the theoretical leadership of the International Working Men's Association, the so-called "First International." Later in their lives, as various workers parties formed which proclaimed themselves socialist, social-democratic, or even "Marxist," Marx and Engels gave no end of useful advice to these groups. Although both men were hugely respected in the labor movement and the object of much hero worship, the advice that Karl and Frederick imparted was more often than not ignored. Little wonder that by the 1870s, Marx was fond of saying, "I know only one thing. I'm not a Marxist." All the same, the ideas of these two German radical democrats would have a profound influence on sections of the European working class. Of these ideas, the thought that all history is the history of class struggle was an important contrast to previous theories of cooperation, or what Marx once called the "Universal Brotherhood Swindle." Even now, in the twenty-first century, the political ideas, philosophical method and moral positions advocated by Marx and Engels have significant influence on large groups of the common people.

In France, the workers' attempt to change their place in society was met with a brutal suppression of their protests. The rebellion was provoked by the dissolution of the socialistic national workshops that in some ways, like medical care, had proven too successful for the rich to tolerate.[14] Physical repression was not the only, or most striking, part of the reaction to the commoners' struggle. Louis Napoleon, the nephew of Napoleon Bonaparte, proved that universal (male) suffrage could be used for non-radical, even reactionary, ends. That voters can sometimes be manipulated into voting against their own interests is not a great revelation of the twenty-first century. In the nineteenth century, universal suffrage was thought to be a magic formula that would abolish tyranny and poverty. Capitalizing on this, on December 20, 1848, Louis Bonaparte was elected president of the French Republic, exploiting his famous name and presenting himself as all things to all people.

He particularly had massive support from France's rural population, in part because of his famous name but also because he promised no more taxes and a vague anti-bourgeois program. Once in office, he systematically planned to establish a dictatorship.[15] He organized a successful *coup d'état* and proclaimed himself Napoleon III on December 2, 1852, Emperor of the Second Empire. In this enterprise, he achieved success by using techniques that would later be expanded upon by Mussolini and Hitler. Like the later dictators, he came to power by craftily combining open and legal political activity with covert illegal activities. He formed his own personal army, a precursor to the later Black Shirts of Mussolini and Brown Shirts of Hitler. He was a master of propaganda that relied on its persuasion, not factual accuracy. Bonaparte claimed to be a man of the people while he served the rich and rewarded friends and cronies.

In Germany, universal (male) suffrage would await Otto von Bismarck and his top-down drive for German unification in the decades to come. Instead, the rulers of German-speaking Europe deployed their armies against the revolution in a way not seen since the slaughter of the Peasants War of 1525.[16] This story was repeated with minor variations throughout Europe, as reaction swept away the hopes of the "spring time of the people." At first look, with the notable exception of the abolition of serfdom in the Hapsburg empire, it seems like little changed despite all the noise and fury of 1848. France went from monarchy to republic only to shortly become a dictatorship known as the Second Empire. The once awe-inspiring rebellion by the Germans ultimately appeared to do little beyond enlarging the number of exiles in the US. Powerful czarist Russia remained largely quiet, while dissent in England was marginalized.

Little wonder that so many have seen 1848 as a failure. This attitude is understandable, but in many ways it is also wrong. Certainly it is true that the immediate results of the 1848–49 revolutions were far from what insurgents had dreamed. The revolutions, at first glance, seem to have done little more than expose dissidents to repression. Thousands had to leave the nations of their birth, at times even crossing the Atlantic in order to make a new life in the Americas. But, when a longer view of European history is taken, the picture that emerges is quite different. Those small changes that at first were deemed insignificant turned out to have lasting effects in the light of history. Many of the demands of the 1848 rebels were in fact later achieved, albeit mostly by non-revolutionary leaders.[17]

One most decidedly revolutionary person who proved an exception to this general pattern was Giuseppe Garibaldi. A hardened radical, nationalist and later a member of the First International,[18] Garibaldi landed in the Italian South in 1860 with a dedicated group of fighters. Their goal was to unify Italy and create a secular, democratic and social republic. Defying conventional wisdom, Garibaldi's ragtag band was able to achieve unexpected victories over professional military forces. These upsets were made possible by the rousing of the peasant masses, who thronged to the rebel army in hitherto unexpected numbers. In and of itself, this enlarged rebel mass ensured little besides a more generous spilling of blood. But the rebel leaders proved themselves to be innovative military tacticians. Rather than give battle to the better armed and trained forces opposed to them, Garibaldi's forces engaged in what has been called irregular warfare, better known today as guerrilla war.

While never minimizing the importance of these martial skills, the genius of this campaign was due to more than this new military science. Garibaldi, and his comrades in the leadership, had the ability to inspire their forces by treating peasants and other commoners as equals; they demoralized their enemies while relying on the popular rising of the common people to help accomplish their goals. In an article in the *New York Daily Tribune* on September 24, 1860, Engels captured some of this campaign's excitement. The co-author of the *Communist Manifesto* noted how along with military victories, insurrections broke out in provinces not yet occupied by the radical army. When the rebels confronted the traditional military forces, the latter often collapsed with only token resistance. In one situation, "whole regiments refused to march against the insurgents and desertions took place in bodies, even among the troops guarding Naples."[19]

The revolution spread northward toward Rome, home of the Pope, whom the rebels hoped to depose because of his opposition to both Italian unification and a republican form of government. Understandably, this was far from welcome news to the papacy nor to its French and Austrian supporters. Even if the papacy had not been an issue, the conservative rulers in Paris and Vienna had no taste for a democratic, republican Italy to their south. Neither did the northern Italian kingdom of Piedmont led by the crafty Count Cavour, who had Piedmont's soldiers occupy northern Italy to check Garibaldi and postpone foreign intervention. This presented the revolutionaries with two disagreeable options. They could compromise with Cavour at the risk of abandoning many of the ideals for which they had fought. Alternatively, they could defy Piedmont and plunge Italy into a civil war that would almost surely have seen foreign intervention on the side of Cavour.

For better or, as some would argue, worse, the rebels led by Garibaldi opted for compromise. Although southern Italy was united with northern Italy by a plebiscite, many southerners experienced the new Italy less as liberation and more as occupation, as northern officials flocked southward to administer the lands. The faith that Garibaldi and so many radicals had placed in the newly created Italian Parliament quickly dissipated. Instead of being a means of reform for the common people, the Parliament was a talking shop where the rich and powerful cut deals for their, not the people's, benefit. With a mere 7 percent of the population entitled to cast a ballot, the new liberal Italy under the King of Piedmont was far from what the radicals had fought to create. Instead of a people's government or a social republic, the new Italy was a failed system created by the liberals forming an alliance with the remnants of the old feudal order.

It would be an error to conclude that the rich and powerful, represented by the likes of Louis Napoleon, Bismarck, or Cavour, were the only forces of significance. There were other agents of change in nineteenth-century Europe. They had little in the way of funds and they commanded no armies. Among the most important was the attempt of the International Working Men's Association (IWMA), also known to historians as the First International, to unite the workers of, if not yet the world, then Europe. The First International provided very real services to the struggling labor movement. The IWMA served as a source of communication and strike support in a pre-Internet age. The minutes of the General Council are rich in detail of requests for help in promoting work actions, notifying workers in other countries not to be tricked into becoming scabs and collecting funds to help workers' struggles. For example, the IWMA minutes from May 23, 1865 included a letter from Lyons explaining how wages were being cut using the argument of cheaper English production. It was resolved that the actual costs and price of labor in England would be researched and the facts sent to the French workers.[20] When London employers sought to import German tailors to break the work action of their laborers, the International warned off many unwitting strike breakers through the German labor press.[21] When boot makers in Geneva planned to fight for higher wages, they requested and received help from the IWMA who alerted workers in other nations.[22] Sometimes, the IWMA's actions were more direct. In fall 1866, Belgian basket makers were brought to London to undercut wage levels in the trade. Members of the IWMA went straight to the workplace and "pointed out to the Belgians the injury they were inflicting on the English ... getting two of them to come out [of work] to have a glass of drink."[23] Within a day, all the Belgian workers in the shop had quit and were on their way back to the Continent.

This is not to say that the IWMA dealt in pure and simple trade unionism. For example, the plight of Irish political prisoners led to a demand for "better treatment for these unfortunate men."[24] The organization made a class analysis of the Irish situation. As one council member noted, "It was our business to show the Irish that it was only a class of the English that wrongs them and that the same class of Irish were as bad."[25] Later in April 1872, the General Council issued a declaration against "Police Terrorism in Ireland."[26] Ireland's relation to England was said to be the same as Poland's to czarist Russia. In other words, both nations were "oppressed nationalities."[27] At the risk of stating the obvious, the IWMA believed, and advocated, for independence and freedom for both.

From its start in 1864, the Provisional Rules of the Association argued, "The emancipation of the working classes must be conquered by the working classes themselves ... [and] that all efforts aimed at that great end have hitherto failed from want of solidarity." This absence of solidarity was seen not only within the working classes of any one specific nation but also "from the absence of a fraternal bond of union between the working classes of different countries."[28] This statement was more than noble words. It was also a guide to action. When war broke out between Prussia and Austria, the International condemned it as "a war for Empire, and as such is not calculated to benefit the peoples, as whichever becomes victor it will be but the substitution of one despot for another."[29] The IWMA advised workers "to be neutral" in such conflicts.[30] When the Prussian kaiser demanded a war loan to fight France, August Bebel and Wilhelm Liebknecht, two IWMA members in the North German Parliament, refused to vote for war credits.[31] The IWMA denounced the war and printed thousands of flyers in both French and German giving their reasons.[32] Later in 1870, in the midst of the Franco-Prussian War, a group from Paterson, New Jersey sent £26 to be split equally between French and German sufferers of the war.[33] This was no mere symbolic gesture, as important as that might be, since according to one calculation this sum represents in 2014 well over

€22,000. Unfortunately for the organization, this size of donation was quite uncommon.

Many activists in the International had clear, if not prophetic, vision. Harriet Law, a member of the IMWA General Council from Manchester, remarked that machines "made women less dependent on men than they were before and would ultimately emancipate them from domestic slavery."[34] All but written out of history, Law had an important career as a public speaker advocating secularism and women's rights. For the better part of a decade, she was editor of *Secular Chronicle* in whose pages she fought for free thought and the liberation of women. It is noteworthy that the IWMA gave Law a platform for her views and that although an ally of Marx and Engels, she certainly appears to have considered herself their equal.[35]

Despite its leadership in many areas, the International led a relatively short life. Certainly, the disputes between Marx and his supporters on the one hand and those of the anarchist Bakunin on the other played a major part in the organization's demise.[36] This is in fact the accepted wisdom on what went wrong with the IWMA. But, there were other systematic difficulties experienced by the association as well.

First, there were certain inherent problems that presented themselves to an organization whose goal was to be international in scope. In an age before the invention of the Internet or other means of global communication, there was a regrettable tendency for members closest to the organization's center, London, to have the most influence. This also applied to the division between those members who could and could not, often for lack of means, attend international conferences and congresses. Frequently, governments prevented or impeded the travel of IWMA members, such as in 1868 when Belgium passed a law allowing the government to expel non-citizens without specific cause. The law was passed with the International specifically mentioned as one reason for the legislation.[37]

More concretely limiting for the IWMA was lack of funds. A study of the financial records contained in the *Documents of the First International* reveal that the organization lived literally from hand to mouth. Despite constant rumors spread by police agents and political opponents that the leaders of the organization were those "who live on the workers' money,"[38] the evidence suggests that being an International activist often meant spending one's own funds.[39] Add to this the costs of arrests, police attacks, confiscation of newspapers and other publications, and the facts underlying the poverty of the organization are clear.

Despite all these limitations, the IWMA directly promoted international solidarity. This was not always easy as the particular nature of each local struggle might obscure the global essence of the situation. Even when the organizational position was thoughtful and farsighted, change did not automatically follow. Thus, no amount of enthusiastic thanks to the International from Polish exiles who agreed with the IWMA stance towards their nation[40] could solve the incredible complexity of the problems facing partitioned Poland, which was divided between Russia, Prussia and Austria. The problems facing the newly united Italy often defied easy solutions, even though Garibaldi was an enthusiastic member of the Association.[41] Recognizing that one solution would not apply exactly the same everywhere, the *General Rules of the IWMA* allowed for local autonomy.[42]

Based in Europe, the organization often could only give advice rather than concrete assistance to radical supporters outside their mainly Western European base of support. Yet the organization was always more admired, and feared than one would imagine, looking at their actual membership, which was never much more than some few thousands, and their financial base in the cold light of hindsight. This was understood at the time by the leadership. Marx, for example, argued against revealing true membership numbers "as the outside public always thought the active members much more numerous than they really were."[43] This meant the IWMA was to get credit, or blame, far beyond their actual strength to control events.

French novelist Emile Zola captured some of the initial, certainly naïve, enthusiasm the IWMA must have provoked in some workers. In *Germinal*, his classic work of fiction revealing the lives of miners, Zola includes a character named Etienne. The author puts these words in Etienne's mouth early in the novel as news of the IWMA is spreading throughout France: the International has

> ... just been founded in London. Wasn't it a superb accomplishment, to have launched this campaign through which justice would at last triumph? With no more frontiers, the workers of the whole world would rise up and unite, to make sure that the worker kept the fruits of his labour.[44]

Although *Germinal* is a work of fiction, it is not difficult to think that some may have had exactly that response.

From the very beginnings of the IWMA, their rules and regulations stressed the need for labor solidarity between workers, regardless of the nation state of residency.[45] Nor was this solidarity extended only to Europeans. In 1867, the General Council discussed the French occupation of Mexico and condemned the official press of Europe for attempting to gloss over the crimes committed by Maximilian in his desire to destroy those Mexicans fighting for their country.[46] One must return to the fact that the very real limitations and weakness of the International were not necessarily generally known at the time. If so, why would a Swiss watch manufacturer feel it necessary to publicly announce he would not hire IWMA members?[47] Or, why would the authorities in Geneva feel that a small number of copies of a paper influenced by the International deserved suppression?[48] Authorities went to great lengths trying to incite ethnic tension between sections of the organization. In 1871, the mainstream press claimed that all Germans were to be expelled from the association.[49] The Pope even weighed in, joining the attacks on the IWMA, claiming it, "would subvert all order and all law … ."[50]

The organization pushed back against the rising tide of nationalism and racism, with admittedly only limited success, in a manner that can only be seen as commendable in a world that witnessed the massacres and genocide of the twentieth century. Despite personal backsliding, the IWMA was committed to a class-based rather than racially or ethnically based worldview. At a time when many, if not most, people accepted racial differences as scientifically proven, the counter-example of the association stands as a sharp exception. Fear of the IWMA's ideologies gaining wider acceptance led an international combination of manufacturers to declare one of their most important purposes was to "spy into the action and working of the International Working Men's Association … and to execute such measures against it as the Government may officially demand."[51]

The IWMA was able to influence working-class movements in those countries that were within their geographical and political sphere. The International relied on influence as their mode of operation rather than giving orders or attempting to control—as opposed to the later Comintern. Through this influence the International, during its brief life, achieved a number of important breakthroughs. One scholar notes the International scored two lasting achievements: it became "the first effective international support for workers on strike … [and was] the medium through which the ideas of Marx penetrated the new labour movements of Europe."[52] Not only did it engage in strike support, the IWMA even pressed for the idea of international trade unions. Even as it was going into decline, Paul LaFargue, Marx's son-in-law and a leading French socialist, was pushing for the Association to organize international trade unions.[53] This First International additionally served to spread political theory, mainly shaped by Marx and Engels to be sure, to rising social movements and radical political parties. A quick look at some of the parties that the IWMA influenced will suggest its European importance.

Of course, scholars have argued that the International ultimately failed even in those locales where it had a short period of glory. So it has been argued about Ireland. Even here, however, the argument can be made that the impact of the IWMA far outlasted its organizational life. As one author comments

> ... any history limited to the organization failure of the First International in Ireland would be incomplete. The IWMA continued and strengthened a tradition of social protest ... elements of Marxist thought, such as the reality of class war and the necessity for working-class solidarity, can be discerned in the speeches of socialists who first learned of them during the existence of the IWMA in Ireland.[54]

Even among the German labor movement, whose leaders so frustrated Marx, the International helped push the evolution of radical thought by stressing "internationalism, class-consciousness, socialist politics and Marxist philosophy."[55] France was certainly strongly influenced both before and after the Paris Commune.[56] Thanks to the hard work of the Dutch police we know quite a bit about the IWMA in the Netherlands.[57] Even the famously conservative trade unions of Britain were unable to completely resist the allure of an international organization devoted to the betterment of their class. While the British may have remained in the main non-revolutionary, they were touched by both the idea of socialism and the idea of working-class internationalism.[58]

That the Association played a part in mobilizing the common people is obvious. Not only were actual members mobilized, but vast numbers of those who never formally took out a membership card were influenced by the group's ideas. This was possible precisely because it was an open organization, not a secret society; the ideas and finances were mainly an open book. Of course, this meant it was easy for police spies to infiltrate the IWMA or for members to publicly go over to the enemy, as did two French comrades who left to support the dictator Bonaparte.[59]

What destroyed the IWMA? Often overlooked for more obscure ideological disputes is the reign of reaction that hit Europe in the aftermath of the Paris Commune. This repression supplemented already existing police intimidation and spying. As one historian comments, "It was the European reaction inspired by fear of the Commune and the International, rather than Bakunin's attempts at a takeover, which wrecked Marx's International."[60] In the wake of the destruction of the first workers' government in Paris in 1871, it became open season on the IWMA.[61] Police in Leipzig warned taverns that their licenses would be in danger if IWMA members were seen gathering within.[62] One chief of police attempted to found an IWMA section so that his agents could intervene as delegates in congresses.[63] Even "liberal" Britain was thrown into the frenzy with Prime Minister Gladstone reportedly thinking of expelling Marx and others from the country.[64] One Member of Parliament claimed leaders of the International had both planned the Commune and ordered the French Communards to execute the Paris Archbishop.[65] The mainstream press bayed like a pack of hounds thirsty for the blood of the International.[66]

But the problems that led to the demise of the IWMA were of little concern to the region we now call Germany. Around the time Italy was born, and slightly after the rise and fall of the IWMA, Germany was still a confusing stew of 39 different kingdoms, duchies, principalities and city-states. Before undergoing a Prussian-led, top-down unification, it was not even generally agreed upon what territories should make up a German-speaking nation. Should a greater Germany be established which included the still-powerful Austrians, or should it be a smaller nation-state that excluded the lands ruled by the Hapsburgs? During 1848, a German national assembly met at Frankfurt am Main, naïvely hoping to convince their hereditary rulers to commit political suicide. But when class and self-interest won the day, hopes for a united Germany with freedom of speech, trial by jury and so forth were crushed. The next attempt at unification, though successful, was undemocratic and authoritarian. It was not the result of popular movements but rather the skillful use of force by Otto von Bismarck of Prussia.

In a series of carefully crafted maneuvers in the early 1860s, Bismarck first allied with Austria to fight Denmark over their southern provinces of Schleswig and Holstein. Next in 1866, the Prussians provoked a war with the Roman Catholic Austrians, uniting most of the Protestant northern German lands in the process. Austria, like Denmark before it, was quickly defeated and forced to pull back from German affairs. Now, the Berlin-based militarists faced a delicate situation. The southern German states were Catholic and had traditionally looked to Vienna, not Berlin, for leadership. Bismarck wisely gambled that, in the final analysis, the southern Germans would prove more anti-French than anti-Prussian. In 1870, Prussia cleverly created a diplomatic incident that provoked the reckless French dictator Louis Napoleon into declaring war. Bismarck successfully painted this misstep by Paris as foreign aggression against all Germans. The southern Germans joined with the Prussian-led northern federation to defeat the corrupt and inept French government in a brief war. Before the other great powers (e.g. Britain, Russia) had time to consider the implications of the German victory, the German Empire was proclaimed in January 1871.

As impressive as this accomplishment was, it had some very negative results. Liberalism was jettisoned along with most of the ideals of 1848. Most hitherto liberal German bourgeois would satisfy themselves with unification, even if it came without a republic. Often overlooked is that at the same time, German conservatives "became themselves the prisoners of the nationalistic sentiment with which they sought to broaden their popular support."[67] As noted before, the bourgeoisie had abandoned their attachment to liberal, republican ideas out of fear of those who actually made change possible: the common people or to be more specific, the proletariat. Why was the business class willing to abandon virtually everything but remained wedded to the concept of the nation-state?

The reason, as is so often the case for those in business, was material gain. The disunity of German-speaking central Europe had been a huge obstacle to the expansion of business and a drain on profits. For all the noble talk that frequently accompanies nationalist movements, for the bourgeoisie it all came down to money. One factory owner-turned-revolutionary observed that it was not any love of freedom that drove the well-off to the flag of German unity. No:

> ... it was the desire of the practical merchant and industrialist arising out of immediate business needs to sweep away all the historically inherited small junk which was obstructing the free development of commerce and industry ... German unity had become an economic necessity.[68]

Out of Louis Napoleon's farcical military downfall, as was noted, came a united Germany in 1871. But, a new nation-state forged by Bismarck's policy of blood and iron was not the only offspring of the French government's debacle. Along with the birth of a powerful new entity Germany, which was more of an army with a state than a state with an army, came its mirror opposite, the Commune. Also, the Commune of Paris, an experiment in popular democracy that still inspires today.

The Commune was the result of neither conspiracy nor preplanned program. It grew out of the demise of the French Second Empire and the grand bourgeoisie's willingness to abandon Paris to the victorious Prussians. As one author observed, "it was the Parisian solution to the collapse of legally constituted authority in the vacuum of defeat that followed the 1870 Franco-Prussian war."[69] The actual nature of the Commune has long been a source of confusion. At the time, even a supportive Karl Marx called it a "sphinx" because it seemed so mysterious. One historian chalks up the difficulty in describing the Paris Commune to the fact that it was a "genuine mass democratic movement, reflecting an abundance of different ideas, [so] no easy definition could suffice."[70] It has been hailed as the first workers' state and said to be a purely local reaction to a collapsed state apparatus. Some have made the case that it was both things at the same time. Many scholars have never really made up their mind.

By March 1871, the citizens of Paris had endured months of suffering, military humiliation and the death of loved ones. When the Bonaparte dictatorship was replaced with the Third Republic, things should have improved dramatically but for most of the common people they had not. The new government capitulated repeatedly to the German-speaking invaders. The entry of Bismarck's troops into Paris, albeit only for a limited and mainly symbolic occupation, was a bitter experience for most Parisians. The National Guard of Paris reorganized itself and elected a central committee. Steadily but without a clear vision of where they were going, the Guard transformed itself into an alternative government that challenged the legitimacy of the Republic headed by Adolphe Thiers. On March 18, this provisional government attempted to disarm Paris by sending in regular army units to seize cannons and arms. The soldiers, however, fraternized with the city's common people and refused to carry out orders. When told to fire on radical crowds, the troops refused and even killed two of their own generals. Most soldiers then peacefully went back to their family homes, although some stayed to fight with Paris.[71] Two days later, Thiers and his "National Assembly" fled to the calm and relative safety of Versailles, the former home of Louis XVI. The Civil War in France had begun.

The richest residents of Paris, who had not fled during the war, followed suit very soon after this and left the capital as well. Paris was left in the hands of what can only be called the common people. A detailed study of more than 36,000 Communards who were arrested later found only 8 percent had been what we would call "white-collar workers" and a mere 4 percent were small businesspeople, with another 4 percent coming from the professional strata of doctors and lawyers. The remaining 84 percent of Paris was mainly from the manual trades and in almost all cases were wage earners.[72] Not surprising, therefore, that so many have viewed the Commune as a workers' uprising. While the Commune attempted to practice liberty, equality and solidarity and, for example, restricted the highest government salary to 6,000 francs, the gathering at the old palace of the French kings was cut from a different cloth.[73]

German playwright Bertolt Brecht captured the spirit of Thiers and his colleagues in the play, *The Days of the Commune*. Brecht penned this fictional, but all too believable, dialogue in which Thiers spoke to Jules Faure in these words:

> … our civilization is founded on property. Property must be protected at all costs. They [Paris] have the nerve to dictate to use what we must give up and what we can keep? Get me sabres, get me cavalry, if it takes a sea of blood to wash Paris clean of its vermin then let us have a sea of blood.[74]

It is true that from a military viewpoint, the Paris Commune probably didn't have much of a chance. After all, the bulk of the nation's military assets were under the control of the Versailles government, not revolutionary Paris. All the same, reactionaries feared that if the ideas boiling up in the capital ever spread to the countryside that situation might change.[75] What was so dangerous about the Communards' ideas?

First, they established a radical participatory form of democracy that was in almost complete contradiction to traditional parliamentary systems. This new democratic experiment relied on the mobilization of the average citizen whereas traditional republics had depended on popular apathy, encouraging an attitude among the common people that governing ought to be left up to the "better sort." Further, the social reforms in the sphere of education were alone sufficient for the Commune to earn a secure place in the heart of radicals.[76] In the same spirit, night work for bakers was abolished and labor conditions improved throughout all branches of the economy, as abandoned workshops were converted into worker-owned cooperatives.[77] One aspect of the Communard experiment all too seldom mentioned is the vital role of women.

Books written by, for and about men typically narrate the events in 1871 Paris as if all the females in the capital were at home cooking. When women are introduced into the story, it is often only as the libel that they ran around (irrationally) setting fires during the fall of the Commune.[78] This depiction is far from the reality, as described by eyewitnesses to female involvement in the rebellion. Of notable significance was Elisabeth Dmitrieff, founder of the International in Russia, who was also a key figure in the *Union de Femmes*, a particularly important woman's organization.[79] Moreover, there were women active in various political clubs throughout the brief lifespan of the Commune. Another important female participant was the anarchist, Louise Michel, who fought oppression in Paris and continued her fight when sentenced to a South Pacific penal colony.[80]

The *Union de Femmes* was arguably the most advanced expression of class-consciousness during the Commune. By mobilizing working-class women into active participation in the life of the Commune, they helped partially overcome centuries of anti-female prejudice. Women achieved positions of power within the new administration. Female Communards administered welfare and worked on educational reform, including increasing schooling for girls. Progressively, old tired clichés employed against the idea of women's equality were dismissed as baseless as arguments in defense of slavery.[81] The radical women of the Commune struggled towards critiques of gender, class, culture and traditional power arrangements. Not surprisingly, different female thinkers came to various conclusions. Yet, all attempted to build bridges to a world of gender equality and social justice.[82]

At first, all this revolutionary activity by women, typically from the lower orders of society, might appear strange or even fanciful. Yet, there is a massive amount of hard evidence that confirms the vital role of the Commune's female members. This mobilization corresponds to a certain cold logic. As Edith Thomas argued decades ago, "it is understandable that women, who are the first to suffer under the social order, would have a hand in a revolutionary movement aimed at changing that order."[83] Throughout April 1871, the women of Paris together with their male comrades proceeded to build one of the most democratic and egalitarian societies ever witnessed in Europe. Obviously, the forces of tradition and order could not stand for this—particularly as it might spread beyond Paris. On May 21, troops dispatched by the Versailles government entered Paris. Despite heroic resistance, the Communards were unable to overcome the heavily armed and professionally led forces. In the actual street fighting, the Commune lost between 3,000 and 10,000 people while the invaders lost only 877.[84]

An even higher pile of corpses was to be erected in the "bloody week" that followed close on to the military defeat of the Commune. Determined to, in Thiers's words, "bleed democracy dry for a generation," the capitalist state took revenge on radical Paris with an estimated 40,000 executed. Women made up about a fifth of these murdered civilians. Another 50,000 individuals were arrested, often on evidence as scant as being found to have the calloused hands of a worker. While many were later released, over 10,000 of these were sentenced with as many as 4,000 transported to a penal colony in New Caledonia. This number was so large that it took the French Navy a year to move this massive human cargo of radicalism.[85]

Given the short life and violent death of the Commune, it is reasonable to ask, why is it still so important? The Commune did not establish a long-lasting government nor did it immediately transform society in any obvious way. Yet, as an example (a myth some might say), of common people rising up not just to protest but to take power and rule, it gives hope to the left and nightmares to the right. It is an exaggeration to say, as one historian did, that the working class in France was made "as a result of the construction of a collective memory, the myth of the Paris Commune."[86] All the same, the Commune was an important part in the consciousness of the European labor movement. The victors understood the power of this example and did all they could to destroy the memory,[87] but it is remembered to the present day. In any number of ways, the Commune is a founding myth, a memory or story for the organized, particularly radical, working class in Europe. In spite of the setback the left suffered when Paris fell and the vicious repression that followed, the commoners were able to organize themselves successfully in the years after the suppression of the Commune and before the great imperialist slaughter of 1914–18.

CHAPTER SEVEN

The Rise of the Working Classes: Trade Unions and Socialism, 1871–1914

Radicals in nineteenth-century Europe devoted themselves to more than grand transcontinental enterprises like the First International or radical insurrections like the Commune.[1] They built up organizations of workers, which could both fight for material improvements (higher wages, shorter hours, better working conditions) and prepare proletarians to take power in the future. Although the origins of trade unions can be traced backed to the medieval guilds, unionism took on a new importance in the period after 1871. The growth of unionism was made possible by broad developments largely outside the movement's control: 1) the economic cycle, 2) technological and social changes, 3) political developments, and 4) the relative strength of employers and workers both organizationally and ideologically.

During periods of widespread unemployment and economic downturn, trade unions were inevitably taxed to the limits of their strength, often crushed altogether. Having no control over the boom-or-bust nature of the economy, workers often despaired of union activity, strikes especially, feeling their positions hopeless in face of ever-changing providence. As the economy improved and employment rose, so did the prospects for unionism. Likewise, the rapid introduction of technological change could render entire groups of workers powerless. Hand weavers serve as one often cited example, for these workers saw their craft skills replaced by machines in a matter of a few years. Yet, once workers became acclimated to the new technology, their self-confidence returned.

Nor was the political system an impartial spectator standing on the sidelines of industrial conflict. Governments throughout Europe actively helped the bourgeoisie accumulate capital and hence control its workforce. As a result, worker's rights were severely restricted for much of the nineteenth century with unions outlawed or, at a minimum, prohibited from striking. Thus, wherever trade unionism developed in Europe, it always did so with a keen eye cast upon the political system and how it could be altered to level the playing field between the bourgeoisie and the laborers. In addition, the conflict between laborers and the bourgeoisie was an ideological battle as well. That is, the capitalists sought to convince workers that theirs was the "best of all possible worlds" while radicals created an alternative worldview.

Given these inherent difficulties, trade unions never succeeded in organizing more than a fraction of those who toiled for wages. With the possible exception of Britain, unionism operated on the margins rather than in the heart of large-scale industry. Trade union members were mostly highly skilled workers employed in small to medium enterprises. Given the heterogeneous nature of the working class, union organizations were usually local or, at best, regional. Trade unions often rejected strikes either for ideological reasons or because they had no opportunity of winning a direct confrontation with the bourgeoisie. By the mid-1870s, a recession hit much of Western Europe; the resulting increase in unemployment rendered most unions ineffective or dismantled them completely. Yet by the end of the nineteenth century, the diverse and often hostile segments of the European working class began to come together, often under at least nominally revolutionary leadership.

As industrial capitalism expanded and, in turn, restructured the labor process, it radically altered the lives of average people. One response to the devastating economic and social subordination so many workers experienced was trade unionism. Trade unions offered a pragmatic way of collectively advancing, or at least defending, proletarian interests in a way that individual efforts could not. With the rise of industrial capitalism, a laborer's skills, which traditionally had protected workers' living standards, became less important. Many a worker who once could count on their skill to guarantee both steady employment and a living wage, now turned to collective organization for help.[2]

Unlike those in the United States, these unions were often socialist in their perspective. Socialism provided a framework that allowed the average person to understand and interpret the tensions of industrial society. Thus, on both the practical and the ideological level, trade unions were to become an indispensable part of organized resistance to capitalist society. This is exemplified by the fact that the majority of trade unions were typically associated with a radical political party. In Germany, the Social Democratic Party had, in fact, created the so-called "Free Trade Unions." Across the Rhine River in France, the national trade union federation, *Confédération Générale du Travail* (CGT), was associated with the doctrine of revolutionary syndicalism.[3] Even in relatively moderate Britain, the unions were typically socialist in outlook and instrumental in the creation of the Labour Party.[4]

The last two decades of the nineteenth century saw a steady and rapid rise in the number of unionized workers. Britain, France and Germany can be held up as paradigmatic of the unparalleled gains trade unionism made during this period. In Britain, the first nation to have an industrial revolution, there existed 674,000 union members in 1887. A mere five years later, in 1892, union membership had soared to over a million and a half, while by 1905, 1,997,000 people carried union cards. Across the Channel on the Continent, the increases were just as striking. In France, despite the relatively slow pace of industrialization and the continuing preponderance of the peasantry, there were 139,000 trade unionists in 1890. This figure more than doubled in three years, and by 1893, there were 402,000 union members. In 1902, less than a decade later, the total had reached 614,000. Meanwhile, the rapid industrialization of the newly united German Empire would result in even more spectacular growth. From the relatively low number of 95,000 workers enrolled in trade unions in 1887, German union membership had skyrocketed to 294,000 by 1890. This swift expansion continued into the twentieth century with 887,000 workers belonging to unions by 1903.[5]

As always is the case with statistics, these numbers say little in and of themselves. But they are indicative of the growth of a mass base for radical politics among the European working class. Further, growing union membership was accompanied by waves of intensive labor struggles and massive industrial conflicts. Not only did more strikes take place,[6] the whole character of the trade union movement changed during the last decades of the century. Whereas trade unions had previously been largely passive self-help organizations, members began to see the unions as the best mode to actively challenge the status quo and advocate for improvement in working conditions and standards of living. Increasingly, trade unions were viewed not only as struggling for immediate concessions to improve labor conditions, but as part of a broader revolutionary process for the working class as a whole. While this was a general trend, not all unionists were revolutionary.

Union membership not only increased in numbers but in scope, as the types of workers who joined expanded to different industries. Much of the boost in membership came from the organization of previously non-union-ized labor. Proletarians such as dock workers, miners, gas workers and transportation workers joined organized labor. What all these trades had in common, besides their previous non-union status, was that they were in key sectors of the industrial economy. Therefore, a strike within any one of these industries would have repercussions reaching much further than that sector alone. After all, miners and gas workers provided the energy that drove the industrial economy, while dock workers and other transportation workers were vital to the flow of goods and services.

During this same period, hundreds of thousands, if not millions, of women were forced by economic necessity to work outside of the home. During the 1880s and 1890s, nearly a third of all females over age 10 worked outside their households in Britain and France, nearly 20 percent did so in Germany. Although domestic service accounted for a large number of these female workers (by 1891 there were 2,000,000 domestics in the extreme case of Britain), women workers also labored in textile, clothing and, increasingly, food manufacture. Of course, even these figures understate the extent of female labor, especially since most working-class women worked at least part-time (taking in laundry, for example) and all but a fortunate few were occupied with socially necessary but unpaid work in the home. Although still concentrated in typical "female" industries, women began to play an even more important role in the labor movement as both their number and the diversity of their employment grew.

Moreover, the trade unions themselves tended to change. Both through mergers and the birth of new unions, the labor movement at the end of the century looked quite different from the fragmented, craft-oriented organizations of earlier days. As hitherto unorganized workers poured into the trade union movement, the conventional wisdom, which held that strikes were usually counterproductive, was soon abandoned. While more moderate craft unions still persisted, in the twentieth century, the "new Unionism" would lead to the development of mass industrial unions. In these unions, all members of a plant belonged to the same union, instead of being divided across numerous craft lines. This change within the trade unions was heavily influenced by a number of trendsetting strikes such as the London dock strike of 1889. These strikes aroused workers to the possibility, if not necessity, of both trade union organization and militant actions in the workplace. These battles were not purely a matter of "bread and butter," although such routine issues were important. In many instances, particularly in certain nations like Germany, strikes helped to satisfy the thirst for action which had been dammed up by years of despotism. Many German workers, for example, failed to differentiate between strikes and unions, on the one side, and the social revolution's political expression— social democracy—on the other. Even where the root cause of strikes was most clearly economic, many saw the conflict in terms of a struggle for power.

While struggles intensified in the workplace, workers viewed politics as a means to improve their condition. Pre-existing radical and republican hatreds of the "rich" and the "plutocracy" intensified after 1871. The bitter ordeal of industrialization ultimately convinced many, particularly manual workers, of the injustice of the social order. As workers felt increasingly distant from the world of the bourgeoisie, the idea of class-based political parties gained wider acceptance. Political parties began to represent specific social groups in society rather than claiming to speak for the entire nation. In Britain, the Labour Party, as the name suggests, saw itself as presenting the interest of the working people while Tories, or conservatives, claimed to represent all British men. Segregated in their proletarian districts (ghettos) like Wedding in Berlin or West Ham in London, workers viewed political issues, such as the fight for extension of voting rights, from the perspective of proletarians, not just citizens.

As even the most modest property qualification for voting would disenfranchise many working-class men (few in power yet envisioned giving women the vote), workers overwhelmingly became proponents of universal suffrage—at least for male citizens.[7] Where universal suffrage was lacking, massive struggles took place. The enormous general strike in Belgium in 1892, which demanded an expansion of the franchise, is just one such example. Since governments were national in scope, any effort to pressure them had to likewise be national if it were to have any hope of success. Thus, the very organization of national states in Europe helped push the working class in each country toward the formation of national, class-based parties. These parties were typically called "socialist" or "social democratic". In fact, these two words were considered interchangeable in the nineteenth century.[8]

The most powerful of these parties was to be the Social Democratic Party of Germany (SPD), formed in 1875 by the combination of two hitherto hostile groupings: the state socialist Lassalleans who attempted to collaborate with the government and the Marxist-oriented Eisenachers.[9] Despite attempts to destroy this party with a series of repressive laws enacted by the German Reichstag in 1878, the Social Democrats, under the leadership of August Bebel and Wilhelm Liebknecht,[10] were to become an "empire within an empire." This is certainly true if election results are any indication. Starting with less than 125,000 votes in 1871, the SPD would gather over 500,000 in 1884. Six years later, in 1890, over 1 million German men cast their ballots for the Social Democrats while this figure doubled to over 2 million votes by 1898.

Not merely an election machine, the German Social Democrats furthermore possessed a press empire. By the end of the nineteenth century, the SPD had 75 papers of which over half were dailies. Besides their theoretical journal *Die Neue Zeit* (The New Age) which advanced Marxist theory, there were a surprising number of non-political publications affiliated with the party. Among the latter were various special-interest publications, many with a circulation over 100,000. Thus, a radical intellectual could spend the evening perusing the pages of *Die Neue Zeit* while less theoretically oriented workers could spend their free time with *Der Arbeiter Radfahrer* (The Worker Cyclist) or the *Arbeiter Turnzeitung* (The Worker Gymnastic) Even socialist innkeepers and stenographers had their own publications.

The party created an entire alternative world for their supporters.[11] If a worker wanted to borrow a novel, there were worker libraries.[12] Those who wished to sing could join "red" singing societies. For those who enjoyed beer, there were frequent meetings and dinners in beer halls, while those with a drinking problem could join the German Workers Temperance Federation. These activities served a number of important functions. They created a sense of belonging, that is, group solidarity among socialist workers who otherwise might have been isolated or demoralized. Meanwhile, the party press and the seemingly countless SPD-sponsored activities served to form an information network where issues could be discussed and news exchanged. Thus, a night at the local *biergarten* might allow debate on controversial party proposals, and be a place for a member to find out about possible job openings from comrades, while also offering casual socializing and entertainment.

Not all Social Democrats were content to limit their agitation to only economic or more traditional "worker" issues. Even topics as controversial as sexuality and sexual preference drew the attention of some in the party. Thus, when Oscar Wilde was arrested on a morals charge for homosexual activity in 1895, an article in *Die Neue Zeit* defended the Irish author and decried the "arbitrary moral concepts" which had led to his detention. Of course, most socialists were loath to add gay rights to their already lengthy list of demands. Still, in 1898, from his seat in Parliament, August Bebel openly championed a petition to legalize homosexual relations between consenting adults over 16 years of age.

Yet even in Germany, where not all workers voted for the Social Democrats let alone belonged to the party, there still developed a remarkable identification of the proletariat with the socialist political parties. So much so that an election analyst in one central German district before World War I expressed amazement that "only" 88 percent of workers voted for the SPD. Germany may have been one of the most extreme cases in regards to worker's allegiance to socialist parties, but the SPD was far from the only socialist party to be born and grow up in the last decades of the nineteenth century.

Pablo Iglesias, who was to be the first socialist in the Spanish Parliament, helped form the Spanish Social Democratic Party in 1879, and a similar party was born in Denmark in the same year. By 1882, France's *Parti Ouvrier* was organized by Jules Guesde, and five years thereafter a Norwegian Social Democratic Party began. In 1888, socialist political parties were established in both Switzerland and the Austro-Hungarian Empire, followed the next year by a new party in Sweden. The Social Democratic Federation in the Netherlands was also formed in 1889. Finally in 1893, in the birthplace of industrial capitalism, Britain witnessed the formation of the Independent Labour Party[13] by Keir Hardie and other socialists.

While other socialist parties could not match the level of electoral success enjoyed by the German party, they were, nonetheless, steadily growing in popularity among the masses. By 1897, the Italian Socialists were to receive 135,000 votes while the Austrian Social Democrats won about 600,000 votes. In 1898, socialists in France saw over 750,000 ballots cast for their candidates while by the end of the century there were 31 socialists in the Belgium Parliament. Even largely rural Finland saw a huge surge of socialist activity by the early twentieth century.[14]

Each party was fashioned within the traditions of its nation and heavily influenced by the leaders who gave it direction. Thus, the French or Spanish parties lacked the iron discipline and significant Marxist influence of the Austrian or German parties. The British Labour Party[15] looked as much to the work of Robert Owen, a utopian socialist, or the Chartists, who thought universal suffrage would solve labor problems, as to the *Communist Manifesto*. It was this identification that led them to create a Socialist International in 1889. For all their dissimilarities, these parties held certain fundamental beliefs in common: all believed in working towards a socialist society, based in democracy and equality. In contrast to non-socialist democrats, they believed in economic democracy and equality, which to them meant the socialization of the means of production. That is, socialists believed in the right to vote but also the right to eat. They felt that political democracy was essential but so was a social equality which would ensure that no one lacked the basic human necessities such as food, housing and health care. As much as their individual notions of socialism diverged, these organizations shared a conviction in the socialist future. Under the careful eye of the scholar, these parties might appear quite different, but to their members such nuances were of little regard.

Socialists knew that this revolutionary process could never succeed if it took place only within one nation. And so they endeavored to coordinate their efforts across national boundaries. On July 14, 1889, the hundredth anniversary of the storming of the Bastille during the French Revolution, two international meetings took place in Paris. In one hall sat representatives of English trade unions and moderate French socialists. In another, sat a gathering of socialists from the European continent who considered themselves Marxists. Many delegates attempted to attend the meetings of both groups while anarchists enthusiastically tried to disrupt them all. Out of this organizational competition and chaos, the Marxist-oriented group emerged the more popular.

Like the IWMA a quarter-century before, this International Workers' Congress held greater symbolic than practical significance. This situation arose because unlike the First International, the Socialist International was to be composed of socialist parties and bona fide trade unions.[16]

Accordingly, argument raged over who was and who was not a "genuine" representative from a "bona fide" association. In fact, most of the first two days of the gathering were wasted in squabbles over who was entitled to vote. After this process was completed and various anarchists, who jumped up on tables to denounce meeting organizers as traitors, were expelled, the congress did make progress. For three days, delegates heard reports on the socialist movement in the different countries represented.

To push for the eight-hour day, it was decided that May 1 should be the occasion for worldwide workers' protests, which would demonstrate the power of the new International. This day had become symbolic for radicals since 1886 when labor protests in Chicago led to a deadly confrontation with the police during which an unknown individual threw a bomb into the crowd. Eight police officers and an unknown number of workers were killed by the explosion and in the resulting police crossfire. In an atmosphere of hysteria whipped up by the press against the "scum of Europe," eight anarchist labor organizers were prosecuted for conspiracy to commit murder. All defendants were found guilty and four were sent to the gallows.

Despite endless disagreements over implementation, the European left almost universally welcomed the idea of May Day protests. When May 1, 1890 came, even the most pessimistic were overwhelmed by the size and spirit of the demonstrations. While it was not astonishing that there were widespread work stoppages in France, strikes also broke out in Austria, Hungary, Belgium, the Netherlands and the Scandinavian nations, as well as in Italy and Spain. By way of contrast, the British trade unions avoided strikes and held their mass meeting on May 4. Even so, the rally held in London's Hyde Park attracted well over 250,000 people, ranging from dockers in their rough clothes to working women dressed in their finest apparel. Likewise, the German SPD thought it unwise to provoke the government and tried to avoid work stoppages. Despite pleas from party officials against "an undue show of spirit," 40,000 workers in the port city of Hamburg stayed away from work.

The next gathering was held in Brussels in August 1891 with 337 delegates in attendance and representing 15 different countries. Immensely heartened by the success of May Day in 1890 and 1891, this congress resolved to make it an annual event while adding the demand for continued peace between nations to the official list of demands. This time the International took the opportunity to call for a labor standstill on May 1. Although this resolution was to apply to supporters throughout the world, there remained an escape hatch for the more timid or vulnerable. Thus, the final resolution called for strikes on May Day "everywhere except where it is impracticable." These varied approaches to May Day foreshadowed differences within the International that would later escalate and finally lead to its destruction in 1914.

Since the socialists had no wish to alienate the unions which were such a critical part of their overall revolutionary strategy, they had no choice but to suffer the occasional anarchist from Italy or even some English unionists who remained wedded to the Liberal Party. Members of the Second International regarded the organization as the overall framework in which radical parties could unite the entire working class. The working class was greatly diverse, with varying levels of consciousness and differing political beliefs, and the socialist parties and their International made every attempt to accommodate these differences. If the Communist motto in the twentieth century was to be, in Lenin's words, "Better fewer but better," the nineteenth-century socialists felt, despite their exasperation with the anarchists, "The more, the merrier."

Throughout Europe, different strata of society increasingly came forward with demands that women be granted equal rights and opportunities. While socialists agreed with the moral arguments made by middle-class feminists that the suppression of females was unjust, they had a distinctive theory on the question of women. For the left, in the words of Clara Zetkin, "the question of women's emancipation is, in the end, the question of women's work."

That is, leftists argued, that the oppression of women was rooted within the needs of a class-stratified economic system. If the institution of private property had dictated the domination of women by men, then women working outside of the home would be a precondition for women gaining equal rights. In the writings of socialist feminists like Zetkin and men like August Bebel and Frederick Engels, there was a common theme: the working-class man cannot be free if he continues to oppress the working-class woman. By the closing decades of the nineteenth century, the Marxist prediction of growing female participation in the labor force seemed to be coming true. Ever greater numbers of women were seeking work outside the home in all the industrialized nations of Europe. However, once in the factory or workshop, the woman worker was exploited even more intensely than her male counterpart. Female laborers commonly received only half (or less than half) of the wages a man was paid for the same work. In addition, unlike men, women had no political rights. They could neither run for public office nor vote. In some countries, there were even prohibitions on women attending political meetings.

As more lower-class women entered the industrial workforce, they frequently found neither their male co-workers nor middle-class feminist "ladies" of much help. The former saw them as unwanted competition for jobs and a downward pressure on wages, while the latter were preoccupied with achieving equality within the existing order. Workers seldom followed the high-minded words of Bebel in *Women Under Socialism* where he stressed female equality, while middle-class women's issues, like female admittance to medical schools, were not a burning concern for factory females. Therefore, working women struggled to build their own unions and organizations—but typically under the general guidance of the socialist movement.

If this failure to build exclusively feminist organizations seems strange, bear in mind that the socialist movement offered one of the few places in a male-dominated society where women could develop their abilities. Further, for all the sexism which remained among male workers, the socialists promised a revolutionary transformation of society which would require a new equality among the sexes. The primary choice was between revolutionary politics and religion. Fighting against the rising tide of secularism, the churches, particularly the Roman Catholic Church, sought to maintain, if not expand, their female base. The Roman Catholic Church postured as the defender of traditional women's rights and attempted to pit pious wife against atheistic husband. The dramatic growth in full-time female church personnel, the papacy's encouragement of the cult of the Virgin Mary, and the creation of additional female saints were all attempts to incorporate women into "Holy Mother Church."

As the number of working women increased, so did their self-confidence. A strike by "match girls" at London match factories in 1888 resulted in a modest pay increase, for instance. More and more women became members of trade unions, although these women remained a minority of the female labor force. Though female membership was still a small percentage, the growth was symbolically quite significant, given that only a generation before trade unionism had been almost an exclusively male institution. By 1913, most industrial countries could boast women within the organized labor movement. Their percentage of trade union membership ranged from a modest number in some countries (5 percent in Sweden) to a somewhat more substantial figure in others (9 percent in Germany, 10.5 percent in Britain, and 12.3 percent in Finland.) Statistics aside, trade unionism was poised for an explosive influx of female members that would occur soon after the beginning of World War I.

It is fitting to address another element inside the movement. Anarchism, like socialism, democracy, freedom, or any other abstract concept, is a doctrine which defies simple definition. This is particularly true for anarchism, as it placed an extreme emphasis on the individual. In general, however, anarchism in the nineteenth century rejected all political authority and, thereby, any participation in elections. Furthermore, anarchists had as their goal the elimination of any state or government, hoping to replace such structures with a self-regulated society of individuals.[17]

While all anarchist theory rests on the intellectual basis of nineteenth-century liberalism, there was a clear dividing line between those anarchists who believed in private property (in the twentieth-first century, these people call themselves "libertarians") and those who rejected private ownership as a source of social inequality. It was the latter—alternatively called "libertarian socialists," "anarcho-communists," or "socialist anarchists"— that were to be important in the European revolutionary movement and in giving the socialists so many headaches.

Although few actually practiced it, anarchists believed in, or at a minimum defended, "propaganda of the deed," a doctrine which held that talking about oppression, organizing protest meetings, or voting in elections all wasted time. What was needed, argued the anarchists, was an illustration to the downtrodden of the weakness of the system. What better demonstration than the assassination of prominent members of the state like czars, kings and presidents? By employing terrorism against the bourgeoisie and their representatives, "propaganda of the deed" was intended to spark popular insurrections. However, while there were a number of political killings and even more unsuccessful assassination attempts, there were no mass uprisings.

After 1878, anarchist "propaganda of the deed," which had previously been limited to Russia, Italy and Spain, spread throughout Europe. Two unsuccessful attempts were made on the life of Kaiser Wilhelm I of Germany which gave Bismarck a long-sought excuse to outlaw the socialist movement. That neither of the men who attempted to kill Wilhelm I were Social Democrats nor the fact that the party repeatedly condemned individual acts of terror was of any help to the soon-outlawed SPD. This incident nicely illustrates one motivation socialists had for hating anarchism. The Social Democrats, not only in Germany, viewed anarchists as frustrated petty bourgeois (or small businessmen) and lumpenproletarian (or habitually unemployed) adventurers who provided the police with the justification they sought to repress the left. That is, the socialists saw anarchists as frivolous, and often unstable, individuals who rejected the hard labor necessary to build a revolutionary movement. In the eyes of socialists, the anarchists opted instead for the emotionally satisfying, but inherently counterproductive, path of violence.

Although the vast majority of anarchists personally rejected homicide as a political procedure, few would criticize assassinations. Indeed, "propaganda of the deed" was approved in principle by an Anarchist Congress held in Switzerland in 1879. That the bulk of those attending did so either as a response to the extreme repression existing in czarist Russia, or out of abstract principle, made little difference to European socialists or, for that matter, the general public. Anarchism's identification with murder made it easy to brand every lunatic who killed a prominent person with the labels "anarchist" and "revolutionary." Based upon an essentially individualistic worldview, many anarchists simply did not believe in democracy. After all, majority rule and representative democracy of necessity limited the liberty of the individual. In essence, political freedom was not the goal for anarchists, but rather freedom from politics altogether.

As a result of their tactics, anarchist groups suffered major repression, and the public's rejection of violence left a limited base for their groups to find support. In response, anarchists began to develop an alternative revolutionary strategy. This new doctrine was known as syndicalism. The word "syndicalism" is the English translation of the French term for trade unionism. Syndicalism's goal was to turn unions into revolutionary instruments which would form the basis of the new society. Rather than promoting "propaganda of the deed," syndicalists believed that a general strike could paralyze society and thus spark revolution. During this general strike, the workers would take over the means of production and abolish the state, replacing it with a new society based on workers' organizations. Thus, syndicalism remedied anarchism's glaring organizational problem with a reliance on union structures.

Like anarchism, syndicalism was never a coherent theory, as the emphasis was on deeds not words. Among key themes, however, was the importance of militancy in the workplace, including sabotage as a means of struggle, and the centrality of rank-and-file initiative. To prepare for the revolution, syndicalists proclaimed the necessity of organizing unskilled workers while arguing that contracts signed with capitalists need not be honored. By promoting direct action, they felt the class consciousness of workers would be enhanced and the bourgeoisie weakened until the day the general strike signaled the beginning of the revolution. The only field of action that mattered was the industrial battlefield. All other campaigns and political activities were at best, to the syndicalists, mere distractions for the working class.

This movement reached its greatest heights in France where the syndicalist *Confédération Générale du Travail* (CGT), founded by an anarchist named Fernand Pelloutier, was to become one of the major trade union federations. Refraining from the more normal union activities like saving funds for pensions, this collection of pugnacious unions devoted itself to direct action. Before World War I, the CGT was to play a prominent role in many militant labor struggles, including strikes among railroad workers and civil servants. The CGT even attempted to organize soldiers within the French Army. Although syndicalism went on to have influence in other countries, notably in Spain and Italy, nowhere else did it achieve such victories.

In the last decades of the nineteenth century, governments looked upon the expanding left-wing movement with alarm. While governments made occasional concessions to improve the life of the average worker, the stick of repression was used at least as much as the carrot of compromise. Even liberal Britain massively expanded her repressive apparatus in the years before World War I, with the number of police increasing 20 percent in the last pre-war years. This enlargement of the British police force did not occur solely to fight common criminals, but rather, in the words of one police inspector, to combat general unrest "too great for its normal strength."

Repression took many different forms and varied in intensity from place to place. Britain, for instance, shied away from the outright use of force, save for exceptional situations. In contrast, czarist Russia elevated the whip and Siberian exile to almost a state religious ritual in its drive to curb revolutionaries. Although few European countries were as tolerant as Britain or as brutal as Russia, all practiced some form of suppression to control those who challenged the status quo. Though their methods varied, their goals did not. One universal method of control was the infiltration of radical groups by police spies. This snooping went beyond national borders. Imperial Germany, for example, went so far as to keep tabs on radicals in the United States. In addition, governments would often trade information on revolutionaries. Thus, details of a Russian exile's speech in New York City could wind up in St. Petersburg via Berlin. Likewise, the usually broad-minded British government was always anxious for information concerning anyone of Irish descent—and other nation's agents gladly provided it.

The best-known and most comprehensive attempt to crush revolutionaries in the nineteenth century was perhaps the anti-socialist law employed by Bismarck in Germany. The law was passed by the Reichstag in 1878, after a press campaign which tried to link the Social Democratic Party with the assassination attempts on Kaiser Wilhelm I. It was, in its time, the most far-reaching attempt to crush a radical party. Lasting until 1890, the law forbade all organizations or publications that attempted to subvert the social system or displayed socialist sympathies. The police had the right to arrest, interrogate and expel suspected socialists. The SPD and the affiliated free trade unions were thus dealt a terrible blow, as many SPD leaders were jailed or forced to flee the country while the socialist press was outlawed and public meetings banned. The only right the SPD retained was the ability to enter elections.[18]

Yet, twelve years later, the party and unions emerged stronger than ever because the socialists refused to give up, and utilized every means at their disposal to continue their fight. Election campaigns took on added significance as the only legal avenue for radical activity. Free to campaign publicly, German socialists used elections (and, when elected, their parliamentary seats) to crusade for their beliefs. In fact, it was said that the SPD speeches in the Reichstag were given "out the window." That is, they were not intended for other Parliament members but for the general public, who might be able to read about them in the mainstream press or the parliamentary record.

Further, SPD members built up a clandestine organization that illegally distributed various party publications including the central newspaper

Sozialdemokrat. Printing their publications in Switzerland or Britain, the Social Democrats would then smuggle them into Germany and distribute them among their supporters. This system of distribution was so efficient and successful that it became known as the "red postal service." At the same time, a network of secret agents was organized to hinder government spies. This network ultimately unmasked hundreds of police agents. Later, secret print shops were created within Germany and only the printing plates were smuggled in from abroad. In 1880, the *Sozialdemokrat* could boast of the thousands of copies distributed door to door, at factories, in the streets and squares, in omnibuses, and even in churches. Local party branches were gradually rebuilt under the guise of being apolitical organizations such as choral societies or smokers' clubs. Frequently, these "non-political" organizations would even have public meetings where lectures were given on some harmless-sounding topic like "The wild birds of central Europe." In reality, the talk would be a coded socialist discourse. (This speaks to the average policeman's lack of imagination for it usually took them some time to see through such transparent ruses.) The workplace was not ignored, as every large factory had trusted men who would secretly collect dues and pass on information.[19]

Hence, the anti-socialist laws were an abject failure. The German Social Democrats and their counterparts in other nations which suffered repression emerged stronger than ever before. Therefore, as the European left moved towards the twentieth century, an overwhelming sense of optimism prevailed among the revolutionary faithful. This optimism blinded many to the critical contradictions developing within their movement.

The movement's talk of revolution and stress on the proletariat made it difficult to win support from other social strata such as the peasantry or the small businessmen. Speeches about the coming socialization of agriculture may have warmed the hearts of many workers, but did little to endear the socialists to peasant farmers, who continued to represent a significant portion of the population. Middle-class progressives may have agreed with socialism's immediate reform goals, but hesitated to back a movement which sought to totally transform society. Some solid, pragmatic trade unionists felt that revolutionary rhetoric needlessly alarmed employers.

Thus within each European society, there developed a group of reformists who desired to jettison radical theories and shift class-based socialism into a more inclusive "people's party." In other words, they thought both the old class-based party model and revolutionary theories were obsolete. These pragmatic politicians argued that the days of revolution were over and that the true goals of socialism could be won gradually through reform legislation and stronger unions. These reformists saw the rising standard of living and increased social welfare laws as evidence against orthodox Marxism, which they felt held back change by needlessly alienating the urban middle class and the peasantry. As socialists expanded their representation in the various parliamentary bodies across Europe, more seats could be theirs if only non-working class and non-revolutionary voters could be reassured. In fact, many legislative seats then held by socialists were only achieved by a small, but vital, crossover by non-proletarian voters.

Further, the growing wealth of working-class institutions like unions, combined with relatively high wages for at least some sections of the working populace (the so-called "labor aristocracy"), produced a material basis for reformist theories. That is, the revolutionary slogan "we shall be all" lost much of its power since many no longer felt "we now are nought." While the economic base for reformism can be overestimated (some groups of highly paid workers remained devoted to revolutionary sentiments), it is important to consider that reformism as a theory only made sense during a period of material advancement. In addition, reformism was strongest in areas where socialists were less concentrated and under heavy pressure from non-socialists, such as in smaller towns or rural areas. The large concentration of workers in cities like Copenhagen, Turin, Berlin, or Paris would force such urban areas, in spite of middle-class residents, to remain radical "red," while smaller towns might turn reformist "pink."

Not surprisingly, the anarchists greeted splits within European socialist movement with glee. For the orthodox anarchist, the growth of reformism within the mainstream revolutionary movement was proof that they had been right all along. For the anarchists, all manifestations of "revisionism" were merely the logical conclusion to socialism's emphasis on electoral politics. While reformists sought to brand their radical socialist opponents as semi-anarchist, European anarchists saw these charges as further evidence that they, not the socialists, were the true revolutionaries. Unfortunately for the anarchists, they were in no position to capitalize on the difficulties confronting their socialist rivals.

In most northern European countries like Germany and Sweden, anarchism flourished among a few cafe intellectuals but lacked any mass influence. Even in nations like Italy and Spain where anarchism could truly be termed a movement, it suffered massive setbacks due to its association with "propaganda of the deed." The cycle of anarchist violence, followed by massive governmental repression, continued throughout the twentieth century. The immediate loser in this political battle was the anarchist movement, which saw its leaders jailed or exiled, and all manifestations of public activity severely attacked. Yet in the early twentieth century, a revived anarchist tendency became instrumental in the birth of a powerful syndicalist union—the *Confederacion Nacional del Trabajo* (CNT).

As with the French CGT, the CNT viewed trade union struggles as the most meaningful method of class struggle. On a day-to-day basis, the CNT promoted strikes and industrial sabotage as weapons to improve the condition of their members. Members of the CNT believed that the first step was the establishment of anarcho-syndicalist organizations across Spain. Then when this structure was robust enough to uphold a new society, a general strike would be called which would sweep away the old institutions. The organization believed that if the overwhelming majority of workers failed to report to their place of employment the economy would collapse along with all the bourgeois political structures.

As events in France would show, this was an illusion. True, the French CGT went on record during its Amiens Congress of 1906 as rejecting all political alliances in favor of complete trade union independence. Rather, the CGT argued, a federation of unions would bring together "all workers who are conscious of the need to struggle for the abolition of the wage system" and not concern themselves with electoral politics or parties. But the most solemn proclamations cannot preclude political pressures in the real world.

Although formed by an anarchist, the *Confédération Générale du Travail* was never of one mind when it came to political ideology. In addition to anarchists, there were "pure" syndicalists and socialists in the ranks of the CGT. There existed a minority reformist current within the organization that wished to avoid not only political affiliations but wanted to concentrate solely on economic activities. Although the revolutionaries had a clear majority, this reformist minority was by no means insignificant. Reformism was so strong in the last years of the nineteenth century that the leaders of the CGT's left wing saw "domestication" or taming of the workers' movement from within as a greater danger than outright repression by outside forces. For the time being, the revolutionaries within the trade unions maintained the upper hand.

The actions of certain socialists confirmed in the minds of many CGT members the folly of hoping for change through the political process. This alienation from politics was increased by the legal status of trade unions. The Act of 1884, which gave workers the right of association, did not apply to government workers. While informal associations of public employees were tolerated, the government reserved the right to dissolve as unlawful any group that sought to act like a trade union. As the CGT organizing efforts began to make headway among elementary school teachers and postal workers, conflict became inevitable. In March 1909, French postal workers went out on strike in hopes of removing the generally detested minister who presided over them. Taken unprepared, the government convinced the postal workers to call off the strike with a number of implied promises. When the unpopular head of the post office stayed in his position, while other promises remained unfulfilled, the workers resumed their work stoppage. But this second strike was less solid and there was little support from other unions, despite the CGT's organizing attempts. Seeing the postal workers' weakness, the government crushed the postal worker union, firing en masse the most militant union members. The CGT was helpless in the face of this governmental onslaught. This defeat created a deep sense of bitterness and betrayal within the CGT who saw politicians, now more than ever, as a plague to be hated and avoided.

So far, this discussion has focused on the social forces that gave rise to these new organizations and the prominent individuals who played key roles in their formation and downfall. What, however, did the average European make of all these political events, proclamations and infighting? In this realm, official political pronouncements, theoretical tomes, and the speeches of famous revolutionaries are of little value. Since there existed few of the modern techniques we now have for discovering public opinion, any investigation into the attitudes of the ordinary European at that time remains speculative. What we can look at, however, is evidence that suggests how the common people reacted to European radicalism.

Also, information can be gleaned from election results from those nations which had more or less free elections (excluding czarist Russia, of course). In addition, since membership figures exist for the various organizations associated with the revolutionary movement, these numbers suggest a certain minimum base of support. Finally, there are some evidence in the form of diaries, memoirs and police spy reports, which help round out the overall picture of everyday perceptions.[20]

Looking at vote totals, it would seem that the left grew stronger with each passing generation well into the twentieth century. This is not only true for the well-known case of Germany where the Social Democrats were the single largest party by World War I,[21] but also for other nations as well. In the Kingdom of Sweden, to cite only one example, the Social Democratic Labor Party (SDLP) garnered 28.5 percent of the votes cast in the 1911 balloting, a percentage that rose to 36.4 percent by 1914. Sweden, which was the scene of alternately bitter strikes and lockouts up until the 1930s, was home to a mere 3,194 SDLP members in 1889, the year the Second International was established. By 1914, this puny number had grown to 84,410 dues-paying party members in a country of under 6 million inhabitants.

Similar numbers could be provided throughout Western Europe to show that the official socialist movement had wide support in terms of both voter support and membership participation. Of course, the movement was stronger in some areas (particularly in the more industrialized nations) than others and support vacillated from year to year. All in all, however, the trend was clearly upward. Likewise, trade unions,[22] considered an integral part of the movement, enjoyed a momentous surge in membership. By 1912, there were 1,064,000 trade unionists in France and 2,553,000 union members in Germany. Meanwhile, the trendsetter in labor organizing, Britain, had 4,135,000 organized workers by 1913.[23]

A careful study of proletarian attitudes indicates that workers were neither the stereotypical revolutionary machines betrayed by corrupt leaders nor the vile racist and sexist creatures of bourgeois caricature. The true picture of workers is far more complex than the one-dimensional views often put forth. Most workers who identified with socialism appear to have considered themselves people of science who rejected religion. That is, they saw the revolution as unfolding according to what they held to be the laws of historical development. Thus, they saw little contradiction between reforms today and revolution tomorrow. Belief in revolution gave them dignity and the promise of a better life. Most importantly, all the available reports from government agents and workers' diaries indicate that it was their hard everyday life with its miserable economic conditions that made revolution appear to them not only desirable, but also inevitable.

Naturally, sentiments among workers were volatile and people would change their mind from one day to the next, as is true today. In one context, a worker would embrace revolution while in another circumstance the same individual would support reform. Yet then, as now, most people's attitudes were conditional not absolute. Although prejudice, racism and bigotry did exist among members of the left, on the whole, the movement was characterized by acceptance. Being oppressed themselves, most workers tended to sympathize with the "underdogs," whether they were colonial subjects or oppressed national minorities. All the same, political viewpoints varied widely.

Where is the transition to this? German police reports on conversations held in proletarian taverns in Hamburg show the response of many workers to the revisionist controversy. Most seem to have rejected Bernstein and his revision of Marxism. This disapproval appears to be based not on hostility to new ideas, but because reformist theory did not correspond to their everyday reality. Huddled over beer after a hard day of labor, these workers thought that the revisionists were "from the bourgeois camp," who wished to destroy Social Democracy as a worker's party. Feelings such as these are not particularly strange, for the progressive changes that Bernstein had suggested were occurring in capitalism made only a slight difference for the average worker. Harassed by police, bullied at work and often short of money, the proletarian radical was far less likely to see compromise or cooperation as viable strategies.[24] Still, other workers, and middle-class socialists, did support a reform strategy.

Of course, not all workers were revolutionary. The story of how one socialist woman attempted to convert her traditionally minded mother illustrates this reality. In her autobiography, Adelheid Popp describes the objections her widowed mother raised to her involvement with the socialist movement. Thinking that her long-suffering mother rejected her logical arguments in favor of socialism because they came from her child, Adelheid was thrilled when Frederick Engels and August Bebel agreed to visit her home. After an evening of explaining to the mother why she should be proud of her daughter, these two famous socialists departed. When mother and daughter were alone, Adelheid's mother asked, "Why do you bring old men here?" Ironically, Popp's mother had focused on the unsuitability of either man as a potential husband for her daughter.[25]

In the end, many workers, like Popp's mother, were too bound up in older traditions of religion and family to consider the socialist movement to be of interest. Perhaps the best way to view the outlook of common people towards social revolution is to emphasize its constantly evolving nature. A once-conservative peasant could quickly become radicalized when forced by economic change to become an urban worker. The revolutionary often looked more to immediate reforms during periods of improvement in the standard of living. Workers could demonstrate for peace one week and support war as self-defense the next. As the revolutionary Rosa Luxemburg remarked, the masses were like the sea: calm and peaceful one moment, rough and stormy the next. The ebbs and flows of the workers' movement in the next decades would confirm this standpoint.

CHAPTER EIGHT

Protest and Mutiny Confront Mass Slaughter: Europeans in World War I

All wars give rise to myths and World War I is certainly no exception. In most Anglophone countries, people "know" that the war was caused by an aggressive and expansionist Germany. Yet much of the evidence suggests a much more nuanced picture.[1] Likewise, it is commonplace wisdom that the conflict was almost universally welcomed by the common people everywhere, with this support only weakening, if at all, at the very end of the fighting. Even a century later, many find evidence contrary to these ingrained beliefs hard to accept.[2] One radical argues that even right from the start, "the popularity of the war was not as widespread or deeply ingrained in the mass of ordinary people [as one might think]."[3] French socialists, in July 1914, agreed to "use every means at their disposal, including the general strike, to prevent a European war."[4] In the week before the shooting started, hundreds of thousands demonstrated for peace in Germany.[5] Many of Europe's leaders, like Kaiser Wilhelm II, thought that going to war would fan the flames of socialism.[6] At the other end of the social pyramid, Berlin metalworker Richard Müller saw no nationalist euphoria among workers and his view seems vindicated by recent research.[7]

Despite the protests, there were also significant pro-war feelings at various times and among diverse populations; one would do well to remember that much of this was orchestrated by ruling pro-war institutions. From the start, the British propaganda against Germany employed highly sexualized undertones. Concluding that legalistic discussions of treaty violations would fail to stir human emotions, the invasion of Belgium was conflated with images of sexual violation.[8] The promotion of the notion that the Germans were setting a new record for heartless atrocities against innocents such as women and children became a major campaign. As early as June 1915, it is estimated that the British government had already distributed 2,500,000 copies of printed material in 17 different languages.[9] Another ironic example of the pro-war propaganda was the recruitment of Mussolini, then working as a journalist in Milan, by British MI5. His job was to publish pro-war propaganda and pay Italian veterans to attack peace protesters. For these services to (another country's) king and country, the British treasury weekly paid the future fascist dictator what would amount to £6,000 in twenty-first-century terms.[10] Of course, some people caught war fever, but as an eminent British historian observed, the "myth that European men leapt at the opportunity to defeat a hated enemy has been comprehensively dispelled. In most places and for most people, the news of mobilization came as a profound shock, a 'pearl of thunder out of a cloudless sky.'"[11] Mass disbelief was followed by fear, confusion and fatigue certainly, but also by resentment and even fury.

Before discussing the war itself, a brief analysis of why it broke out is in order. First, certain possibilities can be eliminated. It was not merely about an assassination, as Europe had sadly seen a number of important people murdered without a war ensuing. The war wasn't about race as it was fought mainly by Europeans and colonial people dragged into the fight by their European overlords. It was not about religion as French Catholic killed German Catholic, German Protestant slaughtered English Protestant, Arab Muslim attacked Turkish Muslim and Jews fought for their nation regardless of its predominant creed. Many other circumstances worked in tandem to spark the war. One enabling factor was that the European rulers had to a large extent forgotten how destructive war could be. With the notable exceptions of the Crimean War (1853–56) and the Franco-Prussian War (1870–71), the European powers had either been at peace or had only fought ill-equipped "natives" in colonial wars since the Napoleonic War ended at Waterloo in 1815.

What had changed in the century since Napoleon's defeat was the industrialization of much of Europe with resulting economic competition. Even US President Woodrow Wilson commented, "… is there any man or any woman—let me say any child, who does not know that the seed of war in the modern world is industrial and commercial rivalry?"[12] Nor did this competition take place solely within national boundaries. By the early twentieth century, there were numerous industrial or financial organizations that destabilized the international political arena. For these companies, there was no limit to their accumulation of capital since "the 'natural frontiers' of Standard Oil, the Deutsche Bank or DeBeers Diamond Corporation were at the ends of the universe, or rather at the limits of their capacity to expand."[13]

Economic warfare had led to imperialism and the search for colonies across the planet. Approximately a quarter of the earth's landmass fell to the onslaught of a handful of dominant nations, while the formerly independent inhabitants were reduced to the status of colonial subjects with few rights. In the period from 1876 to 1915, Britain alone amassed 4,000,000 square miles of new territories with France coming in a close second with 3,500,000. Even tiny Belgium and relatively weak Italy were able to carve out immense empires of slightly under a million square miles each. Germany, only unified in 1871 and a relative latecomer to the scramble for colonies, was still forceful enough to conquer a landmass of over a million square miles.

With the world divided up, the only way to gain more territory was through war. Britain planned on a transition from coal- to oil-fired ships and looked greedily at the rich oil fields belonging to Germany's ally, the Ottoman Empire.[14] The ever-growing importance of oil led Britain's foreign secretary to contend after the war that the "Allies floated to victory on a wave of oil."[15] It may be more than coincidence that World War I was between one side that represented the vast majority of colonial empire owners versus Germany and her allies, who were devoid of overseas holdings.[16] None other than Lloyd George, Britain's war leader, admitted that it was an imperialist war.[17]

Another factor leading up to the war was the alliance system whereby each nation was tied by treaty to other nations. The result was that what might have been a local conflict between Serbia and the Austro-Hungarian Empire snowballed into a global conflict. These alliances deterred compromises that might have prevented the outbreak of hostilities. That is, might not little Serbia have backed down in the face of Austria-Hungary had it not had the backing of the czar's Russia? Wouldn't even France have thought longer about another war with Germany, if they had lacked the promise of British naval and military support, and wouldn't Britain have insisted on serious peace efforts if they had lacked US financial support? Of course, it is commonplace for historians to point to the backing from Berlin that firmed up Austro-Hungarian resolve to punish Serbia as contributing to the pre-war crisis.

Arms races often precede wars and World War I was no exception. Germany's frenzy of naval construction had deeply worried the Lords of the British Admiralty.[18] Some have argued that anxiety about German naval expansion, particularly as regards submarines, led Britain to enter a war they might have avoided, in order to destroy the German fleet. However, it would be a mistake to consider this the only arms race that encouraged Europe to drift into military conflict. All the major powers saw themselves running to keep up with their rivals, as boots on the ground were augmented with new technological innovations: machine guns, barbed wire, heavy artillery, telegrams, airplanes, and so on. War had become industrialized and it would be a race to produce large quantities of the new industrial killing machines as well as develop new and wonderful methods of dispatching the other side (for example poison gas).[19]

To add to all these pro-war pressures was the feeling some had that a war would rally to the nations their troublesome ethnic minorities, like the Irish in Britain, or the Slavs in the Austro-Hungarian Empire. Likewise, socialists or radical labor movements might be tamed with a sizable dose of nationalism stemming from armed international conflict. Failing that, the war would give Europe's rulers the perfect excuse to repress all those who, in a manner of speaking, didn't salute the flag. Before the guns of August began their murderous firing, Basil Thompson, chief of the British politically directed Criminal Investigation Department (CID), feared that "unless there was a European war to divert the current we were heading for something very like revolution."[20] In a very similar mindset, one army officer wrote, "A good big war just now might do a lot of good in killing Socialist nonsense and would probably put a stop to all this labor unrest."[21] What the common people of Europe got was not just war but repression and the suspension of most basic civil liberties. Even in famously tolerant Britain, by the end of the war people were being convicted for their beliefs "almost solely on the basis of military opinion."[22] It has even been suggested that, despite real and important gains, in the process of supporting the war, British feminism "lost its ability to advocate equality and justice for women."[23]

Once the shooting had begun, both sides initially thought that the war would be over if not by Christmas, certainly by the spring. Naturally, most on both sides assumed their own side would win. Reality soon intervened. The war was neither to be short in duration nor heroic fun as so many military recruiters had promised. Because the opposing armies bogged down into trench warfare after the initial German offensive was stopped outside of Paris, the fighting took on an almost otherworldly quality. Living for long periods in trenches, shared with lice, filth, mud and often their dead comrades, soldiers found the misery of everyday life almost as painful as actually fighting. "We are living the life of moles or rabbits," wrote one British major, "the stench is awful, for there must be hundreds of dead never collected ... ."[24] During the lulls, the fighting continued to a certain extent with shooting at the enemy trenches. Given the closeness of the trenches and the lack of real hatred among many soldiers, it appears that direct "communication of friendly sentiments was not uncommon."[25] This often led to what have been called "Live and let Live" agreements, where the uniformed warriors simply refused to provoke firefights. As one scholar commented, "on many occasions tacit agreements existed between the opposing troops to restrict offensive activity."[26]

During the first Christmas of the war, a strange (one is tempted to say surreal) series of events occurred at places all along the trenches. After months of attempting to murder and maim each other, soldiers decided that there should be a Christmas truce. Not only was the fighting suspended for a time, but enemies wandered tentatively into "no man's land" to exchange greetings, gifts and even play sports together. Hushed up at the time and downplayed since, the truce actually took place. Although once called a "latrine rumor," "eyewash" and far less polite things, it is now accepted that it not only took place but was far more extensive than once believed.[27] In 2005, the truce was dramatized in a $22 million European movie called *Joyeux Noel*. By 2014, a United States military collectors' company issued a catalog offering "World War I Christmas Truce Figures" for sale.[28] At the time, the warlords appear not to have taken such a kindly view towards their subordinates' expressions of human solidarity. On December 29, 1914, the German high command forbade all fraternization and made approaches to the enemy punishable as high treason. A few days later, the British warned that informal dealings with the enemy would result in court martial.[29] All the same, there was still some, limited fraternization during the Christmastime of 1915.[30]

Nor was fraternization limited to the Western Front. Often overshadowed by the later, greater drama of the 1917 Revolutions are earlier incidents of Russians communicating with German and Austro-Hungarian soldiers. "We send them sausage, white bread and cognac," one 1915 letter to home reads, "the Germans give us cigarettes."[31] It is, of course, tempting to see all such incidents as isolated and insignificant kinks in the otherwise well-functioning military machines possessed by all sides. Still for the pro-war rulers, these were dangerous seeds that might take root and lead to mutiny as, in fact, happened in Russia, Austria-Hungary, France, Germany and even Britain.[32] "If the truce had gone on and on, there's no telling what could have happened. It could have meant the end of the war," one British veteran remembered, "After all they didn't want war, and we didn't want war and it could have ended up by finishing the war altogether."[33] Not very likely, but still an indication that many combatants were far less bloodthirsty than their rulers at home.

After the war, groups of former officers and some ultra-nationalist veterans attempted to make a great deal of noise about the nobility of sacrifice and comradeship of the trenches. One historian warns that it "would be hopelessly misleading to regard the testimony of literate, educated, upper-and middle-class combatants as descriptive of the war experience as a whole."[34] Some soldiers, particularly socialists, saw the war as merely a harsher version of pre-war bourgeois society. "There was no comradeship in the trenches," one British veteran remembered, "it was simply a case of members of the working classes held down by brutal and iron discipline. Different rations, different pay and different risk. The class line was as clear in France as it is at home ... ."[35] Many argued that the war was the logical extension of proletarianization in civilian life; human beings in both cases being reduced to the handmaidens of machines.

Authors often quibble about the exact quantity of suffering on the battlefields of Europe, yet all the differing figures still point to an almost inconceivable number of dead, maimed and missing. Just look at the numbers in Table 8.1 below.

Table 8.1   Number of troops mobilized, killed and wounded, World War I

	Mobilized	*Dead*	*Wounded*
Germany	11,000,000	1,773,700	4,216,058
Russia	12,000,000	1,700,000	4,950,000
France	8,410,000	1,375,800	4,266,000
Austria-Hungary	7,800,000	1,200,000	3,620,000
United Kingdom	8,904,467	908,371	2,090,212
Italy	5,615,000	650,000	947,000
Romania	750,000	335,706	120,000
Ottoman Empire	2,850,000	325,000	400,000

Source: Susan Everest, *World War I*, Riverside, NJ: Simon & Schuster, 1985: 248.

What these numbers fail to show, however, is that suffering extended beyond just those soldiers killed and wounded, to the qualitative horrors of trench warfare. The terrible emotional and psychological impact of industrialized warfare resulted in scars less obvious, but no less real, than those caused by bayonets. Simply put, some soldiers lost a leg or an arm, while others forfeited their joy of life, their nerves, or even their minds completely. Angst, anxiety, worry became a long-term or even permanent condition for millions.[36]

While pro-war narratives and mainstream cinema have stressed the frontline soldier's noble courage, the reality as seen by the rank and file was often quite different. One French veteran in his 1916 autobiographical novel *Under Fire*, confronts this attitude: "They'll tell you: 'my friend, you were a great hero!' ... Heroes? Some kind of extraordinary people? Idols? Come off it! We were executioners. We did our job as honest killers ... military glory is not even true for us ordinary soldiers."[37] Another Frenchman, Louis Barthas, was a worker and political radical re-minted by his government in 1914 as a corporal. He witnessed an attack order issued in circumstances where it was little short of madness. Rather than viewing this as stoic patriotism, Barthas describes the scene as heartbreaking: "In the trench, the men trembled, wept, pleaded. 'I have three children,' cried one. 'Mama, mama,' said another, sobbing. 'Have mercy, have pity,' one could hear. But the commandant, out of control, revolver in hand, cursed and threatened to send the laggards to the gallows."[38] Barthas goes on to recount that the men were given a reprieve when their commanding officer fell over, a bullet through his head. Barthas says no more, leading the reader to assume it was a German sniper but perhaps it was not.

Even early in the conflict, there were a large number of officers who appear to have been killed by their own men. The military high command didn't broadcast this fact nor, for rather obvious reasons, did the soldiers who shot them. This seems to have mainly occurred to particularly cruel officers who treated their men with hostility and disdain. But it also happened to sadistic leaders who mistreated the "enemy." German soldier Julius Koettgen reported instances early in the war in which officers ordered that defeated French combatants be killed rather than made prisoners. Koettgen wrote:

> ... not all the soldiers approved of that senseless, that criminal murdering. Some of the "gentlemen" who had ordered us to massacre our French comrades were killed "by mistake" in the darkness of the night, by their own people, of course. Such "mistakes" repeat themselves almost daily ... .[39]

In his memoirs, William Hermanns who was a German veteran of the Western Front, reported on the hatred felt towards many officers. Marching on the way to the battlefield of Verdun, "... [he] first heard the whispered slogan 'A bullet from the rear is just as good as a bullet from the front.'"[40]

The war took an almost unbelievable emotional and psychological toll on the people at the front. One French soldier told how, when he

> ... took a couple of steps to the left, I saw, as if hallucinating, a pile of corpses ... At the entrance to the connecting trench, leaning on the slope, was a young German who looked like he was asleep. There was no

visible wound. Death had brushed him with its wing, and preserved the smile which still marked his youthful face.[41]

Little wonder that one author concluded one "should not rule out the possibility that almost half of the survivors sustained more or less serious psychological disturbance."[42] This is famously on display in the war art of German veteran Otto Dix.[43] Jay Winter argues that "Dix represents every possible manifestation of dehumanization: madness, mutilation, horrific wounds, putrescent corpses, rapes, civilian casualties, sexual depravity, wretchedness."[44]

Nor was the pain limited solely to those in uniform. Besides the obvious suffering caused by artillery shelling and the like, the stationing of German, British and other, soldiers outside their home country inevitably led to various crimes, both petty and major, against the occupied civilian population.[45] In the Ottoman Empire,[46] a form of genocide was carried out against Armenian civilians whose Christian beliefs had made them suspect. Even those civilians left unmolested saw their lives turned upside down, as witnessed by women who were thrown into dangerous factory war work.[47] In Britain, many female armaments workers were poisoned by TNT or other materials they had to handle.[48] For Germany and its allies, the war meant civilians would be starved, frequently to death, by the British naval blockade of formerly food-importing nations.[49] If German industrial growth had threatened Britain's claim to economic supremacy, it handed the Royal Navy a potential hostage, "in the form of a German urban working class."[50] The resulting illness and death may have even been decisive in the outcome of the war.[51]

For some people, the war was added incentive to attempt to redress ancient wrongs. In the "jewel in the crown" of the British Empire, Indian rebels hatched a number of conspiracies to promote revolt. One of the more significant was the Ghadar Mutiny, focused on the British Indian Army and planned for February 1915.[52] Troops in the Punjab were detailed to kill their officers and seize arms. This was to be followed by other armed risings by Indian troops. The whole plot, with its connections to overseas Indian expatriates, Irish rebels and the German government, was discovered by British spies and nipped in the bud.[53] About half of the 5th Light Infantry stationed in Singapore actually revolted, but within a week were crushed. Several hundred mutineers were arrested and 47 sent to public execution by firing squad.

"England's difficulty," it was said, "is Ireland's opportunity." During Easter week 1916, there was an armed insurrection in Dublin in the vain hope that it would end British rule. The Easter Rebellion saw the occupation of vital positions throughout Dublin by armed Irish republicans. Hopelessly optimistic, if not naively romantic, the rebels had no real likelihood of seeing their poorly planned project succeed. The British armed forces had little difficulty in suppressing the unrest and they court-martialed and executed the rising's leadership.[54] Hopeless though the uprising was, it sent shock waves through the Anglo-Saxon ruling circles. They feared what an uprising might bring next time, not just in Ireland but maybe elsewhere in the Empire.[55] In the French African colonies, mass recruitment resulted in drawing 450,000 soldiers and 135,000 factory workers to Europe.[56] Immigrant workers who replaced those called up to the frontlines in France made a valuable contribution to war production.[57] Even though no insurmountable problems arose, the French leader Clemenceau feared that these policies could provoke a mass revolt in France's African colonies.[58]

Most scholars agree that given such international carnage, support for the war was tenuous; this went from bad to worse the longer the war dragged on. An Englishwoman married to a German prince, spent the war in Berlin and recorded her impressions in a diary. While such sources are always highly personalized and thus somewhat suspect, they can be useful for understanding the range of emotional responses to World War I and the general outlook of the populations. As early as autumn 1914, Princess Eveyln Blücher records many events that upset her privileged social circle. She reports of German soldiers, after being hit by sniper fire, being ordered to shoot into crowds of fleeing Belgian civilians so "many innocent perished with the guilty." The much-respected Imperial German Army also comes in for criticism as the princess learns from a wounded German officer how "his regiment had been practically annihilated by their own side, through a mistake of his Colonel's."[59] By late 1915, the princess expresses the fear of many of the elite that "Germany will be a very difficult country to live in after the war, as, whether she wins or loses, the Socialists are going to revolt—I feel quite sure of that."[60]

It was not only the German left who would revolt; even Cambridge-educated British officers began to reject the war, as is clear in the following excerpt. After serving in the trenches and being wounded in action, Siegfried Sassoon wrote a protest saying the war had "become a war of aggression and conquest ... I have seen and endured the sufferings of the troops, and I can no longer be a party to prolong these sufferings for ends which I believe to be evil and unjust."[61] The Army decided it would be politically unwise to court-martial a brave and popular officer. Instead, they sent him off for psychological treatment arguing that his mind must have been ill if he opposed the war. Sassoon was told if he resisted he would be locked up in a lunatic asylum.[62] Of course, mutiny would soon grip the French and mutiny would lead to revolutions in the Russian Empire and elsewhere.

What led to such dire reactions on the part of presumably patriotic citizens in uniform? One vital factor was that the class conflict of industrial life was reproduced in the officer/enlisted men split in the trenches. Nor was this only true for such undemocratic societies as the Russians or the Ottomans, it was just as true for the British. "Between the [British] officer and the ranker there stood a gulf," it has been argued, "which had no bridge."[63] This was more than a matter of tradition or class prejudice. The actions of officers reinforced, over and over again, the difference between the privileged and the proletarians.

"What about the way the officers live, when not in action? Pheasant served on slices of pineapple, with champagne, is a mere item in a long menu," wrote Princess Eveyln Blücher in 1915

> ... whilst others are starving. The bread they get is so hard that they cannot bite it, and often there is not even that. The injustice of all this is bound to make them cry out for equality and fairness, not that they should be sent out to fight other men, called enemies, who are just in the same plight as themselves.[64]

It was no different in the French Army, where officers commonly thought the men would work better if you gave them hardly "anything to eat." At the same time, their officers drank, filled their bellies and were warm. In protest, French enlisted men attempted to report themselves sick, only to be refused by the medical officer. As they bitterly retreated from the officers, they began to sing the "Internationale," the socialist hymn.[65]

While the 1917 mutinies in the Russian armies[66] that led to revolution are more celebrated, it is important to remember the mutiny of the French Army as well.[67] On April 16 of that historic year, French General Robert Nivelle thought he could order a successful breakthrough that would take place within 48 hours of the first assault on German lines. Of course, he was wrong. Over a million men were sent to assault the enemy trenches in what has been called "France's go-for-broke gamble to end World War I."[68] The mass murderer, as he was known to some of his troops,[69] was too proud to admit his mistake and after ten days, France had lost upwards of 30,000 citizens in uniform. Next, the unthinkable happened. Units refused orders to attack. The soldiers were willing to defend their own trenches but not throw away their lives in suicidal and pointless heroics. Not all of the army was affected, but roughly 49 divisions of France's 113 infantry divisions were mutinous. Louis Barthas described how one general who dared to harangue a group of mutineers

> ... was grabbed, slammed against a wall, and was just about to be shot, when a much-beloved commandant succeeded in saving the general ... [the next day] they assembled us for departure to the trenches. Noisy demonstrations resulted: cries, songs, shout, whistling; of course, the "Internationale" was heard. I truly believe that if the officers had made one provocative gesture, said one word against the uproar, they would have been massacred without pity, so great was the agitation.[70]

Scenes like that described above doubtless took place throughout the French lines on the Western Front. The replacement of General Robert Nivelle by General Philippe Pétain saw the mutiny broken by a subtle combination of lethal repression and concessions to the troops, most importantly to end the hopeless attempts to overwhelm the enemy's entrenched positions. Good political training for the man who would become Hitler's puppet ruler of unoccupied France after the Nazi victory in the Second World War.[71] The number of those executed may never be known. It appears that of over five hundred death sentences only about fifty were carried out. However, there remain recurring reports of mutinous soldiers shot out of hand and then listed as "killed in action." More may be known if historians gain access to archives on the mutinies, which were scheduled to remain closed until 2017.[72] In any case, the mutiny remained a secret to the German high command or, more likely, they refused to believe intelligence reports saying common people had taken matters in their own hands.

In the months to come, many ordinary Europeans would certainly defy the age-old stereotype of being docile and unthinking. Little wonder when one considers the suffering that almost all sectors beyond the rulers had endured since the outbreak of war. Russia may stand out as the example where mutiny led to victorious revolutions but it was only the weakest link in the European chain. Central Europeans were hardly much better off. Added to the losses on the battlefield, the home front was, by 1916, "defined by food shortage." As early as March, a letter from Hamburg tells how queues of 600, 700 or 800 people formed outside shops whenever butter was delivered.[73] While all urban areas in central Europe suffered, Vienna probably was hardest hit. By 1917, a quarter of million people stood daily in one of 800 food lines spread throughout the city.[74] In Berlin, even the privileged could complain that everyone was "all growing thinner every day, and the rounded contours of the German nation have become a legend of the past. We are all gaunt and bony now, and have dark shadows round our eyes, and our thoughts are chiefly taken up with wondering what our next meal will be … ."[75] By the end of the war, 760,000 German civilians had died because of the food shortages caused by the British blockade.[76]

Friedrich Adler, a radical anti-war socialist, publicly shot a high Austro-Hungarian official in October 1916. At his trial, Adler damningly indicted the rulers for waging war without the people's consent. Although sentenced to death, Adler's sentence was commuted to 18 years because of the wide support the assassin enjoyed among the working class and even beyond.[77] While this act was exceptional, the feelings that motivated it were not. It can be argued that World War I, even allowing for the new industrial technology, was no more brutal or murderous than any number of previous wars. What may have been more unique was the level of collective anti-war opposition to it.[78]

Be that as it may, by 1916, perhaps 1917 at the latest, Europeans in war-locked nations were tired of the conflict. The populace was tired and more than a little angry at those they believed had begun the conflict, as well as those who were seen as profiting from it. Certainly, there were some who still bought into the romantic myths of the extreme right, for example Adolf Hitler, who at this point was an insignificant corporal in the war. Yet, one wonders if these supporters were as common as was later claimed. What is not in dispute is that the war gave birth to anti-war agitation throughout the continent of Europe. In turn, these peace movements evolved towards revolution, as millions came to believe that their rulers wouldn't end the war. In the face of such belief, the response was that they must dispose of the rulers themselves.

CHAPTER NINE

War Leads to Revolution:
Russia (1917), Central Europe (1918–19)

If the war to end all wars was a disaster for the commoners of the West, it was, if possible, even worse for the people of the Russian Empire. Backward economically and as deeply superstitious as it was religious, Russia was a historical curiosity. French financial capital had invested heavily in attempts to modernize this land, as had the British and Americans. Between 1890 and 1904, the total railroad mileage within Russia doubled. In addition, national production of coal, iron, and steel doubled during the last five years of the nineteenth century. The Russian bourgeoisie, with its ties to Paris and London, was European in mindset. Likewise, the radical leaders were far better schooled in revolutionary theory than one might expect. This might in a small way be because czarist censors allowed Marx's *Capital* to circulate freely, their rationale being "few will read it and even fewer will understand it."[1]

The Russian Empire had 126 million inhabitants by 1897, of whom four out of five were still peasants ruled by the hereditary nobility, which comprised 1 percent of the population. Although the serfs had finally been freed in 1861, agriculture remained primitive. For example, by the start of the twentieth century, peasants in the European portion of Russia produced on average only nine bushels of grain per acre compared with the British average of over thirty-five. Yet by 1914, massive capital investments, both private and public, had resulted in dramatic industrial advances. For czarism, an unfortunate byproduct of economic growth was the creation of a modern working class heavily concentrated in a few major industrial areas in atypically large plants. Despite some un-enforced statutes, the workers had no protection. Within factories, "the real law was often the fists of the foremen. Corruption, bribery of officials, cheating by petty merchants, arbitrary treatment by authorities made up the context in which workers made contact with other classes and officialdom."[2]

The czar ruled his domain through a bureaucratized autocracy, which alternatively ignored and repressed the populace. These contradictions would bear strange fruit during World War I. On bad days, czarist officers would order assaults on enemy trenches even if their soldiers were without bullets. There were conspiracies in the general staff and at Court. Russia's war administration was stuffed with even more incompetents than is usual. Rasputin, a "mad monk," became an advisor to the czar and appointed and dismissed ministers with neither rhyme nor reason. This all took place as the holy man wandered from one drunken orgy to the next.[3] This deadly cocktail of political chaos brought about response from an unexpected source. On March 8, 1917,[4] a demonstration was held in Petrograd for International Women's Day. Some striking men joined this demonstration, the size of which amazed both organizers and bystanders. The next day, almost a third of the city's workers marched, with cries for bread being supplemented by the looting of bakeries. Throughout the war, bread prices had risen sharply, and by 1917, inefficient distribution meant that Petrograd saw huge lines of citizens waiting their turn for bread. It was reported that these lines were "often over a mile in length with people waiting four deep."[5]

On March 10, the demonstrations reached an unheard-of size. The city of Petrograd was effectively shut down, without trains, trams, taxis, or even newspapers. The government announced that all demonstrations and rallies were forbidden and everyone must report for work on Monday. Nonetheless, the streets were filled with people as in prior days. When on Monday, troops were told to open fire, they began to shoot their officers instead. Officers fled for their lives while many, maybe half, of the soldiers joined the protesters. In an attempt to control the unrest, Nicholas II, Czar by Grace of God, headed back from the war front towards rebellious Petrograd. Tuesday saw government buildings torched as the sailors at the Kronstadt naval base rose up and killed many of their officers. On Wednesday, the czar's train was halted by mutinous troops and he was forced to flee to a military base southwest of the capital, only to find that there was no army present to support him. After a period of confused bewilderment, Nicholas II abdicated. When his brother refused the throne, the Romanov dynasty came to an end. A Provisional Government was established by members of the previously tame parliament, the Duma. It immediately faced a competitor in a popular assembly known as the Petrograd Soviet of Workers' and Soldiers' Deputies, which consisted of 2,500 delegates elected from workplaces and army units.[6] Worse was the fact that the new Provisional Government, faced with direct, unbearable pressure and more than a few threats from their Western allies, felt compelled to stay in the war.

At first, the new government was greeted with outpourings of joy and wild applause. After centuries of autocratic rule, it seemed as if Russia was at last to enter the modern era. Things almost unthinkable only months before—freedom of speech, an independent press, women's rights—were proclaimed by the czar's replacements. As one women's organization excitedly, if naively, proclaimed,

> ... [the] great Russian revolution has realized women's boldest dreams. The first Provisional Government has acknowledged the civil and political equality of the women of Russia. This equality, which as yet has been realized nowhere in the world on such a scale, lays upon the Russian woman a huge responsibility.[7]

Despite male resistance, all-female combat units were created.[8] In this heady atmosphere, even many among the most radical groups, like Anarchists and more than a few revolutionary socialists, such as the Bolsheviks, supported the Provisional Government. Despite whatever good intentions the latter may have harbored, the reality was that the country had all but collapsed and what remained functioning was typically under workers' control,[9] with more support for the soviets.

Early enthusiasm for the new government soon vanished, as the continued butchery of the war front combined with ever-worsening shortages on the home front, alienating the bulk of the population. Not only was everyone hungry, but at the front, food shortages combined with a scandalous lack of armaments for soldiers. One historian later commented:

> Short of food, and short of clothes, the Russian soldier with any guts left to fight in 1917 often found himself without weapons to fight with. One-third of the number of rifles required at the front were lacking in 1917. In order to obtain rifles, those who had no weapons waited for their fellows to die, desert, or get wounded.[10]

Things were hardly better from an economic standpoint. The dearth of manufactured goods was severe, with basics "like kerosene, soap, textiles, paper, leather and metal products" in short supply: "By October the cumulative effect of these shortages was taking its toll of human patience."[11]

Bolsheviks who had flirted with support for the Provisional Government were knocked back into line by their leader V.I. Lenin, who returned from exile in April. Despite endless rumors to the contrary, there is "no evidence of any secret agreement between Lenin and the Germans."[12] A delegation of Russian moderate left-wing Soviet members ventured to Western Europe in the summer of 1917 to rally support for reuniting the Second

International and ending the war. British and French labor leaders and Western governments refused to support the peace initiative altogether. Likewise, peace attempts initiated by the Pope also failed.[13] The failure of these moderate socialists to make any progress towards ending the war gave more credence to the Bolshevik argument for the necessity of a unilateral Russian-German peace agreement. The failure of the delegation "contributed to and symbolizes the failure of the moderates in 1917."[14] For all the various anarchist groups, "the great hopes stirred up by the February Revolution soon turned into bitter disappointment." In fact, they would soon join the Bolsheviks in promoting a second revolution.[15]

Thus, it is not surprising that the Provisional Government was overthrown. In a sense, it is a sign of the Russian people's patience that no one did so sooner. Leaving aside other mistakes that were made, the lack of supplies alone would have brought down even a strong government.[16] The government formation led by liberal lawyer Alexander Kerensky was many things, but it could not be accused of being strong. It failed to deal with the two basic problems undermining Russian society: the war and economic chaos. This resulted in further radicalizing the workers and within a period of a few months "compelled the workers ... to give their support to a new leadership—that of the Bolsheviks."[17] The picture often presented of Lenin, Trotsky and the Bolsheviks as an isolated clique does not fit the facts.[18] Throughout 1917, this party's influence grew as more moderate revolutionary groups lost influence, particularly among the workers of Petrograd.[19]

Thus it should have come as little surprise that in October 1917, the Provisional Government was deposed and a Bolshevik-led government based on the Soviets was proclaimed.[20] Although the hopes of that revolution would be dashed on the rocks of civil war, foreign embargo and the rise of a dictatorship under Stalin, it is useful to look at the initial reasons why it succeeded. The October Revolution was a success not because the party of Lenin and Trotsky were superior manipulators or cynical opportunists, "but because their policies ... placed them at the head of a genuinely popular movement."[21] Legend would have us believe that the revolution was led by a handful of conspirators when in fact, the strength behind this revolution was the common people of Russia, most of all, urban Russia.[22] After all, the Second All-Russian Congress of Soviets, which represented millions, voted to approve the formation of a new government with a majority of Bolshevik commissars. Moreover, the masses immediately got what they had most wanted in the form of an armistice with Germany, recognition of peasant land seizures and confiscation of privately owned factories. Still, neither revolution was able to fully overcome the legacy of Russian backwardness.

For example, while the situation of women ultimately improved, in the early years, little actually changed due to both male prejudice and lack of resources.[23] Of course, the nature of revolutions frequently leads to such heightened expectations, thus leaving some aftermath of frustration.[24]

Revolutions also serve to embolden those, like many German workers, already predisposed to rebellion.[25] Not that other Europeans involved in the bloodbath of the trenches or the sufferings at home needed external examples to tell them things were bad. In Austria-Hungary, flour rations were slashed in half, resulting in strikes around Vienna on January 14, 1918. The strikes spread throughout the Hapsburg Empire and around 700,000 workers of various ethnic backgrounds took part in the strikes, which lasted ten days. Early the next month, there was a naval mutiny that lasted for three days: sailors flew the red flag, demanded a peace without annexations and killed an officer.[26] On January 28, 1918, Berlin, the German capital to the north, saw the region's entire armament industry come to a halt as hundreds of thousands of workers organized by the Revolutionary Shop Stewards demanded peace without annexations, as well as more radical demands like the democratization of the entire state structure.[27] This strike could not be dismissed as merely a knee-jerk reaction to food shortages as earlier work stoppages were.[28] It would be a mistake to think that only the common people of the Central Powers were suffering. The mutiny in the French Army and the revolutions in Russia made Europe-wide unrest apparent. Even Italy, although on the winning side, was in a disastrous economic crisis by the latter stages of the war. As one historian explained the conditions in Italy, "[livestock] had been slaughtered without replacement. Wood had been substituted for coal in industry, and forests had been cut down to meet industrial and military requirements ... Workers in town and country, unable to live on their former wages ... struck."[29]

Within the Imperial German Navy, disaffection with conditions and treatment led to riots in August 1917. It was only through brutal violence that discipline was restored; rioting sailors received heavy sentences and over a dozen were executed.[30] Nonetheless, the suppression proved a grave mistake for the admirals, and a valuable lesson for German sailors. By October 1918, with peace seemingly at hand, the latter were in no mood to listen to their officers, be they right or wrong. On October 28, the High Seas Fleet began to assemble outside Wilhelmshaven Naval Station in the North Sea. What the German Admiralty had in mind was an assault against the British fleet; what the sailors had in mind, however, was altogether different. One sailor recalled later:

Rumors circulated to the effect that it had been decided to engage the enemy in a final encounter, in which the German fleet would triumph or die for the glory of the "Kaiser and the Fatherland." The sailors of the Fleet had their own view on the "Glory of the Fatherland"; when they met they saluted one another with a "Long Live Liebknecht," [Karl Liebknecht's vote against war credits in the Reichstag having made him a symbol of anti-war resistance to large sections of the populace.][31]

Even if this perception was not universal, it is certainly indicative of the mood of large numbers of the fleet's rank-and-file sailors. Thus, when ordered to sea, the crews on the Thüringen and Helgoland mutinied. In a vain effort to prevent the spread of mutinous sentiment, the squadrons of this battle fleet were separated and the third squadron was dispatched to Kiel. But, as soon as these ships docked, radical activity began anew. Petitions were circulated demanding the release of imprisoned comrades as the thin veneer of discipline began to crack, and officers' orders were ignored with greater and greater frequency. On November 3, a crowd estimated at 20,000 moved in on the detention barracks and street fighting broke out when the crowd encountered a line of armed sailors with orders to disperse the demonstration. Within minutes, eight people were killed and twenty-one more were wounded.

When news of the events at Kiel reached Berlin, the shaken government headed by Prince Max resolved to send a reliable but well-known Social Democrat to the port city to calm the revolutionary waters. Before this could happen, a crowd mainly composed of sailors seized numerous buildings and set up a Sailors' and Workers' Council.[32] The authorities had estimated that as many as a third of the sailors were radicals.[33] It has even been claimed that there was a secret revolutionary organization among the members of the North Seas fleet:

[Under] seamen's yarns in the lower deck, in the lockers, the munitions rooms, crew's nests of the fighting masts, even in the lavoratories, an underground organization was built up which did its share towards stopping the imperialist war, and sweeping away the semi feudal monarchy.[34]

All along the coastal area, the working class took the events at Kiel as the signal to rise up. On November 6, a Workers' and Soldiers' Council seized control of Hamburg, with the *Hamburger Echo* reappearing as *Die Rote Fahne* (Red Flag).[35] A hundred naval mutineers, being conducted under guard to a prison camp, passed through Bremen, where they were freed by proletarian crowds. Another Workers' and Soldiers' Council was established and soon in command, with guards being posted to ward off any government assault. By the end of the first week of November, not just Bremen and Hamburg, but Lubeck, Cuxhaven, Rensburg, Restock and other smaller towns were in the hands of the working class. As the empire that Otto von Bismarck had so carefully built was tottering under the blow struck from the north, the *coup de grâce* was delivered by a revolutionary uprising in the kingdom of Bavaria.[36] Over one hundred thousand people assembled in Munich on November 7 to hear speeches demanding the kaiser's abdication. After the rally broke up, revolutionary soldiers joined with the city garrison, and all strategic points—railroads, telephone, telegraph offices, army headquarters and government agencies—were occupied.

By November 8, the major urban areas of Saxony, Baden, Hesse-Darmstadt, Wurttemberg and the Thüringen states were all in open rebellion. One by one, the old ruling dynasties were pushed off the stage of history by the rising tide of revolution. All these regional revolutions awaited word from Berlin as to the end of the kaiser's political reign and the proclamation of the long-awaited republic. Following the lead of Friedrich Ebert, the SPD bureaucracy gained increasing influence in the liberal monarchical government of Prince Max of Baden. Right-wing Social Democratic leader Ebert and his close associates not only refused to consider any radical alternatives, but concentrated on derailing the speeding train of revolution.[37]

When Ebert later learned of countless reports of meetings and protests, which suggested that the revolution was about to hit Berlin, he was forced to demand the kaiser's immediate removal. On the morning of November 9, 1918, 39 unit commanders were ordered to report to Army Headquarters at Spa as to whether or not their men would fight for the kaiser against the revolution. The verdict was clear: most officers reported their troops unwilling to risk their lives for Kaiser Wilhelm II and doubtful that they would fight "Bolshevism." That morning, the streets of the Reich's capital were filling with large crowds. Increasingly, shouts of "Long Live the Socialist Republic!" echoed through the air.

As the day went on, the crowds grew. One non-socialist Reichstag deputy recorded his perceptions of the day in his memoirs. Returning to the Reichstag from a restaurant on Potsdamer Plaza, he saw throngs of people on the streets in larger and larger numbers while "red flags, revolutionary songs, and shouts for the Social Republic were seen and heard everywhere."

Reaching the doors of the German Parliament, he was surprised to observe "a score of fully equipped riflemen and above them a huge red flag. Sailors with cartridge belts across their shoulders and rifles in their hands stepped forward, ready for battle."[38] The kaiser fled into exile and a German republic was born. However, though the kaiser departed, ominously the generals remained. Two in particular had been the de facto rulers of Germany since 1916: Paul von Hindenburg and Erich Ludendorff. Both these generals were placed on a list of suspected war criminals, and then quickly removed from this list by people more interested in order than justice. Ludendorff became an early supporter of the Nazi Party and Hindenburg, later in 1933 as president, appointed Adolf Hitler as German chancellor.[39]

Within Berlin's working class, nerves grew strained and tempers began to flare. Finally, the raw nerves of common people were sparked by Emil Eichhorn's dismissal as Berlin's chief of police. He would later become the Communist Reichstag deputy. Impatient and angry workers viewed this dismissal as a counter-revolutionary putsch and fighting raged in Berlin during January 5–13.[40] By the time the battle ceased, thousands of workers were dead and the proto-Nazi *Frei Korps*[41] marched through the old imperial capital in triumph. Various right-wing units serving under the general direction of Gustav Noske seized upon the previous week's fighting as an excuse to decapitate the German revolution.[42] Around 9 p.m. on January 15, Rosa Luxemburg, Karl Liebknecht and Wilhelm Pieck, later first president of the German Democratic Republic, were arrested by *Frei Korps* troops in the Berlin suburb of Wilmersdorf. They took the three KPD leaders to the Eden Hotel for questioning. That same evening, Luxemburg[43] and Liebknecht were murdered while Pieck escaped under circumstances that have never been fully explained.

One should not see this as a conflict between the military and civilian radicals. As the following incident suggests, many in the armed forces had switched their allegiance from the old order to those fighting for a new Germany. Going to see Eichhorn for an exit visa from Germany in the midst of the fighting in early 1919, an English woman describes waiting in a room with a huge sailor standing guard. He was the head of the radical police chief's guard. When the woman noticed a "smart military cap on his head," the sailor responded "The Kaiser gave me this as a souvenir. He used to wear it, and now I wear it. I was his bodyguard on the *Hohenzollern* for years, and now I guard Herr Eichorn [*sic*], and I will guard him with my life and soul to the last."[44] Before leaving Berlin, she found out that although Eichhorn had been saved, the sailor she had met died defending him.

The radical elements of the German populace would struggle on, but the rise of right-wing paramilitary units, combined with Eichhorn's dismissal, dealt decisive blows.[45] In Munich, there arose a radical regime led by left socialist Kurt Eisner, which had taken power peacefully in November 1918. There the revolutionary group had taken over the army barracks. As one author noted, "without any resistance the soldiers went over to the revolutionaries; even the military prison was stormed without bloodshed."[46] The resulting government contained a bewildering collection of anarchist and semi-anarchist writers and intellectuals, yet it survived the collapse of the revolution in Berlin. Then in February 1919, Eisner was assassinated by an ultra-reactionary aristocrat. In a context of political chaos, the proclamation of the Hungarian Soviet Republic on March 21, 1919 led to a wave of utopian hope across Munich. This resulted in the proclamation of a Soviet Republic in Bavaria, despite the lack of support among the ranks of conservative peasants outside Munich.

This short-lived experiment was drowned in blood on the first of May and the Communists led by Eugen Leviné were heavily blamed, although they had opposed the initial Munich proclamation. Before being sentenced to death, Leviné famously told the court that, "We Communists are all dead men on leave. Of this I am fully aware ... And yet I know, sooner or later other judges will sit in this hall and then those will be punished for high treason who have transgressed against the dictatorship of the proletariat."[47] Although there have been numerous disputes over who is responsible for the failure in Munch, this seems like a fruitless debate. One historian is probably correct in saying that it "was not the failure of the Räterepublik that led to the resurgence of right-wing radicalism, but it was unrepentant German nationalism, unshaken even by military defeat, that led to the bloody suppression ... ."[48]

The situation elsewhere in Central Europe was a series of strikes, revolts, abdications and reactions as, for example, in the Austro-Hungarian Empire. This once seemingly mighty empire had melted down under the pressure of the war, internal agitation by national minorities, and anti-war resistance by socialists. The summer of 1918 saw the majority of Hapsburg subjects in a state of advanced misery, particularly as food shortages worsened. Vienna's food supply was all but non-existent and

> ... mass starvation had only narrowly been averted by the desperate expedient of confiscating barges carrying Romanian grain belonging to Germany up the Danube ... [by the beginning of October, Austria's

situation] was summed up by the head of its Food Office, Hans Loewen-feld-Russ, as "utterly desperate."[50]

Hunger drove even the apolitical into action and the last Austrian kaiser abdicated on November 11, 1918.

Revolution gripped Hungary, particularly Budapest, and Austrian socialists seized a degree of power in the erstwhile capital Vienna.[51] In March 1919, the Hungarian government was turned over to the Communist Bela Kun. June 1919 saw the emergence of a Slovak Soviet Republic, which quickly "issued a number of decrees nationalizing industrial plants, banks, large estates and other private property. It ordered the payment of old age and disability benefits. Everybody who worked was eligible to vote."[52] Within a few months, both radical experiments were suppressed by reactionary armies with the help of moderate Social Democrats.[53]

In the years after World War I, it often seemed as if Italy was bent on following the example of Soviet Russia. The Socialist vote rose from 18 percent in 1913 to 31 percent in 1919. Socialist leagues won an eight-hour day from landowners and the right to unionize. Socialist radicals even called for land collectivization.[54] This growing movement even penetrated into the ranks of loyal Roman Catholics.[55] In a more direct show of power, there were worker occupations of important factories in northern Italian cities, such as Turin.[56] This was all part of the "two red years" in Italy that followed the war, promising but not making a revolution. With the failure of the left to transform Italian society, the road would be left open to counter-revolution that would take the form of a new right-wing movement, fascism.[57] Led by Mussolini, this violent and racist organization

> ... was brought to power by a conspiracy of high military authorities, nationalist politicians, and big businessmen not because a way out of economic disintegration had to be found but because big business wanted to break the backbone of working-class organizations ... .[58]

Before the birth of fascism, an organized assault was already being made upon "Bolshevism," "reds," and Soviet Russia. During what the West has usually called the Russian Civil War,[59] fourteen foreign nations provided guns, funds and troops to try and, in Winston Churchill's words, "strangle the Bolshevik baby in its crib."[60] Although intervention was originally framed as part of the war against Germany, it soon became clear—particularly after Germany's surrender—that anti-communism was in fact the main motivation. To be fair, Churchill never hid his antipathy, calling Bolshevism the "worst tyranny, the most destructive and the most degrading. It is sheer humbug to pretend it is not far worse than German militarism."[61] Of course, he also thought Jews were behind every revolution from that in France in 1789 to Russia's in 1917. In an article in 1920, the man who would later be feted as a great leader of the Free World, warned that the Jewish "world-wide conspiracy for the overthrow of civilization and for the reconstitution of society on the basis of arrested development, of envious malevolence, and impossible equality, has been steadily growing."[62]

From the start, the foreign intervention or invasions of Soviet Russia were quickly recognized (by France, Britain and the United States at least), as being motivated mainly by a desire to roll back radicalism rather than fight Germany.[63] This motivation was not publicly stated, certainly not until the war was over and often not even then. The fear was that many in war-weary Europe might look at revolutionary Russia with sympathy. US President Woodrow Wilson, memorably called the "servant of the capitalist sharks" by V.I. Lenin, was haunted by "the susceptibility of the people of Europe to the poison of Bolshevism."[64] So were others among the rich and powerful. Not only were guns and money deployed, but also food. The Allied blockade starved Soviet areas, while food was dispatched to areas held by the counter-revolutionaries. Thus it could be argued that the Cold War started in 1917, not after World War II.

All the same, the West's intervention was not purely ideological—it was also economically motivated. In a November 1919 speech to the House of Commons, Lloyd George noted not only Bolshevik Russia's "infinite possibilities for mischief," but also stressed that "Russia is one of the great resources for the supply of food and raw material."[65] In fact, Britain had hopes for separating Siberia from the rest of Russia, if necessary with allies like France and the United States. As one scholar comments, Britain "wanted to keep Siberia separate from the rest of Russia ... [and turn British presence there] to protracted economic advantage. Britain failed, but that does not negate her attempts."[66]

It is important to bear in mind that it was not only the Russian people who suffered massive violence in the aftermath of World War I. Large-scale and systematic repression was the order of the day, as nervous ruling classes turned to repression to prevent revolution or, for that matter, even radical reforms. This period of class war from above is all too often forgotten. Not only is it an important corrective to the mainstream narrative that violence comes from the left, it establishes the context for the growth and development of fascism.[67] Nationalism had been a major card that the old rulers played against insurgent movements from below.

As the common people grew angry at the war, many looked towards the day when the world would be one unified federal social republic consisting of all nations. This republic would eliminate national conflicts and eradicate war forever. Anarchist and syndicalist thinkers,[68] while rejecting even such a benign form of government, also looked forward to a world of peace. It would also be a mistake to think that these sentiments were only the product of defeat in Germany and her allies. Consider what one French soldier said after the fighting ended:

> … they lied, cynically, saying that we were fighting just for the triumph of Right and Justice, that they were not guided by ambition, no colonial covetousness or financial or commercial interests. They lied when they said that we had to push right to the end, so that this would be the last of all wars.[69]

The right reacted to these visions of peaceful unity, and fought back the tide of revolution that came at the end of the war; they crafted a vision starkly in contrast to that of the left. The right wanted a world of war where the strongest, or the "master race(s)" would rule, and everyone else would be little better than slaves. The property owners wanted order and, naturally, the continuation of profit and privilege. This conflict of visions between revolution and reaction, while political movements saw struggles of popular democracy fighting traditional hierarchy, would set the stage for the inter-war period in Europe.

CHAPTER TEN

Economic Collapse and the Rise of Fascism, 1920–33

The "war to end all wars" didn't eliminate war, but it did hasten the destruction of many pre-war empires. The once mighty czarist regime collapsed in 1917 and the Austro-Hungarian Empire was swept onto the proverbial dust heap of history the following year. Both these transformations were, to one extent or another, the result of uprisings from below by those who had had enough of war, oppression and exploitation. The Turkish revolution that came from within the ruins of the Ottoman Empire was much more top down. The Ottoman Empire was the last great Islamic empire and had been in crisis long before 1914. In fact, it was referred to as the "sick man of Europe" for many years before its final collapse.

Allied with Germany during World War I, the multinational, religiously diverse Ottoman Empire suffered military defeats and internal decline. In addition, the Ottomans were beset by nationalist uprisings of their Arab subjects, who were financed by the British and directed by the famous "Lawrence of Arabia." After the Ottoman defeat in the war, the British, French and their minor power allies, like the Greeks, sought to dine on the territorial remains. The British and French partitioned the oil-rich Ottoman provinces, while ignoring promises made to the Arabs living there. The British and their Greek allies attempted to seize parts of the Turkish heartland of Anatolia.[1] The reaction was a Turkish nationalist revolution led by Mustafa Kemal, who was known after 1935 as Atatürk or "Father of the Turks."[2] The hero of the Turkish resistance to the Allied invasion of the Dardanelles in 1915, Atatürk was a modernizer who led those who wished for a modern Turkey to replace the discredited Ottoman Empire.

Atatürk reasonably accepted that the lost Arab provinces were beyond recovery and concentrated on defending the Turkish heartland. He and his co-thinkers had little nostalgia for the old Islamic monarchy; they wanted to create a modern secular republic, albeit built from the top down. From 1919 until 1922, Atatürk and his forces fought Allied armies that occupied major parts of the country, including the capital Istanbul. Further, Sultan

Mehmed VI and his supporters thought the monarchy might survive under a British mandate or American protection. In the end, the invaders were expelled, the previously dictated peace treaty was revised and the last Ottoman sultan fled into exile aboard a British ship. Thus, in 1922, the office of sultan was abolished and a republic proclaimed by 1923.

Although there wasn't much democracy in this new republic, Atatürk did launch a program of radical social and political reform. Whereas the Ottoman Empire had claimed spiritual leadership of the Islamic world, this new Turkish republic was fiercely secular. Within a decade, the republic had adopted the Western world's calendar and metric system, switched from the Turkish language to the Latin alphabet, and prohibited religious attire in public. Further, women gained the right to vote and serve in Parliament.[3] Not surprisingly, the abolition of all Islamic institutions and separation of the state from religion has been resisted by many conservative Turks, up to and including the present century.

Not all those defeated in World War I were as immediately successful at resisting allied demands. The Austro-Hungarian Empire was completely destroyed and broken into its various ethnic components. Germany was presented with a harsh treaty that stripped it of all colonies as well as a tenth of its European territory; it was also forced to take the burden of guilt for the war and thus required to pay for all the damage done. The war guilt clause and the reparations payments were poison pills forced on the new German republic. This treaty was a far cry from the promises President Woodrow Wilson had made of a just peace. Why then did representatives of the new Germany sign it? Simply put, they had little choice, as the British continued to blockade Germany, leaving growing numbers of people dying of starvation. The Treaty of Versailles, as the peace settlement is known, was likely a factor (among many) leading to the rise of Nazism and World War II. The treaty enacted numerous measures that would surely provoke hatred among large sectors of the German population,[4] but did not destroy Germany as a nation-state. The treaty was unjustly harsh, yet the victors wound up unable or unwilling to enforce it. It was, in one way of thinking, the worst of all possible worlds.

In Germany, the captains of industry and their political supporters remained unreconciled to any significant level of reparations.[5] This is not terribly surprising given that the peace treaty was imposed on, rather than negotiated with, Germany. From 1921, the German rulers' strategy, through the *Reichsbank*, was to ruin the nation's currency in order to reduce reparation payments and roll back the gains workers had achieved during the revolution.[6] The magnates of Germany industry seemed to think that runaway inflation would wipe out the German debt and render meaningless labor contracts and wage agreements, as the situation generally exhausted the working people. Early in 1922, a dollar was worth 1,000 marks—by November, a dollar bought 6,000 marks. On January 4, 1923, a dollar fetched 8,000 marks, less than a week later it was worth 10,000 marks, and by January 15, it took 56,000 marks to purchase one US currency unit. From then on, the mark skyrocketed with little relation to anything approaching economic reality; reaching 60,000,000 marks to the dollar by the first week of September.[7] Inflation was such that a typical Hamburg dockworker was paid 17 billion marks a day by fall 1923.

Before 1923 came to an end, transactions were no longer conducted in marks but with hard currency or gold, or by barter. The exception, of course, was wages that were still typically paid in nearly worthless paper marks. The money was of so little value that people often used it for heating their apartments or as wallpaper. At the beginning of that same year, the French sent 60,000 troops into the Ruhr, Germany's industrial heartland, to force reparation payments from an unwilling Germany. There was an immediate reaction from the common people of Germany, who participated in demonstrations, strikes and work slowdowns. Under pressure from below, the government organized a campaign of passive resistance to the French occupation. It was a confusing time: it was hard to tell if workers were striking out of nationalist passion or class hatred for their employers, like Krupp and Thyssen, who continued to amass greater and greater profits. The German Communist Party (KPD) planned and then cancelled an uprising in October 1923. The cancellation failed however, as the messenger sent to Hamburg didn't arrive in time, and on October 23, over a thousand KPD members seized police stations and erected barricades.[8] Although they held out for a few days, the uprising soon collapsed[9] because most workers did not rise up. Many, particularly SPD members, did not participate because they still believed that gradual reforms would be the best road to improving their lives. Some were passive simply out of despair. Moreover, there is evidence that the split between those workers ready to rebel and those who pinned their hopes on gradual change was at least partially generational.[10] That is, older workers were influenced by pre-war socialist gradualism, while the rebellious disposition of younger workers tended to be the consequence of war and revolution.

If the "War to make the World Safe for Democracy" didn't, the question remains, how did average Europeans fare after the guns finally fell silent? Not only did the great depression of 1929 sink the hopes and happiness of many average people, the fact is that the period before the crash wasn't so wonderful either. The economics of labor conditions can be measured many ways. One of the most common methods is to compare the level of real wages. Real wages means "nothing but money wages corrected according to the price changes."[11] Using this tool, one finds that if 1900 is taken as the base year [1900=100] then real wages fell almost 10 percent by 1924 in the United Kingdom.[12] In Germany, real wages fell twenty percent by 1924 although the decline was somewhat reversed the following year.[13] If we leave real wages aside and look at relative wages, the picture is even bleaker. Relative wages show the relative movement of the purchasing power of the worker vis-à-vis the rest of society. It more clearly shows that if productivity climbs more than the purchasing power of labor, workers can only buy a smaller share of the national product. Thus, in the United Kingdom during the economic cycle of 1924–32, real wages were only 7 percent below 1900, but *relative* wages were 22 percent below 1900.

In Germany, during the 1924–1935 cycle, real wages were 77 percent of 1900, but *relative* wages were a mere 44 percent of the pre-war benchmark.[14] In France, after the end of the war, "labour conditions undoubtedly became worse, real wages decreased, intensity of work increased immensely—especially owing to the reconstruction and rationalization process applied to French industry."[15] Not only were wages a problem for workers, in many places inadequate housing contributed to a decline in living standards. In the Ruhr coalfields, for example, the number of people crowded into already small dwellings increased after the war. From 1912–1925 in the city of Bochum, the average number of occupants per room jumped. While in 1912, one-room housing had an average of 1.09 persons and two rooms 1.65, by 1925 there was an average of 2.30 people living in one room and 1.80 in two rooms.[16] Housing became another tool for management, "to gain an element of control and stability over a chaotic situation."[17]

What neither the Treaty of Versailles nor the new German government did was purge the old monarchical leaders from the military or the government administration. This may well have been the biggest flaw in the Weimar Republic. On the positive side, there was healthy political participation in the new republic, as shown by party memberships and an electoral turnout higher than many modern Western governments today. On gender equality, the Weimar Republic compares favorably with other European nations. Not only were women given the right to vote, unlike in France or Italy, but females served in the Reichstag in greater numbers than in the British House of Commons. On the other hand, from the outset, right-wing anti-democratic militants used violence to achieve their goals. Note the murders of Karl Liebknecht, Rosa Luxemburg, Kurt Eisner and many more by German "patriots". One key weakness of the new republic was that while the kaiser was forced into exile, the generals, judges and all the old monarchist officials remained. The result was a socio-political environment that accepted violence on behalf of the far right who, from 1918–1922, committed 354 murders. Meanwhile, murders committed by those on the left numbered only 22. Yet, of the latter, 17 received harsh sentences including 10 condemned to death. On the other hand, right-wing murderers were typically released (326 out of 354) or, if convicted, received on average only a 4-month prison term.[18]

Still, one should dispute the conventional narrative that presents a republic, without republicans, as notable almost exclusively for the level of decadence on display in urban centers like Berlin and Hamburg. This negative narrative sees a straight line from Prussia, famously called 'an army with a country rather than a country with an army,' to the Third Reich, with the Weimar democracy as little more than a speed bump on the road to militarism and war. This standard view oversimplifies not only the complexity of the Weimar Republic but also that of Prussian/German history. It is important to look beyond the cartoon version of German history that fascists presented in the twentieth century, which has also been largely accepted at face value by anti-fascists.

For example, Frederick the Great, a man of the Enlightenment and not merely a military leader, once observed that "all religions are just as good as each other, as long as the people who practice them are honest, and even if Turks and heathens came and wanted to populate this country, then we would build mosques and temples for them."[19] Such sentiments are unlikely to have come from the mouths of early twentieth-century German rightists. Another myth is the alleged bloodthirstiness of traditional Prussian courts. In fact, the number of persons executed in England and Wales exceeded that of Prussia by a factor of sixty-to-one in the nineteenth century. Moreover, most of the condemned in British courts were charged with crimes against property, whereas most Prussian executions were for homicide.[20]

The post-war rise of the extreme right was certainly not a phenomenon isolated to defeated nation-states. Horrified by the Bolshevik Revolution, Europe's ruling classes sanctioned "paramilitary mobilization against the perceived menace. This occurred not only where the threat was plausible—in the Baltic states and Ukraine, in Hungary and in parts of Germany—but also in more peaceable victor states such as France and Britain."[21] Particularly on the extreme nationalist right, old leaders were often eclipsed by brutalized ex-officers and a young generation both of whom were furious about revolution and in some places, military defeat.

Militias, such as the German *Frei Korps*, provided a chance to live a romanticized warrior life. An explosive subculture developed throughout Europe in which "brutal violence was an acceptable, perhaps even desirable, form of political expression."[22] Seeing themselves as political soldiers, these paramilitary fighters often lacked anything approaching a clear program. Rather, they defined themselves as being against "reds" and ethnic minorities, while searching for a return to a mythical masculine past. But this movement was far from marginal in many cases. Often, as was the case in Italy, the old liberal ruling class found it opportune to ally with the far right to gain fresh vigor. Also, they typically had the illusion that they could control and use movements like fascism and Nazism. In fact, they were the ones who were used.[23]

In Poland, newly independent after World War I, the republic lasted only a few years. The new Poland was fractured between the conflicting traditions previously learned in Russian, German and Austrian pre-war partitions, as well as the ideological visions to be expected in a new nation-state. The Polish military was a battleground between both different political views and cliques based on personality.[24] Moreover, the economy often undermined the new republic, as in 1923, when the Polish mark went from 53,375 to one US dollar, to 6,050,000 Polish currency units to one dollar.[25] Even after this financial disaster was resolved, the republic's government increasingly lost public confidence, while some on the right, and the left, looked for a strongman.

In May 1926, Marshall Pilsudski, who like Mussolini was a former socialist, seized power in a *coup d'état* against the elected government. At first, Pilsudski had the support of the moderate left, who then were disappointed to find that the marshall had no intention of shifting the balance of power in favor of workers. Instead, he set up a dictatorship that had a whiff of fascism about it. Despite his well-known lukewarm belief in Catholicism and political support from anti-clericals, Pilsudski's regime enjoyed, like Mussolini's, warm relations with the Vatican. Knowing the dictatorship would guarantee the interests of the Church, the Holy See "conferred its blessing on the new leadership in Warsaw even though it was hardly Catholic in spirit or program."[26] Until his death in 1935, Pilsudski had a close relationship with Pope Pius XI even if the latter, by 1933, saw Hitler as the only man ready to take on bolshevism.[27]

In 1926, the same year that Pilsudski seized power, there is alleged to have been an attempted coup against the republic in Czechoslovakia. Radola Gajda, acting chief of staff of the Czechoslovak Army, was fired and convicted of having committed treason against the government. The details are murky and some issues are in dispute.[28] What is clear is that Gajda harbored fascist sympathies. After being dismissed from the army, he became the leader of the National Fascist Community and, in 1929, was elected under their banner to Parliament.[29] Although he was never to seize power, he was implicated in political intrigue, including a 1934 raid on a military barracks. He was never punished severely, either because of lack of evidence or the government's desire not to create a martyr for the fascists.

In Greece, an authoritarian dictatorship led by Ioannis Metaxas came to power in the interwar period, proclaiming the only true Greeks were Orthodox Christians and those of Greek ethnic background.[30] Whether this should be considered a fascist regime or merely a right-wing dictatorship is a matter of debate. The fact that it was openly anti-parliamentary, racist, and crushed all dissent is not. Like Mussolini, Hitler and others before them, Metaxas claimed the Greek Communist Party was about to seize power and thus forced him into action to save "Greek civilization." Even before the dictatorship, the post-World War I government was fiercely anti-communist, and almost openly hostile to labor.

One government official told a meeting of tobacco workers, in 1929: "Let us make it clear, if you are communists, you are enemies of the state and we shall dissolve your organizations as hostile. We do not recognize your right to band together to become stronger and more threatening to the state."[31] It is worth noting that it was bourgeois politicians who paved the way for the dictatorship by agreeing to let Metaxas become head of the government.[32] This followed the same path as had already been paved in Rome and Berlin. Established in 1936, the Metaxas dictatorship banned a wide range of authors from Marx and Kant to Tolstoy. Despite ties to Mussolini's Italy and Nazi Germany, Britain retained enough influence to force the Greek dictatorship to align with the Allies.

Even Britain, one of World War I's victors and perceived by many as an island of tranquility, faced widespread challenges to the propertied classes who dominated the national government. Trade union membership had almost doubled during the war, from 4,189,000 in 1913 to 8,081,000 by 1919. Furthermore, the three strongest unions—the miners, railroad workers and transport workers—formed the Triple Alliance in 1916. This organization held the power to shut down the British economy. By war's end, working-class militancy at home combined with turmoil in Ireland, the Middle East and armed intervention in Russia to cause a crisis for British rulers. In January 1919, Winston Churchill, acting in his capacity of secretary of war, directed the military leadership to "prepare a complete scheme and organization of Military Forces throughout the United

Kingdom to act in aid of Civil Power in the event of a national strike of a revolutionary character."[33] The military mandarins were not very keen on the idea and urged that police forces be made ready for strike breaking, without making this the duty of the army.[34]

Little wonder that the field marshalls and generals felt that way, given the situation in Britain. The British Army was "war-weary and unreliable. The men still in uniform were restless; those leaving the forces faced unemployment; those at work had low pay, while prices were rising. General disillusionment with a post-war world that offered them few rewards ...."[35] By the spring of 1919, the tension between classes was so great that some even feared Britain was on the edge of social revolution.[36] With the raising of the red flag on the city flagpole during the Glasgow general strike of late January 1919 and the seemingly irrepressible power of the Triple Alliance, people can be forgiven for what now may seem like unjustified fear, or hope. After all, the government certainly thought revolution was in the air. Ten thousand English troops, tanks, machine guns and a Howitzer were deployed in Glasgow's George Square, while nearby Scottish troops were kept in their barracks, as their loyalty was suspect.[37] Still, even after the defeat of the 1919 strikes, the government was not about to take chances. An innocently named "Supply and Transport Committee" (STC) was established. This was actually the British government's strike-breaking organization. From autumn 1919 until November 1921, the STC met 46 times and defeated the most important immediate post-war industrial disputes.[38] While the STC was pared back for budgetary reasons after the immediate crises had passed, it was later revived in new form to attempt to break the 1926 General Strike.

During the same period, things were going from bad to terrible for the British rulers in Ireland. Attempts to grant limited home rule in order to divide the Irish independence movement had failed. In December 1918, the pro-independence Sinn Fein took 73 out of 105 seats in the Irish elections and declared a republic. When the republican Parliament met in 1919, half of the elected Sinn Fein MPs were in prison. In this context, and with the memory of the Easter Rebellion firmly in view, the Irish Republican Army (IRA) launched an armed struggle in 1919. To crush the IRA guerillas, the British government deployed paramilitary groups comprised mainly of war veterans known as the "Black and Tans." Violence was high in 1920 with the IRA assassinating British intelligence officers, while the Black and Tans shot to death 15 civilians at a football match in Dublin. The following year brought roughly a thousand more deaths, but also a compromise treaty in which the IRA dissolved the Irish Republic of 1919, in return for British recognition of 26 of Ireland's 32 counties as the Irish Free State. A civil war followed as more radical IRA supporters felt this agreement, which left Ireland divided, was unacceptable.

When the story of the Irish revolt against the British Empire is told, it is often a narrative that is relentlessly male dominated. The reality is that women were an integral part of the rebellion from the beginning. During the independence war, Irish women engaged in not only what might be thought of as "women's activities" like first aid, fundraising and visiting IRA prisoners, but also labored in arms movement, communications and spying on enemy activities. In her diary, Eileen Cunningham tersely recorded her activities. Her handwritten notes, from 1920, record:

> Carrig Barracks was burned. Military lorry was to be attacked in Macroon. Raids on Crikstown and Dooniskey Mails. After this, Volunteers expected reprisals at Macroon, and took up positions in and around town. These positions were held for nearly a week and meant much work carrying arms, intelligence etc. ... .[39]

In recent years, more and more diaries and letters of female rebels have shown that the defeat of Empire was far from an all-boy show.

The facts surrounding the May 4–13, 1926 General Strike in Britain are generally available and need detain us only briefly.[40] The causes leading to the General Strike varied from the loss of export markets for coal, falling coal prices, a glut of coal on the world market, and a large number of inefficient pits. Furthermore, the return to the gold standard made British coal uncompetitive, which led mine owners to attempt to maintain profits by reducing wages and lengthening hours. When the miners rejected this attempt to prop up dividends at their expense, they were locked out and the Trade Unions Congress (TUC), very hesitantly, called a general strike that caused millions to stop work. For nine hard-fought days, poverty-stricken workers battled peacefully against a state apparatus that called upon both their traditional police forces and specially mobilized middle- and upper-class men. Over 50,000 came forth in London seeking to become "special constables," as trucks full of soldiers crisscrossed the central section of the capital.[41] On May 13, the TUC, terrified that the strike might collapse (or maybe equally terrified it might not and thus turn into a power struggle), called off the strike during a meeting with Prime Minister Stanley Baldwin at 10 Downing Street. To the right, this was a victory, while many on the left saw it as a betrayal.[42]

A more complex but still radical interpretation of 1926 is that this was a troubled period in terms of the transition from the pre-1914 forms of social control to new mechanisms. A new strategy being developed by the British ruling class had scarcely had a chance to coalesce or establish itself by 1926. This was, in part, because it was threatened by widespread shop-floor militancy that had begun during World War I, and persisted into the economic crisis of the 1920s. Because the government plan to build up the right wing of the labor movement was less established than anticipated, the confrontation over wage cuts did not spur the collapse of organized labor resistance, as hoped. Surprised by the strength of worker response in 1926, the rulers had to back off their more extreme attacks on wages and conditions in hope of recasting their strategy to co-opt the TUC leadership, and build up the Labour Party's right wing, while isolating the left.[43]

Descending from the heights of theory, it is important to ask what 1926 meant for the strikers, most of all the miners. It is agreed by almost everyone that the miners suffered unspeakable privation both before and after the lockout. During the General Strike, although the suffering was perhaps greater, there was at least the sense that things might change for the better. Although portrayals of the strikers predictably depict the strong and proud male worker, it is good to remember that strikers were part of a larger proletarian community. True, this was a male-dominated world that was deeply patriarchal, but social dynamics were more complex than stereotypes suggest. As one historian studying South Wales discovered, general roles "could be a good deal less rigid than many imagined."[44]

During the 1926 struggle, gender roles were challenged, even if they mainly reappeared unaltered after the defeat of the General Strike. In Durham, where almost a third of the adult men worked in the coalmines, community did not mean a bland occupational homogeneity. Instead, the community was able to subsume and integrate various identities in order to maintain solidarity with the miners.[45] In addition, the family unit and traditional gender roles were subverted by the need for collective action. Since everyone must eat to survive, and miners hardly had enough to eat even before the lockout, the role of collective communal eating is well worth noting.[46] This collective experience reduced gender segregation, even as it maintained the masculine identity of male miners. Despite the ultimately limited nature of these changes, the process of collective food provision and consumption showed how quickly people can change in the course of social struggles. Of course, the most immediate task, and a vital unifying force, was the need the community felt to maintain a united front of solidarity with the miners. One female participant, Lilian Lawrence, was asked about the reaction to those men who carried on working in the mines. Lawrence told how her mother and aunt broke the windows of her uncle's house because he was a scab. When asked if her mother broke any other windows, she responded, "Oh, yes, the ones that was scabs, yes."[47]

Unlike much of the rest of inter-war Europe, Sweden did not suffer the same revolutionary or reactionary fever. In Sweden, the Social Democrats, for all their faults,[48] steered a middle ground between workers' revolution and upper-class repression. Often called "the third way," Swedish Social Democrats used electoral success and trade union might to construct a welfare state without abolishing capitalism. When Swedish Social Democracy took control of the government in 1932, a class compromise was reached with the old ruling class. In a program that contrasts sharply with the limited achievements of FDR in the United States and the central planning that characterized the USSR, the new Swedish government fought for a society where "no longer would private calculations of profit and loss alone determine the level of employment and production; now the state would intervene to rectify the flaws of uncoordinated capitalist enterprise."[49] The Swedish Social Democrats were able to maintain their political dominance and their class compromise program until well after World War II.[50]

Meanwhile, the Russian Revolution, that had been a source of so much hope for European workers in 1917, suffered a counter-revolution during the 1920s. Gone were democratic systems, new artistic styles and attempts to eliminate the old patriarchal structures that oppressed women.[51] Instead there was return to a parody of the old czarist system, with its rule by terror. A newly ascendant bureaucratic regime led by Joseph Stalin increasingly seized more and more power until almost all of the old Bolshevik leadership had been arrested and executed. In their place came a new group, with the Bolshevik Party becoming a hollow shell that merely functioned as a political ornament worn on the shirt of the new Soviet dictatorship. Before his death, Bolshevik leader V.I. Lenin had struggled unsuccessfully against the abandonment of the socialist experiment.[52] Until his assassination in 1940, Leon Trotsky, one of the most important leaders of the revolution likewise fought a losing war against the collapse of the hopes of 1917.[53]

This turn of events begs for the question to be asked: why? Without entering into a belabored examination of every theory that has been put forth, and enough books have been written on this subject to fill a small college library, a few basic facts should be considered. The Bolshevik, later renamed Communist, Party, being a Marxist organization had always stressed the centrality of the working class to their party and any future revolution. Yet, for most of its pre-revolutionary history, the Bolsheviks had been a party of intellectuals who believed in the working class without receiving overwhelming support from that class. Then in 1917, their hope became a reality and the Bolsheviks actually had the impressive support of massive numbers of workers, soldiers and sailors. Although the peasants made up the vast majority of the Russian Empire's population, by 1917 the industrial working class was over 4,500,000 strong with an additional 7,000,000 people in the military, whom Russian Marxists considered as workers.

Within a year, by 1918, this working class began to disintegrate. Hunger became rampant in the cities and factories closed because of a lack of materials, driving people back to their family villages. Then, as discussed earlier, the country endured foreign invasions and Civil War for the next three years; during this period as many as a million workers returned to the peasantry. Other workers were coopted into the Red Army or the governmental apparatus, thus becoming former workers. By the end of the Civil War, there remained roughly a million industrial workers in Soviet Russia. This was reflected in the class composition of the party:, at the time of the February Revolution, 60 percent of the membership had been workers. Despite their best efforts, this same organization had only a 40 percent working-class membership by the end of the Civil War, as the rest of the party were either peasants or middle class.[54]

The party leadership, for all their brilliance, had no real idea about what to do. On many occasions, leaders tried to blame objective conditions for their situation. As one Bolshevik oppositionist bitterly remarked at a meeting in which party leaders claimed that the working class no longer existed, "Permit me to congratulate you on being the vanguard of a nonexistent class."[55] One historian summed up the Bolsheviks' dilemma, "Against all odds, they had made a workers' revolution. Then, in the hour of victory, the Russian proletariat had disappeared—leaving only its vanguard, like the smile of the Cheshire cat, behind."[56] Some, like Stalin, concluded that, without a working class or a worldwide socialist revolution to help under-developed Russia, all that was left was to substitute the party apparatus for socialist democracy. For this, one needed trained cadres; a new elite was educated and went on to run the USSR until its demise towards the end of the twentieth century. As there was both a desire and need for the USSR to industrialize, particular emphasis was given to producing competent engineers who understood the value of political conformity.[57] This goal of modernizing Russia was a gain of the October Revolution and was actively pursued, while other ideals like gender equality[58] and civil liberties were abandoned.

When the Great Depression of 1929 hit the countries of capitalist Europe, workers (particularly industrial workers) were hardest hit. This was especially true in Germany where the bourgeoisie saw the chance to cripple, if not destroy, the working-class movement. Unions lost members and their bargaining power to the widespread joblessness. Workers' wages and standard of living fell drastically. In 1931, a Berlin satirist noted, "[that] workers must receive wages for their work is a theory that has been generally abandoned today."[59] By 1933, 40 percent of all male industrial workers were unemployed, as contrasted with only 13 percent of white-collar workers. Mass unemployment ate away at the "basic substance of the working class movement. Anxiety about keeping a job, worry about finding a job, was not in the long term compatible with militant opposition to the existing social order."[60]

Despite various lightly documented attempts to claim that workers willingly joined the Nazis, there is little evidence to support this whether measured by voting patterns, membership figures, or political logic. Even had the Nazi Party been sincere in its rhetoric about being for the German worker, this was an organization with a social base and financial backers who were "fundamentally and totally hostile to the workers—and this not only in an ideological and political sense, but also with respect to the central economic interests of the working class."[61] After all, one of the most central appeals of fascism, most of all for the vitally important bourgeois portion of their base, is that it will destroy all proletarian organizations and institutions. Facing a working class bitterly divided into Social Democratic and Communist camps, German fascism was able to use violence and a mass mobilization of petit-bourgeois and lumpen elements to crush the left. The battle between the left and Nazis took place in the streets, but also increasingly in sophisticated propaganda.[62] It is useful to remember the unique features of fascism as distinct from those of the traditional right. Whereas most right-wing dictatorships content themselves with using administrative, legal and economic pressures to weaken opponents, fascists seek to quite literally destroy all working-class organizations and murder all resisters among the common people.[63]

Naturally, the onset of the Great Depression left many Germans open to appeals to nationalism and racism. Yet, the most Hitler and his Nazis could muster in a free election in July 1932 was 37.3 percent of the votes cast. A few months later, in November 1932, support for the Nazis had declined another 4 percent, they had lost 34 Reichstag seats and were facing bankruptcy. In order to spread fear, and justify the arrest and murder of political opponents, most of all the KPD, Hitler had the Reichstag building torched. Using an underground tunnel that connected Nazi leader Hermann Göring's residence with the basement of the Reichstag building, Nazi storm troopers fanned out and spread incendiaries. Having set the fire, they hurried back through the tunnel. With Germany's Parliament building in flames, Hitler proclaimed that a Communist uprising had been launched. He then demanded, and received, emergency powers from his cabinet and President Hindenburg. With these powers, all civil rights were eliminated and truckloads of fascist thugs rounded up thousands of Communists and Social Democrats, along with anyone else thought to be an important anti fascist.

What was the popular response? Hans Werner Richter, a German in his twenties when the Nazis began their murderous crackdown, recalled his shock that

> ... nothing moved, nothing happened, no strike, no general strike, no call to battle in the streets—nothing ... Socialist and Communist youth, ready to take the fight to streets, waited in vain for order that never came, except for the instruction of the Communist Party to creep into the underground.

Along with many other young people, Richter awaited direction to "strike out," only to be told to wait or go home.[64]

This set the stage for the election the following month. It is hard to think of a more undemocratic election. The opposition to the Nazi Party had no opportunity to campaign; even simply hanging an anti-fascist poster became a criminal offense. Likewise, those individuals on the Nazi "red lists" were kept from polling places through a combination of violence, murder and imprisonment in one of the new concentration camps for political prisoners. Amazingly, the common people, particularly the working classes, continued to resist the Brownshirt plague, as the election results prove. Despite resorting to political violence, vote stealing and rigging, and having generous financial backing from Krupp munitions and I.G. Farben, in March 1933 Hitler's legions still took only 43.9 percent of the vote. Why then were the Nazis able to seize power? In the end, it was not the popular vote that mattered but the support of the old ruling class. Hitler was given power, as one historian contends, "as a result of political intrigues among the ruling elite just as their electoral support was on the wane."[65] In all the understandable fascination with the obscene genocide, mass murder and horror of German Nazism, one thing usually gets forgotten. That is, for the ruling class of Germany, their support for fascism was not merely a response to crisis, it was rather a way of utilizing the crisis.[66] Big business, the army and other remnants of the German Empire gave the Nazis power and a job to do. The problem was the German fascists got carried away, started a war and then lost it.

CHAPTER ELEVEN

Against Fascist Terror:
War and Genocide, 1933–45

The Weimar Republic's brutal destruction in 1933 gave hope and strength to the ultra-right throughout Europe, while it awoke the left to very real danger of fascism. A year after flames had leapt from the Reichstag, signaling the death of freedom in Germany, a movement from across the Rhine arose with the same ideas. On February 6, 1934, war veterans and right-wing extremists descended on central Paris nominally to complain about government corruption. It seems likely that many came to do fundamental damage to parliamentary government. The demonstration quickly turned into a riot as police fought back wave after wave of assaults on the French Parliament. Over a dozen were killed and hundreds wounded. The next day, the center-left government resigned. Although there was no clear blueprint for a *coup d'état*, this served as the start, not the end, of a fascist march to power. The ultra-right forced one leftist government to resign, and their repeated extra-parliamentary tactics destabilized every subsequent Parliament elected until the German occupation in 1940.[1]

In the United Kingdom, Sir Oswald Mosley formed the British Union of Fascists (BUF) in 1932. Supported early on by the *Daily Mail*[2] and claiming 50 thousand members,[3] the BUF never really gathered much electoral support and is mainly noted for well-crafted rallies and street fighting with left-wingers and Jews. When war came, the government easily interned their leaders and core supporters. In the other major Anglo-Saxon power, across the Atlantic, pro-Nazi groups had thousands of supporters, and help from industrialist Henry Ford and aviation legend Charles Lindbergh. At one point, they filled New York City's Madison Square Garden for a Nazi-style rally.[4] Of course, this does not even consider the vast and powerful, native fascist Ku Klux Klan that held sway in so much of the southern US. It would seem that fascism was on the march worldwide.

These developments did not go on unnoticed. In spring 1934, following the fascist attack on Parliament, the French Communist Party (PCF) proposed a Popular Front against Fascism. The left had previously discussed and, on occasion, entered into "United Fronts" between left, working-class parties. The Popular Front was different in that it included not just leftists but liberals and even, at times, conservatives, as long as the parties were committed to fighting fascism. It was a cross-class, multiple ideological grouping, rather than a clear program based on parties of the working people. The Popular Front policy was supported, many say initiated, by the Communist International and the Soviet Union. Another clear source of support for this new coalition was the pressure from below, as average Europeans, and most of all workers, wanted unity in face of the rising fascist threat. Of course, many have argued that the average people wanted labor unity, not an alliance with capitalist interests who would tie their hands in the fight against fascism. Trotsky, for one, believed that a united front without bourgeois allies was the only road to victory over the extreme right.[5]

In any case, after tough negotiations, the PCF and the Socialist Party joined the center-left Radicals while the previously splintered French trade union movement achieved some significant level of unity. On July 14, 1935, Bastille Day, the Popular Front was proclaimed, with a rather moderate social democratic program. This timid approach resulted from both PCF leaders and the Socialists not wishing to frighten middle-class allies or would-be supporters. The following year, in May 1936, the Popular Front was victorious at the polls and a government led by socialist Léon Blum took office. This victory sparked off a seemingly spontaneous workers' movement, with shop-floor militants organizing strikes and factory occupations. The strikes were unplanned, joyful and completely illegal. This was not only a response to the Popular Front victory, but also the release of pent-up anger over half a decade of lowered wages, employer indifference and terrible working conditions.[6] Although the strikes began in the provinces, they quickly reached the capital.

The largest and most profitable factories were the first hit by these unarmed workers' rebellions. Estimates say between 1,500,000 and 1,950,000 strikers walked out and that there were, literally, thousands of factory occupations. This peaceful uprising from below was demo-cratically organized through average worker militants at the plant level. Unprepared or unwilling to make a push for revolution, the Communists and their Socialist allies decided to restrain the strike wave and then end it completely. But the workers did not come out of this empty handed. The agreement ending the strike recognized unions and their right to strike. Workers gained wage increases of at least 7 percent and in some cases gains were as high as 25 percent. In tandem, the Blum government legalized collective bargaining, set two-week paid vacation standards and a 40-hour workweek, among other concessions.

The French Popular Front also impacted intellectuals and cultural workers. New cultural organizations were established with direct government funding. Communist leaders argued that culture should become one with politics; they believed that art, plays and concerts should be presented to the public as social services.[7] Among others, composers were rapidly involved in this politicized process, which was aided by Communist-funded cultural organizations and an interest in the Soviet cultural model.[8] Moreover, Paris became a magnet for many talented anti-fascists after the Nazi seizure of power in Germany. German leftists who fled to France produced Popular Front propaganda, much of it of an innovative nature.[9] Of course, the fascist regime in Berlin was likewise attempting to use culture to consolidate its power. It even tried to create a new "German" style of dance.[10]

French film was not exempt from the impact of the 1936 strike wave or the initial enthusiasm generated by the Blum government. By the 1930s, film had become the most popular form of entertainment and France produced over a hundred films yearly. Although not always a direct result of the Popular Front upsurge, it is interesting that a couple of films released in 1936 reflected the "aspirations of the urban working class as well as the political tumult linked to the rise of fascism and the threat of war in Europe."[11] Moreover, young filmmakers, often independent of and hostile to the "commercial film industry, produced films for the emerging Left culture."[12] For leftists in the film industry, a unifying issue was the overtly political bias of film censorship. That censorship protected the French populace from the subversion of Soviet films such as *Potemkin*, *Mother* and *The End of St. Petersburg* was a constant source of anger for the left. This frustration and anger was not limited to PCF supporters. Particularly galling was that, at the same time, commercial newsreels of current events were solidly right wing and untouched by censorship.[13]

Of far more immediate and concrete importance for the French common people was the Popular Front's promotion of paid vacations. One not very sympathetic historian has argued the Popular Front "became the birthplace of the weekend, not of revolution."[14] On June 21, 1936, a bill was passed into law granting a two-week paid vacation. This was part of the government's policy of establishing the right to a vacation for workers. It is interesting that in the summers of 1936 and 1937, the left-wing press reported extensively on the Spanish Civil War, but alternated this coverage "with articles recommending seaside and country resorts and featuring

French provincial towns worth visiting."[15] Union papers began to shift from reporting purely on political and economic matters to discussing sports and radio, and publishing "women's sections." The Communist press emphasized that vacations allowed the family to have time to get to know each other. The PCF daily, *L'Humanité*, even got into this "family feel good" trend by featuring a story on the home life of Lenin and his family.[16] The French left hoped that by promoting popular tourism, workers could seize control of participant sports and cultural activities, and in the process free themselves from bourgeois paternalism.[17]

The Popular Front government failed to both follow up on their early success and consolidate their popular support. As a result, by 1938, the Popular Front had collapsed. A new right-wing member of the Radical Party became prime minister and supported a counter-attack by big business against the workers' recent gains. Workers reacted with strikes and factory occupations and in response, the new government engaged in the most brutal strike suppression of the inter-war period. Hundreds were arrested and tens of thousands were fired, while just under a million workers lost the protection of a union contract and were forced to be rehired in non-union plants. The 40-hour week was replaced by a 45-hour week, as militants found themselves blacklisted from their profession. Despite these losses in 1938, the dreams of 1936 remained alive in the memory of the people. The Popular Front, workers' strikes and occupation, combined with major reforms, had given the French common people an expanded sense of what life could be like.

Increasingly, life for average Europeans included the consumption of spectator sports. The industrial revolution had destroyed traditional popular culture to a large extent. With the growth of organized labor, more and more workers had the time and money to participate in sports. This increasingly led to not just playing sports but to watching them. The mass popularity of sports as a leisure-time activity is such that one scholar could reasonably comment that "Marx might well have been nearer the mark had he referred to sport rather than religion as the opium of the masses."[18] In an attempt to come to grips with this reality, left-wing workers' groups attempted to establish independent working-class sporting events in an attempt to compete with the bourgeois culture promoted by commercial sports. By 1928, there were two workers' sports Internationals, one Socialist and the other Communist, which "counted well over two million members, making the sport movement by far the largest working class cultural movement."[19] In 1931, the socialist-affiliated workers' sports movement met in Vienna with tens of thousands of worker athletes. On the last day, a quarter of a million people watched the festive march of 100,000 men and women from 26 nations. The same day, 65,000 watched the soccer championship game and 12,000 watched the cycling finals.[20]

Of course, the fascist movement had long understood the power sports had for the average European. Upon coming to power, the Nazis found Germany committed to hosting an international event that grated on their ultra-nationalist passions, the 1936 Olympics.[21] They cleverly turned the Berlin Olympics into a propaganda event by projecting the image of Nazi Germany as powerful but peaceful.[22] The fascist propaganda orgy that was 1936 Berlin was magnified and preserved by Leni Riefenstahl's film *Olympia*.[23] The workers' sports movement planned to hold counter-Olympics in Barcelona, but these plans had to be abandoned once the Spanish Army rose in revolt against the elected Popular Front government. Still, in 1937, a third (and final) Workers' Olympiad was convened in Antwerp. Not as impressive as 1936 Barcelona had hoped to be, it still drew 27,000 worker participants, both male and female, from 17 nations along with hundreds of thousands of spectators.[24] However, if it proved difficult to compete with fascist sport spectacles, it seemed near impossible to overcome the advantages of commercial sports. The power of bourgeois sport culture was shown, for example, in the Soccer World Cup held throughout France in June 1938.[25]

The appeal of forming a Popular Front against the rising surge of fascism was not limited to France. In Greece, the All People Front, an alliance of the Communist Party and other leftists, won 9.6 percent of the vote in the 1935 election. The following year, the Front won a smaller percentage but elected 15 MPs. This was but the electoral tip of a broad movement that hoped to ultimately topple the monarchy and the conservative parliamentary government. Worried about a possible decline of British power in the Aegean, the British ambassador encouraged General Metaxas to make a preemptive strike. When the general seized power, the new right-wing dictatorship was warmly, if somewhat discreetly, welcomed by the UK's rulers.[26] The most well-known and significant Popular Front movement would, however, take place far to the west of Athens.

The Spanish Popular Front government that won the February 1936 elections was a loose coalition of liberal republicans, socialists and various flavors of communists, both pro- and anti-Moscow. Though the name "Popular Front" was attached to this coalition, it was not formed mainly by the policy of the Comintern. The Spanish alliance and its component parts began to come together early in 1934 and owe more to internal dynamics than external exhortations.[27] In fall 1934, a revolt by Asturian miners united middle-class reformers and working-class militants; it was this unity that later would take on the name "Popular Front." The defeat of the miners using troops from Africa was accompanied by brutal reprisals against strikers, press censorship and the arrest of thousands of political opponents who had had nothing to do with the events in Asturias.[28]

The 1936 elections gave a clear victory to the left, who won in all cities of over 200,000 people. The extreme right made accusations of vote fraud, later using this as a justification for military uprising. Despite these claims, the vote counting included all parties and even the rightist press at the time analyzed the results in terms of issues and emotions, but not fraud. From the beginning, the new government had to deal with pent-up frustrations on the part of many sections of the common people, particularly anarchists and leftist socialists. From the start, monarchists and other rightists openly plotted against the elected government. In July, the military rose up in an attempted *coup d'état* to restore the old order. Although they had some success, Franco and his generals faced unanticipated resistance. The quick military strike bogged down in the face of massive resistance by leftist militias and the Spanish counter-revolution became the Spanish Civil War.

From the start, the Popular Front government was crippled by lack of trained officers and supplies, and was riven by ideological conflicts among its base. The then-aspiring dictator Franco and his apologists pointed to the murder of priests, monks and other religious personnel as proving the Satanic evil of the elected government. Particularly useful for the fascist propaganda machine was that in many places the bodies of saints, priests and others were dug up and put on display. Not only was this universally opposed by the elected government, it was part of a tradition of bitter anti-clericalism that had appeared before, in 1834, 1868, 1909 and 1931.[29] This was not so much an attack on religion per se as an assault on the Spanish Church as an institution, which was seen by the poor as protecting the wealthy and powerful.[30] In any event, there is no denying that supporters of the Republic did commit crimes, especially during the initial fury provoked by the military uprising. The fact must also be remembered that what the pro-fascist military did was thousands of times worse. Moreover, crimes in Republican areas were *in defiance* of governmental policy whereas the bloody outrages committed by the so-called "Nationalists" *were a matter of policy*.

The defeat of the military rising was not merely a ratification of the existing parliamentarian government. The example of the vital Catalan city of Barcelona was a very significant example. The victory over the fascist rebels also "represented the critical moment when power was transferred to the streets—in other words, when the popular movement took effective control of Barcelona."[31] These were people who didn't believe the revolution had to wait until an unknowable future. The anarchists among these people also wished to end the oppression of Spanish working-class women. They hoped to do this by ending formal marriage, eliminating prostitution, and providing training programs and medical care for women.[32] However, anarchist men did little to try and realize these programs. Using excuses like female illiteracy[33] or the influence of priests among women, the anarchists seemed as little anxious to make fundamental changes in gender relations as more moderate Popular Front supporters. Because of this, the traditional relationship between men and women was carried over into revolutionary Spain, despite the obvious contradiction to stated beliefs.[34]

By May 1937, there was bloody fighting between the Popular Front government, which was backed by the Communists, and popular power in Catalonia, which was backed by anarchists and other anti-Stalinist leftists. From the start, the division was between those who thought that republican legality must be maintained so as to not alienate the middle class or foreign powers, and those who believed that the revolution should not be postponed to some future date. This ultimately led to the brutal suppression of the far left by the very government that spoke in their name. Further, the Popular Front government was assisted by Soviet agents who wielded great power, partially by virtue of their control over Soviet military aid.[35] Regardless of one's position on this dispute, it is hard not to see the tragedy of Spanish jails being crammed with populist revolutionaries at a time when the people were supposedly in power via the Popular Front government. For many, May 1937 marks the end of the Popular Front in any meaningful sense of its original purpose.[36]

Still, it is necessary to recognize that the Spanish Republic had been betrayed by the Western so-called democracies. While Mussolini, and later Hitler, poured troops and military resources into the camp of Spanish fascism, the British, French and American governments refused to even sell arms to the elected government. The conventional apology for this behavior is that London was afraid of war, Paris was afraid of war without Britain, and Washington didn't care about Europe. There is some truth in these assertions but they miss the larger picture. Fearing a lurch to the left, the British government aggressively promoted the abandonment of Spanish democracy. While the Spanish Communists were weak, and before the Soviet Union had gained any real influence, London was already pre-disposed towards the right as a barrier to "Bolshevism." After the Spanish generals' revolt, the British leaders were clear that Franco and friends were preferable to elected leftists. One senior official even got carried away and suggested it "is not inconceivable that before long it may pay us to throw in our lot with Germany and Italy."[37] Shortly after the start of the Civil War, the British consul general wrote that if the Popular Front suppressed the revolt, "some form of bolshevism" could be expected. The consul despaired that the Popular Front was "a government sold for long time past to [the] proletariat."[38] So, as early as August 1936, it is undeniable that "Whitehall clearly believed that republican Spain was better dead than red."[39]

Most of those in republican Spain dissented from the viewpoint of the British government. Though neighboring governments would not help the Republic, tens of thousands of ordinary people did. Foreign volunteers, mainly German, French, Italian and American, came to Spain in late 1936 to fight fascism.[40] Ideology was certainly a big factor, but many joined out of impulse or opportunity. Of course, for anti-fascist Germans and Italians living in exile, the International Brigade offered a chance to actually fight fascism rather than merely talk about fighting it. As one German veteran noted, political work in exile seemed "too conventional, too small."[41] In memoirs, many former Internationals talk about the importance of their political beliefs, but also highlight the significant role emotions and nostalgia played. In the face of boredom, the desire for adventure, and a desire to escape leftist political and individual personal circumstances, foreign volunteers found meaning. Especially for exiled anti-fascists, there was often a yearning for a meaningful, active masculinity.[42] Regardless of differing motivations, they fought bravely until fall 1938, when the Internationals were withdrawn from battle in the vain hope of receiving help from the Western powers. The courage of the Spanish people fighting the fascist "nationalist" army is legendary.

In the end, even those who thought the Republic held the moral high ground had to admit that ideals alone were no match for fascist steel. On March 28, 1939, the Spanish military entered the capital, Madrid. For generations, the crimes and true motivations of the Spanish fascists have been overlooked and excused. A close look at what transpired shows that Franco and his followers were every bit as murderous and fascist as their sponsors in Berlin. At his Victory Day celebration on May 19, 1939, General Franco declared: "Let us not deceive ourselves: the Jewish spirit, which permitted the alliance of big capital with Marxism and which was behind so many pacts with the anti-Spanish revolution, cannot be extirpated in a day and still beats in the hearts of many."[43] Nazi anti-Semitic laws were held up as examples to Spain, while the notion of a Jewish-Marxist conspiracy was expanded to include freemasons.

Nor should it be thought that Spanish fascism used words alone against their enemies. A common misconception is that the dead in Spain were purely the result of the Civil War. In reality, once the Spanish far right assumed power, they continued to murder, jail and torture in much the same way as Italian or German fascists. More people died from repression after the fall of the Republic than during the actual Civil War. Many were jailed and denied trial, while those who were given the pretense of a trial were accused of the most fanciful things. One man was charged, post-execution, with, among other things, wearing a red tie. The accused was convicted, though dead, and the man's widow was forced to pay a 500-pesatas fine.[44] Often overlooked is how the military rebels concentrated their wrath on liberal and left-wing women. Not only were they murdered like their male counterparts but, in addition, rape and other forms of sexual abuse were used as a generalized punishment for embracing gender equality. The opportunity to rape was even promoted as an implicit recruiting tool by Franco.[45] Statistics alone can never tell the depth of emotional, physical and psychological damage done to those women who survived fascist abuse. While respect for women was a part of the Popular Front's reform program, hatred for female independence was part of the right-wing program.[46] Women were even persecuted for having married in a civil, rather than Catholic, ceremony.[47]

A victory for Republican Spain might have changed what we now know as World War II. It might have served as a warning to the Nazi and fascist aggressors.[48] Moreover, the impact within Germany is hard to determine. It may well have revitalized the anti-Nazi underground among the working class. It might have even given courage to the cowards of the allegedly anti-Nazi wing of the German Wehrmacht's officer corps. One must question how this group of highly decorated professional soldiers with access to the Nazi leadership and presumably knowledge of firearms and explosives, could not pull off a decisive assassination or two—a task that would not have been too challenging for most Chicago gangsters. But then again, no one could accuse either the German aristocracy or bourgeoisie of being premature anti-fascists.

While the tragedy of Spain played out to the west, Stalin was embarking on a series of murderous purges that weakened Soviet society from the Red Army to the factory floor.[49] Just two years of Stalin's purges, 1937 and 1938, account for 85 percent of all death sentences ordered from 1921 until 1953. According to recently available data from the Soviet archives,

"790,665 [1937] and 554,258 people [1938] were indicted respectively for political crimes. Of them, 353,074 and 328,618 were sentenced to be shot."[50] The political elite were disproportionally represented among the victims but ordinary citizens remained the bulk of those arrested. Historians still debate the reasons behind such a massive, and apparently senseless, bloodbath. Some sort of perverse chivalry appears to have spared many women, who apparently were less than 4 percent of the executed, at least in major urban areas.[51] These horrific mass murders disoriented the left and anti-fascist movements, many of whom had thought of the Soviet Union as a workers' state. One should remember that, in spite of attempts by the right to say Stalinism was as bad, or worse, than fascism, the Soviet purges killed far fewer people than Mussolini and Franco combined, and certainly fewer than the German Nazi death machine that gave the world the Holocaust. To say Stalinism and fascism were identical, as opposed to stating both were evil, is intellectually lazy and dishonest.[52]

As if the purges were not bad enough, in 1939 Stalin again did the unthinkable. On August 23, 1939, the Soviet Union and Nazi Germany signed a non-aggression pact. This treaty had a secret protocol that divided Eastern Europe between Germany and Russia. It gave the green light to the Nazi war machine to invade Poland, an act they undertook on September 1 of the same year. Apologists for this pact have argued that the USSR needed to play for time to prepare for the inevitable Nazi invasion. Interestingly enough, this argument was absent at the time and was not used until after the Nazi invasion of 1941.[53] Moreover, evidence shows that it was the German fascist regime, not the Soviets, who used the extra time to best advantage.[54] What the so-called "Hitler-Stalin Pact" did do was disorient those who were fighting against fascism.

The French PCF, then the largest Communist movement in the West, was confused, sometimes angry, and a number of members quit in disgust. With the PCF press banned as a result of the Pact, the party found itself unable to even communicate effectively with many members and supporters. The party leadership was largely paralyzed and the non-Communist left pulled away from Communist militants in fury.[55] The exiled Italian, Giorgio Amendola, argues that the non-aggression treaty completed the break between Communists and other anti-fascists. He went on to say the "German-Soviet pact aggravated the existing antagonisms and the confusion within the organized anti-Fascist movement."[56] The impact was, if anything, greater among the German anti-Nazi ranks. A young Communist, Franz Loeser, recalls being furious upon hearing the news. The anti-Nazi militant exploded: "How could an anti-Fascist stay out of the war? Should I wait until the Fascists had killed my family? Should I watch the Nazis land in England and send me to a concentration camp? What kind of anti-Fascists were these who didn't want to fight with the Fascists?"[57] By fall 1939, fighting fascism increasingly became not a matter of choice, but of self-survival. As Brecht put it:

ON THE WALL IN CHALK IS WRITTEN:
They want war.
He who wrote it
Has already fallen.[58]

World War II was the largest tragedy in European history.[59] It lasted almost six years and resulted in some 60,000,000 deaths and untold suffering on the part of countless millions who didn't die. The physical and economic damage is difficult to comprehend. The military history of the conflict has been documented in almost mind-numbing detail. Thus, there is little need to visit debates about the quality of Axis versus Allied strategic bombers, the quality of German tanks versus those of the Soviets, the impact of fascist submarines versus Allied naval prowess, or the importance of Nazi Werner Von Braun's missile program. Those matters can safely be left to military historians who have felled whole forests to produce books, articles and essays, while any number of specialized television stations can be counted on to produce 24-hour visual accounts of the war.

Still, it is important to remember that this was not just a war that took place on distant battlefields. This was a war of extermination by the fascists against all their enemies, both real and imagined. The unthinkable "final solution" meant the cold-blooded murder of millions of Europeans of Jewish lineage.[60] In addition to this genocidal attempt to destroy European Jews,[61] the Roma and Sinti (often called Gypsies) were exterminated simply because of their heritage.[62] Other targeted groups included the mentally challenged, the physically disabled, and, despite their earlier importance in the Storm Trooper faction of the Nazi movement, homosexuals.[63] Jehovah's Witnesses, a group termed "bible students," were also sent to the camps. Often forgotten is the fact that the first targets of Hitler's murderous wrath were his political opponents, be they Communists, social democrats, trade unionists, or anti-fascists. While not all political prisoners were marked for execution per se, they were subject to forced labor with the intention that they be "annihilated by work." Thus, many prisoners died of hunger, disease, violence from guards, or accidents. Located just outside Berlin in 1936, Sachsenhausen is a good example of a political camp, although it later contained "racial criminals" and was used for the mass murder of Soviet POWs.[64]

Discussed here is the struggle of Europeans against fascism, whether they were motivated by ideology, nationalism, or the simple instinct to survive. While leaders like Winston Churchill were fighting to save the British Empire, and Stalin to preserve his dictatorship, most people were not fighting for empire—they were fighting for themselves.[65] Space will not permit but a few selected examples of this resistance but they are vital to a more complete understanding. It can even be argued that the Nazi decision to begin the war before their military was at full strength represents constraints imposed by the passive resistance of German workers and fear of a popular rebellion.[66] Even later, anti-Hitler conspiracies within the German High Command were often motivated by a belief that only the Nazis "violent overthrow could prevent the danger of a social revolution from below."[67] That this revolution did not take place is at least partially due to Allied policy as shall be seen. In the popular culture, anti-fascist resistance is often told as stories of heroic men.

Yet the resistance, be it small or great, was a movement across all of Europe. There were exceptional individuals, but to focus exclusively on them overlooks the bulk of anti-fascists, particularly women. While it may be exciting to hear about shoot-outs between anti-fascists and the Gestapo, most resistance work was much more routine. One Dutch woman, who was a courier for the resistance, remembered her work as "going for ration books ... all kinds of things, the whole lot—take it away, get it, and take it to a contact address ... and carrying arms, of course."[68] Resistance could also be of a more spontaneous nature. One Italian female anti-fascist told how a female comrade decided on a risky individual act. The woman named Giglioa was eating at a restaurant when she noticed a German officer had hung his coat and sidearm on a clothes hook. Thinking quickly, she covered his coat with hers. She quickly finished eating before the Nazi, retrieved her coat and slipped his gun into her purse and quietly left.[69] Certainly, traditional gender roles predominated within the resistance but even women who did not enter the underground struggle with a feminist consciousness often developed an awareness of gender oppression as result of their activities.[70]

Women participated in at least parts of the French resistance in traditional ways. By fall 1941, French Communists had begun systematically undermining the morale of German occupation troops. It was young German or Austrian female exiles, or other women who could speak German, who established contact with these troops. They distributed a printed newspaper called *Soldat im Westen*, later subtitled *Organ den soldaten komitee im Frankreich*. It passed on stories of brutal officers, unfair treatment of enlisted men and sought to promote internationalism instead of the fascist nationalism. While the importance of this work should not be overemphasized, it is noteworthy that in some Wehrmacht units, loud complaints were made after agitation about food and treatment by officers. Anti-Nazi propaganda was brought back to friends in the Third Reich and many Germans used "safe conduct passes" given to them by the French to facilitate their desertion to the Soviets, once posted to the Eastern Front.[71]

In the Balkans, the armed anti-fascist movement of Yugoslavia and Greece was a real military problem for the Nazi occupiers.[72] Although supposedly blood brothers according to Nazi mythology, Denmark saw little support for the fascist occupiers while Danish anti-fascists were able to smuggle almost all of the country's Jewish population to neutral Sweden. In 1942, Jews in the Warsaw Ghetto organized armed self-defense units despite little or no help from the Polish nationalist "home army." When the Nazis began the liquidation of the ghetto in order to deport the inhabitants to death camps, the lightly armed Jewish resistance shocked the Nazi forces by driving them back. Although the Warsaw Ghetto fighters had no chance of military success, some resisters fought on for a month.

In a certain sense, the strangest act of resistance came from within the heart of the Third Reich, in central Berlin. Early in 1943, Joseph Goebbels, Nazi Party leader for Berlin, decided to make the capital "Jew free" as a present to Hitler before his birthday in April. Jews previously given exemption were to be rounded up and sent to camps including around 2,000 who had "Aryan" wives. These men were sent to a provisional collecting center on Rosenstrasse 2–4 in the heart of Berlin. As word of the arrests spread, the German spouses of the arrested men gathered by the hundreds at the gate of the detention center and a cry broke out: "Give us back our husbands!" Armed guards threatened the women ordering them to clear the streets or they'd shoot. Women would run for cover only to return and continue their protest. This continued for days. Finally, the elite Nazi SS aimed their machine guns on the women but instead of fleeing, the almost completely female crowd just hurled abuse at the Nazis. Goebbels could have had the women mowed down, but he feared the average Berliner's reaction to the mass slaughter of unarmed women in the middle of the capital. He remembered the 1918 revolution. This women's action on Rosenstrasse was remarkable and shows what could have been, if more Germans had risen up like these women.[73] Why didn't they? For that matter, what about the French? How about the Italians?

Historians have correctly pointed to how twentieth-century technology helped fascist regimes crush any sign of dissent.[74] Not often discussed is how the Allies' conduct played a major part in preventing revolution from below against fascism. It is often noted, and at times even condemned,[75] that the British and Americans rained death from the sky onto European civilians. Thus, something like 600,000 German non-combatants had their lives terminated, not to mention the bombing deaths by "friendly fire" of 58,000 French citizens.[76] In fascist Italy, "only" about 60,000 civilians are documented as victims of the air war.[77] In addition, there is evidence that Anglo-American bombing raids killed an undetermined, but very large, number of foreign slave workers and POWs in the Third Reich.[78]

Although many of these dead were the unintentional victims of the bombing of military targets, most lost their lives because the Allies, most particularly the British, chose a policy of indiscriminate terror bombing. Bomber Harris, of the British Royal Air Force, bragged that he wanted to bomb the German working class out of their homes. The Americans generally aimed for actual military targets, but often engaged in carpet-bombing as well. Rather than hasten the end of war, this bombing diverted considerable resources to wanton butchery; these resources could have been used more effectively to actually fight fascist armies.[79] While the aerial slaughter may certainly have reduced fascist morale, it also preempted popular anti-fascist resistance. In May 1943, in the vital French port city of Marseilles, a cut in the bread ration provoked a series of strikes. As the struggle spread and a general strike broke out, the Nazis and their French collaborators were forced to confront a massive, popular uprising. An eyewitness tells what happened next:

> American planes filled the skies and emptied their bombs on the population which was contesting control of the streets with the occupier! The working-class districts were hit first ... more than ten thousand homes hit; some five thousand victims under the rubble. No enemy operation suffered even a scratch.[80]

Within Germany and Austria, even those anti-Nazi groups that supported the Anglo-American bombing found that this tactic made it more difficult to organize resistance. In Catholic Cologne, anti-fascists from the Catholic Center Party claimed the air raids were so severe that the population did little but try to stay alive. Meanwhile, the Communist and Socialist resistance groups in Hannover stressed that much of their time was taken up finding lost comrades and helping bombed-out workers find a place to stay and something to eat. Austrian resistance movement members, who had managed to escape to neutral territory, protested the bombing of Vienna. While evidence shows that most people understood, and resistance groups generally supported, air assaults on industrial targets, they felt betrayed and alienated by the carpet-bombing of working-class residential areas.[81] In May 1945, the war in Europe ended, not with the bang of popular revolution but with the whimper of conventional military victory.

CHAPTER TWELVE

A New Europe? 1945–48

Even before the blood of battle ceased to flow, the Allied powers began to plan their division of the world. At a meeting with Stalin in the Kremlin on October 9, 1944, Winston Churchill offered a deal on the Balkans. With this deal, the United Kingdom would retain 90 percent influence in Greece although the specifics were never spelled out, and in return Russian predominance in Rumania and Bulgaria would be recognized, with a sharing of power in Yugoslavia and Hungary. Of course, this was partially an exercise in make-believe, as the United States had announced that it intended to be an equal partner in all international matters. In return for British support of the Russian "allied states" in Eastern Europe, Churchill sought (and received) Soviet assurances that Moscow would allow the Greek resistance to be crushed by the Greek right with the support of the United Kingdom and would hold back western Communists from attempting to seize power,[1] as for example in Italy. Despite elaborate efforts to deny the obvious, the British and Russians intended to divide southeastern Europe into spheres of influence. Their agreement was shortly put to the test when the British Army suppressed leftist resistance in Athens and Stalin installed a pro-Soviet government in Rumania in February 1945. Although Washington complained, Churchill and Stalin held fast to their agreement, at least until Britain proved too weak and was replaced by the Americans in Greece and the Balkans in March 1947.[2]

There are myriad examples of the freedom-loving Allies acting like traditional imperialist powers. During the war, the sweet voices floating into Nazi-occupied Europe via the BBC, Radio Moscow and other Allied radio broadcasts, reassured the average people that this was a different type of war. It was a "crusade for freedom"—which later became the title of US General Dwight D. Eisenhower's autobiography. In reality, nationalism was used to whip up Allied soldiers, with the result that civilians, most of all those of "enemy" nations, were treated with neither respect nor dignity. The end stages of the war saw an orgy of rapes of female non-combatants, most notoriously in Berlin by Soviet armed forces.[3] It is also estimated that as many as fifty thousand women were raped in Budapest by Russian soldiers.[4] We may never have a definitive number for the sexual abuses that occurred during the war. When it came to reports on these abuses, those who supported a given Allied power tend to minimize the statistics on rapes while those who opposed the occupation, like anti-communists in Hungary, often exaggerated.[5] But no matter the specifics, the misconduct of the Soviet troops gives further proof that the USSR was acting in a self-interested nationalist manner, as opposed to demonstrating the left-wing internationalism they sometimes claimed to uphold.

What is often not discussed is the behavior of the Western Allies towards women. It seems a rather murky line between rape and prostitution when well-fed American GIs offered food in return for sex to women with starving children. In fact, the treatment of German-speaking women under American occupation was often the source of considerable backlash.[6] Recent scholarship suggests that American soldiers forcibly raped up to 190,000 women in Germany alone. Although evidence of this widespread sexual violence against women has existed for decades, it was ignored for political reasons; an image of the fun-loving, friendly American GI giving chocolate bars to children was promoted instead.[7] While scholars continue to quibble about numbers, the fact remains that sexual violence was common at the end of World War II. The average woman was vulnerable to suffering severe retribution and served as the target for the frustrations built up during the fighting.

Turning away from the atrocities committed against women during the war, one might ask what became of the men who actually put fascism in power and benefited from it? At the end of the war, particularly the (Western) Allies quickly began to use Germans and other Nazi Europeans to fight the new war against the Soviet Union. That they turned to Nazi rocket experts, such as SS member Werner von Braun, to jump-start the US missile program is well known. However, the recruitment of lesser-known fascists is often forgotten. This often meant that Western intelligence services saw their competition with the Russians through the eyes of these dedicated anti-communists and genocidal Nazis.[8] In a later CIA review of US post-war policy, the agency acknowledged that this practice laid West Germany and her intelligence service open to the charge of being a "shelter for Nazis" due to their employment of former SS officers. Further, the CIA admitted that West German intelligence was not the only "agency to lure former NSDAP [Nazi] members or war criminals. The historical amnesia that settled over the Federal Republic [West Germany] in the 1950s had long ranging impact on all levels of German society."[9]

While the Soviets were less forgiving towards fascists, the governments they installed in their areas of occupation were far from democratic.[10] One difference between East and West was that the Soviets tended to expropriate the large industrialists who had funded Hitler, while the Western nations mainly looked the other way. This was not a matter of naivety on the part of the Western Allies. On August 2, 1945, the US Office of Strategic Services (OSS), forerunner to the CIA, issued their monthly report on Germany. Within this report, the OSS noted their discovery of a "secret memorandum circulated among Ruhr industrialists providing a uniform cover story to whitewash their activities under Hitler." Rather than plan any actions that might aim at punishing these industrialists, the report said, "a number of high-level German business contacts will be explored as possibilities for long-term penetration of renascent German 'big-business.'"[11] A year later, US intelligence reported large harvests of detailed material on the expropriation of formerly Nazi-owned industry in the Soviet zone of occupation and concluded, "Russian policy intended to eliminate large private enterprises."[12]

Still, it would be a mistake to think that the Soviet Union was the only source of capitalist hostility or the only target of Western intelligence services. If the threat posed by the Russians as a rival power were a source of concern to Wall Street and the City in London, so too were left-wing movements of non-communist citizens in the West. Witness the US spy report on how British intelligence reacted to the 1945 victory of the Labour Party. First, they noted that this was "not enthusiastically welcomed" by British intelligence agents as they are "a more or less self-selected and self-contained elite, traditionally recruited from traditionalist classes ... nearly all of its staff officers have private means, and indeed, they must as a rule." At first, the Labour landslide caused great alarm but this soon dissipated once they saw "little evidence of any more willingness on the part of Mr. Atlee and Mr. Bevan to liquidate the British Empire that there was on the part of Mr. Churchill."[13] This in no way precluded the CIA from making sure that the right wing of the Labour Party continued to follow policies that did not challenge the fundamentals of corporate capitalism. Borrowing techniques from their Soviet rivals, the Americans carried out a sophisticated program of subversion within the Labour Party that would have made Stalin's Comintern proud.[14] In the end, the British Labour Party may have moved to the right to a large extent because of its own internal dynamics, but that is not to say that "Washington Gold" wasn't spread about.[15] In private, America's rulers became dismissive of the United Kingdom. US President Eisenhower saw Britain as a weak, exhausted power unlikely to recover on its own. Although it must have hurt British pride, the US former general told the British they had little future on their own so they "must either join the Continent or join the U.S. as about three states."[16] Apparently, Eisenhower thought that making England, Wales and Scotland separate US states with each having the right to two members in the US Senate would adequately compensate the United Kingdom for the loss of political independence.

Yet, neither the European ruling classes nor the Americans had been excessively fearful of the situation in Britain; whether or not the Labour Party took office, there was little danger that the people would take power. It was different on the European continent where local bourgeois collaboration with the Nazi occupiers had mainly discredited the old rulers in the eyes of the common people. It is now hard to remember, and rarely discussed, but there was a historical period running from roughly 1942–43 until the Cold War began in earnest in 1947–48 in which there existed widespread anti-fascist unity.[17] The almost unbelievable brutality of fascist occupation, widespread genocide, fierce repression and the massive human suffering during the war caused the development of a new popular front. As the defeat of fascism became a possibility, resistance quickened. One Italian anti-fascist reminisced how with

> ... a violent face-off in sight, the underground organizations in all German-occupied countries turned from hiding to active fighting. In France, Belgium, Holland, Hungary, Albania, Yugoslavia, Greece, Italy, people took up arms and, like hornets, came out of their nests for painful stings to the enemy, then rushed back into hiding.[18]

He might have added that even within the Third Reich as the Nazi murder machine weakened, common people rose up: witness the famous revolt in the Buchenwald concentration camp as the Allies approached. But outside the camps there was also a powerful resistance in Germany that seized power from the fascists, most importantly the "Antifa." This was "an *ad hoc* instrument of the Left for the mobilization of all possible mass support for the assumption of governmental power in the community on the basis of an immediate action program." The movement tended to be led by KPD members but for "adherents of the Antifa, the decisive factor was not the party tie but that it was new, promised radical change, and offered action now."[19] The Antifas did the unthinkable in some places. In Bremen and Leipzig, they seized control and took over administrative powers "without waiting for military government and continued them, even after occupation, without consulting it."[20] Not surprisingly, Allied intelligence services like the US OSS spied on the Antifa.[21] Since Germany was divided into four zones of occupation: British, French, Soviet and American, they were soon attacked. Sometimes these attacks came from club-wielding police, while other attacks came via gray bureaucrats denying resources such as paper for their publications. And, the occupation allowed leeway for Antifas to be tossed into prison as needed without much regulation on the process.

Far more than just an organizational maneuver by the Communist parties of Europe, this and other anti-fascist unions included not only the right's traditional opponents such as communists, socialists and anarchists but also newly radicalized people. These newcomers had previously been non-radical, conservative and often religious. In some nations, these movements were heavily armed, as was the case in Greece, France and Italy. In Yugoslavia, the partisan movement came to power. Despite mainstream history painting these as exclusively male movements, women were essential participants.[22] These movements posed a potential threat to the victorious Allies, both East and West. Stalin did not want leftists or Communists, who thought for themselves, running Dresden or Yugoslavia. The West didn't want the left-wing Antifa running Bremen, or resistance fighters running Greece. What all the Great Powers could agree upon was that popular democracy and movements from below had to be contained, destroyed and, if need be, physically crushed. With the taming and elimination of these anti-fascists came "giving up the sense of agency in a changeable present; of forgetting what the victory over fascism had been expected to bring; of shedding the optimist's skin, the sense of history being made; of living fully inside the moment of the antifascist liberation."[23] True, it was to be a different Europe from the one the fascists had attempted to forge. But, it would not be the Europe that most common people had dreamed of and fought for.

For one thing, the liberation of 1944–45 was glaringly incomplete. Portugal and Spain remained untouched despite the fascist tendencies of the former and the Nazi-like regime of Franco in the latter. Anglo-Americans propped up both these regimes as solid "anti-communist" allies. But this favor was not always reciprocal, as a CIA report from November 21, 1946 makes clear. Not only did Spain resist any modification of their fascist regime by rejecting American advocacy of "political evolution" but also challenged their overlords. If the US wanted Spain to scale back political witch-hunts and executions of political opponents, the Franco government was "worried by evidence, even in the UK and the US, of Communist penetration."[24] And, Americans feared that a weakening of the repressive apparatus might open Europe up to influence by the Soviets. At the end of 1949, American intelligence worried that owing to the "lack of effective internal security forces in Iceland, Communists have the capability of seizing power by a coup d'état."[25]

Remember that this repression extended beyond continental Europe; the continent's old rulers wanted to keep their colonies, too. In what has been called the "Jewel in the Crown" of the British Empire, India, there was strife as well. Though food production had risen since 1941, in Bengal in 1943 there was a great famine that killed approximately 3 million Indians.[26] How could this be if food production had risen? The answer: Churchill and the British Government exported food during the famine and stockpiled it as a potential weapon for crisis elsewhere. When Australia offered Bengal needed emergency grain shipments, Churchill prevented them. The British had calculated a minimum caloric intake for Indians; alarmingly, this calculation was below what the Nazis had set for prisoners at Dachau.[27] Although the details may be a bit more murky as regards the British responsibility for bloody Partition only a few years later, the vast loss of life and senseless violence that took place, if not wholly resulting from generations of divide-and-conquer tactics by Britain, certainly was in part the result of their ill-planned and hasty sundering of what had been a whole for centuries.[28] What under other circumstances might have been a joyful celebration of liberation became, under British oversight, what many have labeled a type of "genocide."[29]

Colonial liberation movements were of great concern to the United States, the dominant superpower at the end of World War II. On the one hand, Washington and Wall Street wanted to enjoy access to previously closed markets in the European colonial world. Yet, they feared that the Western European economies might collapse if their colonies were lost too quickly. The CIA opined on September 26, 1947 that the greatest danger to the US was economic collapse in Western Europe. Their analysis concluded that European economic recovery was threatened by revolts or instability in colonial, or semi-colonial areas that contained

> ... the resources of which several European powers (the United Kingdom, France and the Netherlands) have hitherto been accustomed to depend ... The continuance of unsettled conditions hinders economic recovery and causes a diversion of European strength into efforts to maintain or reimpose control by force.[30]

For France, the first priority after the war was to re-establish control of their colony, Indochina. However, the French greatly exaggerated Vietnamese support of this effort and underestimated the power of the anti-colonial movement. That the government in Paris had no understanding of Vietnamese nationalism doomed their approach to failure.[31] Nor is there any evidence that US aid and advice did anything but postpone the ultimate Vietnamese triumph.[32]

In order to maintain influence, the strategy developed by the European colonial powers was to give independence to a native, but pro-western, bourgeoisie. This strategy was moderately successful in some cases, while in others it proved a failure. Take, for example, the French attempt in the late 1940s to keep control of Indochina by dusting off Bao Dai, a fun-loving playboy who served as the last Emperor of Vietnam. Years later, the US would similarly fail at this attempt in Vietnam by means of a clumsy, fraudulent election in which the US-backed candidate won 98.2 percent of the official vote, thereby putting in office a severe, humorless Catholic in a predominantly Buddhist nation. Another failed example was in Africa's Ghana, previously called "the Gold Coast" under the British Empire. When repression failed to stamp out their movement for independence, the United Kingdom was forced to allow elections that brought Kwame Nkrumah to office. Despite his British education, Nkrumah was a leftist who declared Ghana independent and was a thorn in the West's side. In 1966, when Nkrumah was on a state visit to the People's Republic of China and North Vietnam, an army coup backed by the UK and organized by the CIA removed Nkrumah[33] and Ghana's new rulers became, unsurprisingly, pro-Western. Also witness the colony of the Congo, where Europeans created an indigenous bourgeoisie and petit bourgeoisie who, by and large, accepted the ideas of their Belgian overlords. The Congolese elite tried to emulate Belgian ways and admired European culture. They were willing to defend their privilege; developing various theories and discovering African "traditions" they justified the "exploitation of the great mass of the people: the working class, the lumpen-proletariat, and the peasantry."[34] When the first leader of the Congo following their independence appeared troublesome to Europeans, he was murdered.[35]

In the immediate postwar years, the United States harbored a serious, even hysterical, concern towards France. Failing to understand that Soviet policy was not interested in creating potential rivals who might resist their tutelage, US policy makers were convinced that France was about to fall to communism. An extreme example of this paranoia was what can only be called crazed reports flowing from the Federal Bureau of Investigation in Washington. On October 15, 1946 J. Edgar Hoover sent a report to the State Department that, at least in retrospect, seems irrational. In it, Hoover claimed that:

1. The actual French Intelligence organization, late D.G.E.R. is under the absolute control of Communists ... .
2. The Republican Party M.R.P has secret agreements with the Communist Party. Many of the members of the M.R.P. run on such a ticket to be elected by 'Bourgeois' but are in fact Communists.
3. The key posts in the civil service, in the Air Force, in the Gendarmene [*sic*], are in the hands of the Communist Party. This Party who represents less than one-third of the House of Representatives could paralyze the whole country on J Day.
4. J Day is the day chosen by Moscow to act ... At the chosen time the Russian Army would peacefully and without resistance, occupy the South of France to invade Spain and strike, from Marseille, to Gibraltar and if necessary to Algiers."[36]

The following month, the Central Intelligence Agency presented a slightly more balanced report but still argued that the "Communists have sufficient strength to seize power in France whenever they may deem it desirable to do so." Unlike the FBI, this report contends that the French Communist Party (PCF) would prefer to obtain power by elections and that any coup "would be contrary to the present policy of the Kremlin."[37]

The reality was that the USSR was no more interested in Popular Front movements from below than the West. Stalin ordered Communist parties to make conventional electoral alliance with other parties with the view to creating a foreign policy acceptable to Soviet interests. As party leader, Duclos told the PCF central committee in November 1947 that it had been a mistake to seek agreements with other parties rather than building committees from below and strengthening ties with the masses.[38] Things were the same in Italy, where the powerful Italian Communist Party (PCI) turned in their weapons and soon became no more than the official party of opposition. As Italy approached the April 1948 elections, many thought that the PCI-led coalition would sweep to power. One female comrade active in the Milan branch of the PCI probably spoke for many when she recalled, "We, the grassroots of the party, and not just us, thought that we would gradually gain ground and therefore power; history would be on our side."[39] If the US embassy in Rome can be believed, the Vatican was "deeply concerned" and wanted the government to take a hard line against the left.[40] Washington was quite concerned about the 1948 elections and had the CIA prepare a study entitled, "Consequences of Communist Accession to power in Italy by Legal Means."

Interestingly, the authors of the CIA report were calm about the prospect of the PCI winning the parliamentary elections. They asserted that even if the PCI and their People's Bloc coalition won, they might be prevented from taking office by "falsification of the returns or by force." The report further suggested that even if the left did take governmental control, not much would change. While it would be a public relations disaster for the Western powers, Italy would remain "almost entirely dependent on the West for essential imports of scrap iron, steel … fertilizers required to maintain domestic production of foodstuffs." A PCI-led Italy would do all in its power "to avoid a denial of US dollar credits." In fact, the PCI had been arguing for more US economic aid, not less. On the other hand, the ability of the Italian Communists to help leftist movements in neighboring countries "would not be appreciable" while the specter of a red Italy might actually strengthen the anti-communists in Europe.[41] Whether US intelligence was dreaming or truth telling will never be known, because the PCI lost the 1948 elections. Afterwards, they patted themselves on the back for having prevented a red takeover.[42] Average Communists were shocked at the results and soon after "a huge anti-socialist wave engulfed everything. We were in opposition, out of government forever," wrote one woman.[43]

One major institution that had some power to improve wages, working conditions and the life of the common people in general were the trade unions. On the European continent, trade union leaders were often Communists or radical socialists. In a proverbial killing of two birds with one stone, government intelligence agencies, such as the CIA, used money and pressure to split the trade unions in France and Italy.[44] These divisions and attacks weakened Communist or radical political influence, while at the same time diluting working-class power. Many in ruling circles were absolutely deranged on the subject of Communist trade unions. One CIA report claims that the large French Trade Union Confederation (CGT) was on the verge of revolution in 1948. They quote (misquote?) one CGT leader as saying, "the commencement of the insurrection is scheduled for the very near future," while a CGT Docker's union leader is said to have admitted "that airborne Soviet partisans have arrived in France."[45] If there indeed had been "airborne Soviet partisans" in France, it is strange that neither Paris nor Washington was ever able to discover their whereabouts.

The Anglo-Saxon ruling class was also able to use the US trade union federation, the AFL-CIO, to make contacts and cover the source of funding for conservative business unionists.[46] This is not to say that British trade unionists covered themselves in internationalist glory any more than their fellow English-speakers across the Atlantic. The Trade Union Congress (TUC) was an active partner in defense of the British Empire and battled against radicals within the United Kingdom. The British trade union leadership was not satisfied with fighting domestic radicalism. They fought Communists, socialists and other assorted radicals who appeared anywhere in the world's trade union movement.[47] One Italian activist noted that "workers had been badly burned by the collapse of union unity."[48] For the rulers, however, worker disunity was just what they wanted. Socialist parties increasingly returned to their reformist practices and did little to effectively challenge these policies. Meanwhile, in almost all European nations, Communists tailored their policies to suit the interests of Moscow, rather than that of their own workers.[49]

There was an exception: Yugoslavia. During World War II, Yugoslav partisan forces had mounted the most effective armed resistance to fascist occupation. In addition to Soviet aid, the Yugoslav anti-fascists received Western military support. By 1943, the partisans had as many as 300,000 troops under the leadership of the Communist Tito.[50] These forces liberated Yugoslavia without significant Allied intervention. The result was that Tito's Yugoslavian Communist Party was unique, as the CIA admitted, "in that it is of local development and self-contained. It is rooted in the Yugoslav Partisan movement, which was genuinely patriotic in its appeal, for all its Communist leadership."[51] Moreover, the Yugoslav Communists rejected the Moscow strategy of coalitions with conservative or moderate but anti-fascist parties. Both during and after the war, they instead stressed a Popular Front from below. That is, a direct appeal to the mass of the common people rather than an alliance brokered by party leaders.[52] This more radical policy put the Yugoslavs on a collision course with the Soviet Union.

Another matter of great importance is the role women played in the Yugoslav resistance. Upwards of a hundred thousand women were active in the Yugoslav liberation army.[53] Unlike elsewhere in Europe, the centrality of women to the anti-fascist struggle was openly acknowledged. On December 6, 1942, Tito expressly noted the role of female comrades in the resistance. The women of Yugoslav, the Communist leader noted

... are entitled to expect one thing, today, tomorrow, and forever: that this struggle too must be productive for the women themselves ... They have demonstrated that not only do they have it in them to run the home, but they can also fight with arms and are capable of governing and exercising power.[54]

While far from the ideal of equality, Yugoslav women were given not just the right to vote but also more real power than they had before. This has all but been lost in histories that erroneously paint active resistance as largely a masculine affair. The truth is that in Yugoslavia, and elsewhere in Europe, women were fundamental to the fight against fascism.[55] Of course, this did not mean that sexism or traditional patriarchal male attitudes vanished overnight, even still.

All the same, Yugoslav and other Eastern European nations evolved differently than the West after the war. Although characterized by the West, correctly, as lacking many democratic freedoms, Yugoslavia, and even nations in the so-called "Soviet Bloc," allowed women more freedom sooner than the European lands to their west. While women were systematically excluded and segregated in post-war capitalist societies, to the east, women had a high degree of economic independence although certainly not complete gender equality. By and large, the female portion of these populations enjoyed reproductive rights not granted till generations later in the "free world." This in no way excuses the corruption, unrepresentative nature, or other failings of most of the Eastern European governments. Yet, even if it was a "forced emancipation", to many women it was emancipation all the same.[56] As it has come to pass, these modest steps towards women's liberation would come under assault when the Stalinist regimes collapsed towards the end of the twentieth century.

If the new Yugoslavia was deformed in any number of ways, it was still a unique example of an attempt to embark upon an autonomous "road to socialism." Moreover, the independently minded southern Slavs were not willing to jump at the slightest word from the Kremlin. The Yugoslavs' unrealized plans for a Balkan federation, in cooperation with Bulgaria, threatened to create a center outside Russian control that might compete for the affection of the Italian left and others. According to the Yugoslavs, the Bulgarian leader Georgi Dimitrov supported the idea of an independent federation.[57] That prospect and the face of Tito continued to aid the Greek leftists in the Civil War, which made the Communist Party of the Soviet Union furious, as it feared that the latter would give the West the occasion to negate the Churchill-Stalin carve-up of southeastern Europe. In 1948, Yugoslavia was expelled from the Soviet Bloc and threatened with invasion. The result was that the Yugoslavian People's Army drew up two different defense plans, one in the case of an invasion by the capitalist Western powers and a second in the case of a Soviet invasion.

Many were surprised to discover that the Yugoslavs were able to stand up to Stalin's threats and, standing outside of Moscow's shadow, experiment with workers' self-management in factories.[58] Given Yugoslavia's lack of industrialization, the small size of the working class and lack of democratic political culture, it is little wonder these workers' councils were never a complete success. On the contrary, given the impossibility of building socialism in one country, let alone in a small and ethnically divided nation, it is amazing they accomplished as much as they did. While the self-management of industry always was contained within clear bonds by the government, workers did have actual influence. Workers' councils were elected by all members of the plant for a one-year term and could be recalled, a process that was in sharp contrast to the national government itself.

Many studies have suggested that this moment of history contains valuable lessons for any future democratization of the workplace.[59] Still, how did average Yugoslavs feel about this experiment? The evidence indicates that Yugoslav job satisfaction was quite high and workers viewed their workplaces more favorably than either the Soviet or American models.[60] There is some irony, then, that the West helped Yugoslavia economically. The answer to this apparent contradiction is rather simple. As US intelligence services saw the Yugoslav rift with the USSR as causing "a schism comparative only to that between Trotsky and Stalin … This process will probably complete the elimination of Communism as a formidable political movement in Western Europe."[61] Once this prediction began to actually transpire, the capitalist nations would wreck the Yugoslav experiment. But long before that could come to pass, there was the problem of Greece and those annoying leftist revolutionaries.

The German Nazi-Italian Fascist occupation of Greece in 1941 quickly resulted in the destruction of the Balkan nation's economy. Before occupation, Greece had been poor; under the heel of fascist occupation, a famine overcame the Greeks. The impact was horrific, with roughly 100,000 deaths in Athens alone and many more in other urban areas. The final total counted 250,000 dead from a pre-war population of 7 million.[62] From the start, there was bitter resistance to the occupation and Greece was one of the few occupied nations to successfully resist sending slave labor to the Third Reich. With Italian fascism collapsing by 1943, the Nazis beefed up efforts with "Security Battalions" comprised of right-wing Greeks, who swore an oath of allegiance to Adolf Hitler and followed German orders.[63] Although there were numerous resistance groups, the largest was the left-wing National Liberation Front (EAM) and its military wing, the National Popular Army of Liberation (ELAS). Although mainly led by the Greek Communist Party (KKE), both these institutions had broad political support, particularly as a result of the British insisting on backing the Greek King George II and his unpopular government-in-exile based in Egypt.

Unlike the monarchists who often seemed more alarmed by left-wing reform proposals than the Nazi occupation of their country, EAM and ELAS fought successfully with almost no outside aid. Differences between the king's government-in-exile and Greece-based resistance groups grew steadily. The refusal of the former to form a broad-based coalition government led to mutinies in the Greek armed forces in Egypt and even criticism by the Americans in secret briefing papers.[64] The radical EAM and ELAS, by contrast, transformed the condition of women in liberated areas. Although traditionally treated like chattels and overwhelmingly illiterate, women created schools and were given the right to vote. The EAM Provisional Government granted women political and civil rights.[65] In 1944, the German Wehrmacht alarmingly reported how in occupied Greece

> ... the formation of women's sections has been broadly confirmed. These are almost always crack groups of twenty to twenty-five women. They are trained in the use of rifle and machine-gun ... [they] mount guard on villages and distribute antifascist propaganda.[66]

The KKE membership had leapt to 350,000 by 1945, and although the group built a broad-based movement for national and social emancipation, it continued to follow Moscow's lead. This meant that they committed themselves only to anti-fascist struggle, and not to continued opposition to the monarchy. For many average ELAS fighters, the anti-fascist struggle was closely associated with the liquidation of the monarchy. That is to say, the common people had no interest in the German puppet government being replaced by a British one.[67] In March–April 1944, mutiny by Greek soldiers in Egypt resulted in swift British repression and 20,000 anti-monarchists, republicans and leftists were put in concentration camps. Discontent even surfaced within the ranks of the Greek Navy.[68] Still, when German forces fled from Greece in October 1944, there was no plan or attempt to set up a new government based on the common people who had fought the Nazis. Many observers argue that as the Nazis were leaving Greece, ELAS could have seized power as happened in Yugoslavia. Rather, the British brought back the king and suppressed the left. The situation quickly deteriorated as fascist collaborators were released from prison by British troops. This resulted in a civil war that the Greek left was neither prepared for nor expecting to win. By not supporting Tito in his schism from Moscow, the KKE leaders needlessly threw away an invaluable ally as well as the use of Yugoslav base camps. For their part, the British, and the Americans soon after, sent massive amounts of cash and armaments to destroy the Greek left. The Americans quickly replaced the British, as their empire tethered on the brink of bankruptcy. Despite the usual US macho posturing in public, the Greek rebels gave the capitalists from across the Atlantic some uncomfortable moments. For example, US agents drew up a secret report entitled: "Possible Consequences of Communist Control of Greece in the Absence of US Counteraction" in early 1948.[69]

A secret US Central Intelligence Agency memo, dated January 19, 1949, complained of Greece being, "in a dangerous state of war and political and economic instability despite almost two years of extensive US military and economic aid totaling approximately 750 million dollars." The American disgust with their Greek lackeys is barely disguised in this same report. Despite US pressure to have a broader and more popular anti-communist government, all Washington and the Greek populace got was:

> Selfish partisan interest, political bickering, and an unwieldy bureaucracy have deprived the Greek people of competent government and of a source of inspiration ... [meanwhile] the Athens political merry-go-round continues, with the same faces appearing and reappearing, and popular confidence in the government continues to decrease.[70]

In the end, the power of the Greek people was no match for the massive capitalist financial and military onslaught. The cost of this defeat was great; over 150,000 Greeks died in the civil war, another 50,000 to 100,000 ELAS members fled into exile, and countless thousands of others rotted in prisons.[71] In response, the Russians did exactly ... nothing.

CHAPTER THIRTEEN

Europeans in the Cold War: Between Moscow and Washington

The expression "cold war" has a long history. Used by the ancient Greeks, Spanish crusaders and popular into the twentieth century where it was employed by the likes of George Orwell and Winston Churchill, a cold war is when there is a state of conflict that stops just ever so short of direct military combat. Instead, the fighting mainly takes the form of economic competition, political maneuvers, propaganda and, at times, proxy wars between nations allied to one of the more powerful nations. It is a widely held belief that the post-World War II cold war started in 1946 or 1947 and was largely a result of Soviet aggression. As is so often the case, pinpointing the actual date and catalyst of conflict is not that simple. Some have argued that the Cold War started with Churchill's welcome, but not acceptance, of the USSR as part of the anti-Hitler coalition in 1941.[1] Others have persuasively argued that the Cold War between Russia and the West actually started with the Bolshevik Revolution in 1917. What followed was the inevitable ebb and flow of relations between nations and rival social systems that were in fundamental contradiction.

No matter the date, it is clear that relations between the Soviet Union and the Western powers were not the best for a number of years after the defeat of fascism in 1945. One theory put forward is that the division of Germany was not so much a result of the Cold War as a cause. Having been invaded twice by Germany in the first half of the twentieth century, the Russian government wanted a key voice in any post-war settlement. Failure of the USSR to reach agreement with the West, and vice versa, was a key source of tension.[2] This was part and parcel of the general move to cut the Soviets out of the post-war world. The US may have shared the atomic bomb with the United Kingdom but not with Russia. Of course, that the United States chose not to share military secrets with the USSR, or any other ally for that matter, was hardly a surprise to anyone. More of a surprise, and a major source of animosity for the Russians, was the US reneging on their previous promise of financial assistance for reconstruction. After all, not only had the Soviets endured the largest number of causalities, the European part of their country had been relentlessly destroyed in fighting and they were dead broke.

Before the final defeat of Nazism, the US ambassador to Moscow cabled the State Department that the USSR placed "high importance on a large postwar credit as a basis for the development of 'Soviet-American relations' ... [the implication was] that the development of our friendly relations would depend upon a generous credit."[3] The Russians reasoned that they had suffered disproportionate casualties in the war and had further pledged to sacrifice even more of their people in the finale to the war against Japan, something that was not needed because of the development of the atomic bomb. Therefore, the Soviet Union thought the promises of economic assistance were just. After the war, Britain was granted a handsome loan at below 2 percent interest. But when it came to the Soviet Union, Washington insisted on a political and economic open door in Russian-occupied Europe, in addition to Moscow accepting US multilateral trade regulations. When the Soviets balked at what they thought was a capitulation of national interest and security, the Americans deployed the prospect of a loan as a weapon to make the Russians submit to their will.[4] When they refused to give in to the dictates of the United States, the Western press had a field day painting the Soviet Union as closed, unreasonable and dangerously aggressive.

There are other plausible reasons and theories to explain the Cold War. Maybe the military-industrial complexes of West or East were simply looking for excuses to prevent peace from breaking out and ruining their business. No matter, by the late 1940s, there was a very real Cold War between the USSR and the capitalist West. Now, it is clear that this Cold War was not necessary for the "survival of the west," as bourgeois propaganda claimed. In fact, as the leader of the capitalist world, the United States was in a uniquely dominant position in 1945: it controlled half of the world's GNP and most food surpluses, along with nearly all global financial reserves. As well as economic superiority, the Americans had the nuclear bomb, a planet-wide network of military bases, and an air force and navy, both of which were unchallengeable. Having expanded their industrial and economic base during the war (while others' were destroyed), the US seemed to control the fate of enemies and allies alike.[5] The US concluded that it should go from being *a* world power to being *the* world power.

The Soviet Union, by contrast, had seen much of its industrialized areas destroyed in fighting, had lost tens of millions of lives, and was worried about its ability to feed and house the common people. In addition, the Soviet Union was now occupying territories with millions of inhabitants, who hated the USSR because it was Russian, Communist, or both. Moscow was not in the best shape beyond the prestige they gained from having defeated Hitler. The problem was that prestige didn't feed hungry people in the largely destroyed Soviet cities. Still, the Cold War served Stalin well in that it provided a better excuse to continue the repression of political opponents, whether real, potential, or imagined. Soviet officers who had been concerned for their careers as the military was scaled back could now breathe a sigh of relief as rearmament was ordered, despite the poverty of the average comrade. The West created the North Atlantic Treaty Organization (NATO) as their military alliance; Russia responded with the Warsaw Pact. While the US and Russia did not engage directly in battle with each other, their proxy wars killed millions in Korea, Vietnam, Afghanistan and many other places. Both sides continued to build bigger and more lethal atomic bombs and ever more effective ways of getting them to the "enemy" heartland. In the middle (literally and figuratively) was Europe. More importantly, it was the commoners of Europe who daily lived in fear that one side or the other could start an all-out nuclear war that would destroy the planet. In the West, it was common to hear people say that the Americans would fight the USSR to the last European.

The reality that the Cold War was an imperialist fight between the rulers of two class-based societies is often forgotten. From the East came a flood of claims about how peace-loving the Soviet Union was and so on and so forth. From the West, particularly from the Anglo-Saxons, came a new political Christianity that was part of the "struggle to save civilization." With this new religious rhetoric, the Russians became not just economic or political competitors to the capitalist world, they became the godless seeking to destroy all that was good in the world.[6] This politicized religious fervor that took hold in the capitalist West grew beyond their response to Russia and influenced the social and political scenes much more broadly. For some Englishmen, that meant saving the Empire, while for some white Americans it meant retaining racial segregation.

The view from the Kremlin's windows saw the Cold War and Tito's split as evidence that there were traitors everywhere. If not, it was still useful to pretend there were. Throughout Eastern Europe, the local Communist Party leadership found themselves victims of witch-hunts that often resulted in a show trial, followed by execution. One infamous example was the purge of Rudolf Slánský, general secretary of the Czechoslovakian party. Slánský was among fourteen leaders arrested in 1951 and charged with high treason. The following year, in a mass show trial, eleven of the fourteen were sentenced to death and Slánský was executed on December 3, 1952. Meanwhile across the Atlantic, Julius and Ethel Rosenberg were in New York's Sing Sing Prison awaiting the president's response to their appeal against their conviction for high treason and their accompanying death sentences. Despite such recourse to the American justice system, after two years spent filing appeals they were executed.

In June 1953, the workers in East Germany (aka the German Democratic Republic or DDR) showed that they would not be passive subjects of their government nor their Russian overlords. Resentment grew as workers tired of hearing so much about socialism without ever seeing it put into practice. The straw that broke the camel's back was an increase in work norms that would have cut the average workers' standard of living. The first response came from building workers along Stalinallee who stopped work. They were soon followed by a substantial number of metal workers. Even the CIA seemed surprised, that "spontaneity large-scale uprising unquestionable ... [DDR government] harping on themes such as 1917 Soviet uprisings and analyzing the reasons defeat German Workers' Movement 1933 and prior thereto backfired."[7] In other words, the DDR talked about the glorious history of workers resisting oppression which actually encouraged workers to resist oppression. Nor was this the aimless rioting so often depicted in standard capitalist and Stalinist narratives. In a secret US briefing, it was conceded, "that shop stewards and the revolutionary tradition played a vital role in providing leadership and unity ... East German developments have demonstrated that an uprising from below is possible."[8] These are surely not the sort of comments that the upholders of property and privilege would make in public, at least not about workers under their control. Following 1953, the DDR security apparatus was on alert for organized or politically motivated strikes. Therefore, DDR workers "quickly adapted to this danger, and it became a widely adopted practice to stress that one had decided to down tools spontaneously just this morning and could not remember who had thought of the idea first."[9]

The 1953 revolt was an unplanned, spontaneous revolt directed not against socialism, but against the lack of *real* socialism, which depends upon worker control and democracy. It is interesting that many participants belonged to the Socialist Unity Party (SED), East Germany's ruling party. Even the official SED party paper, *Neues Deutchland*, admitted the justice of the workers' demands. For a few days, the workers felt that power was in their hands.[10] In the end, the tens of thousands of workers flowing into Berlin simply had insufficient planning or organization, and were repressed with the help of Soviet occupation troops. The fact is that the June days had been unforeseen in the West, but agents provocateurs were dispatched to spread rumors, commit sabotage and give the workers revolt a pro-Western facade.[11] Despite the deep pockets of the CIA, they had limited success. The Soviets and their SED allies attempted to rewrite the history of these events into a Western-orchestrated provocation without mass appeal. No one believed them. Bertolt Brecht, living in the DDR, wrote a biting poem about this called "The Solution":

> After the uprising of the 17th June
> The Secretary of the Writer's Union
> Had leaflets distributed in the Stalinallee
> Stating that the people
> Had forfeited the confidence of the government
> And could win it back only
> By redoubled efforts. Would it
> Not be easier
> In that case for the government
> To dissolve the people
> And elect another?[12]

This was not to be the only popular uprising in the Soviet Bloc. Before then, however, the biggest blow would come from within the orders of the Kremlin itself. On February 14, 1956, the 20th Congress of the Communist Party of the Soviet Union (CPSU) opened in Moscow, with 1,500 leaders from 56 nations in attendance. Nikita Khrushchev, by then clearly the top leader in the USSR, made a "secret speech" attacking Stalin and his purges. He condemned the dead dictator's paranoid determination to maintain power for causing the distortion of Marxism-Leninism and the deaths of innocent, loyal, party members. Khrushchev advocated reform and a peaceful coexistence with the capitalist West. Although the speech was meant to be private, it leaked out almost immediately. It hit like a bomb within the ranks of world Communists and their sympathizers. The speech helped encourage protest in Poland in the summer and fall of 1956. These protests escalated when Poland's ruling party overreacted by sending in the military to suppress the protesters.

In October 1956, student protests in Hungary gained widespread support. Before long, there was a revolt against the Soviet-allied government, military units mutinied and the border with Austria was opened. Reform-minded Communists in Hungary hoped to use this movement to recast their country in a more popular mold. Responding to the protests, Prime Minister Imre Nagy declared that his country would leave the Warsaw Pact and pursue an independent path to socialism. On November 7, 1956, Khrushchev told the Swedish ambassador that the USSR had "originally agreed to support Nagy and had decided to use troops in Hungary only when it became apparent that Nagy had lost control."[13] Regardless of the truth of this statement, the fact is Russian tanks crushed the uprising and Nagy was executed by the Soviets. These events significantly impacted the morale of supporters around the world. One Italian Communist remembers that "things were never the same in the party after that. Trust in the USSR was broken or wasn't the same."[14]

A new, more reliable government was installed in Budapest at the point of Soviet steel. Western agents and propaganda from without Hungary's borders, such as the CIA's Radio Free Europe (RFE), called for a revolt and implied that Western military aid would back it. Naturally, once people rose up, nothing was done except to excite further violence with the view to embarrass the Soviet Union.[15] This reckless incitement to cause needless bloodshed was so controversial that the CIA felt compelled to conduct a secret investigation of Radio Free Europe's actions. RFE denied the charges while admitting that some of the broadcasts "sounded emotional." Their defense was "a) Hungarians are basically emotional, and b) this was an emotional occasion [and] ... sentences or phrases could possibly be taken out of these broadcasts [to support the idea] ... that RFE 'incited.'"[16] In any case, it is fair to say that the common people in the Warsaw Pact nations did not live altogether wonderful lives. It was clear to all but the most myopic eye that Eastern Europe was under the heel of the Russian government.

Yet, was it so wonderful in the West? Of course, compared with Stalin's Russia, almost anything looks good. Obviously after the war, Greece was far from the ideal of freedom and democracy.[17] The best to be said about Portugal was that it was an ageing dictatorship: as the US State Department concluded in 1959, after thirty years, Portugal's "carefully managed dictatorial machine is showing signs of breaking down." There was rising dissent as the government failed "to raise the standard of living for the vast majority of the population." The same report concluded that the armed forces, backbone of the regime, "resent the generally low pay levels and the inequitable promotion policy." Accurately, the Americans predicted not an immediate "major national revolt," but warned of increasing boldness on the part of the opposition and the high likelihood of a military coup.[18] Meanwhile, the ruling circles in the West were far more concerned about Spain.

Spain was still run by the butcher Franco, buddy of the dead mass murderers Hitler and Mussolini. Although the Spanish regime found the rest of Western Europe far too left wing for their taste, their hatred of Russia drove them to back an accommodation with London and Washington. Franco's government was backed by the UK and the US as reliably anti-communist despite the continuing stench of fascism that clung to the regime; Franco sided with the West since there was no longer a fascist alternative alliance. There is a mountain of testimony by Spanish exiles, political opponents and victims of this vicious dictatorship that condemns it as no better than its late fascist allies. Anti-fascists universally condemned Spain's government, but they would, wouldn't they? It is perhaps more interesting to see what Franco's de facto allies in the US thought about this government. According to a secret report, US intelligence saw a regime "unable to capture the genuine mass support of the people." Franco's government "has utilized corrupt means to consolidate its power and is now unable to overcome the corruption in the government ... The regime which took power by force has suppressed all civil and political liberties." It wasn't even a successful dictatorship in that "undernourishment has slowed down labor's output," while almost half the budget was consumed by the military and security forces upon whom Franco's "own tenure so much depend[ed]."[19] This situation worried Washington, not because of any professed ideological conflict between Spain and the US, but because the latter was nervous about what would replace Franco. When strikes and demonstrations broke out in 1955–56, the Americans were clearly concerned[20] and this concern continued for decades as Franco hung on to power (and life).

For those capitalist countries herded into NATO, the United States, in a kinder and gentler way perhaps, became the overlord of Western Europe, just as Russia had seized the eastern part of the continent. American forms of control were subtle; the wealth of the American Empire allowed them to purchase consent, as well as punish resistance. In the 1948 Italian elections, it was $10 million that helped the US's allies in the Vatican defeat the left in the vote. Yet, when there was a dockworkers' strike in the key French port of Marseilles, the US hired Corsican gangsters to break it.[21] If it was in some way inconvenient for Washington or Wall Street, European democracy was refashioned to suit American interests. For example, in 1951, Allen W. Dulles of the CIA noted that "electoral mechanisms had been manipulated so as greatly to reduce Communist representation in the French Chamber and in Italian municipalities ... [US economic aid] may well have saved these countries from Communist control."[22]

Not surprisingly, any and all US measures had to "be presented to the people as independent French and Italian moves. It should not appear to come under U.S.A. pressure and our support should be covert not overt."[23] Washington also pressured European governments to repress those Europeans it considered subversive, even at the cost of violating basic freedoms. The 1951 Dulles report noted with satisfaction the actions of the French government in: 1) removing four elected PCF mayor and 29 Communist deputy mayors in Paris, 2) firing all public employees who stopped work to demonstrate against the visit of General Eisenhower, 3) outlawing international and foreign Communist fronts headquartered in Paris, 4) prohibiting the sale and distribution in France of five French-language Soviet periodicals, 5) banning three Communist-organized public demonstrations and 6) "discreetly" encouraging splits in the PCF and the CGT trade union. But even this was not sufficient for Dulles who recommended that Paris be pressured to institute a host of other measures such as limiting the PCF press's access to newsprint and lifting the parliamentary immunity of elected members of the Chamber of Deputies. Even so, the CIA admitted that low real wages were a fundamental cause of the PCF's appeal, and thus trade unions had to be tolerated as the most effective "method of bringing relief to that third of the French working class which is underpaid even by low prewar standards."[24] Needless to say, there is a certain contradiction in attacking militant trade unions, like the CGT, and then conceding that poor living standards are one of the keys to Communist strength.

More effective at controlling Western Europe than the cloak-and-dagger schemes of the CIA was the Marshall Plan. This massive economic aid program, begun in 1948, pumped \$12 billion dollars into Europe to reconstruct and update its economy. By 1951, Europeans began to see the start of what many have called the "golden age of capitalism."[25] Real wages soared, as did industrial productivity. Of course, relative wages were mainly stagnant as productivity rose as fast as wage levels. Still, using the 1890–99 average as a basis of 100, the index of real wages jumped from 1950— United Kingdom (169), France (168), West Germany (174)—till 1959, United Kingdom (207), France (274), West Germany (262).[26] Combined with low unemployment, the common people of Europe enjoyed a real upturn in their standard of living. Despite the lack of capital and a history of economic backwardness, this could also be said, in a lesser sense, for people living in the Soviet Bloc. By the mid-1950s, Eastern Europe had "devised its own variant of the Marshall Plan social contract—citizen enfranchisement through consumer rewards."[27] But all this came at a price.

In Eastern Europe, full employment and other social security measures were purchased with political freedoms.

In Western Europe, the same trade-off occurred, albeit with more subtlety. Along with all those US dollars came the Marshall Plan, with its own ideology: consumerism. It has been argued that the American ideology of a "Consumers' Republic" was a fundamental assault on long-standing European ideas of social citizenship. Without the context of the Cold War, this would make little sense, but the Americans were putting forth a rival ideology to left-wing ideas like equality or solidarity.[28] The old Enlightenment notion that "I think therefore I am" was replaced by "I consume therefore I am." Most Marshall Plan historians agree that "a distinctly political transformation was attempted in Europe in the post-war period: the citizen was reconfigured as a consumer, whose individual prosperity and satisfaction spelled the triumph of democracy."[29] One study of Austria has argued that this was all part of a deliberate "Coca-Colonization." As with the armaments industry, the endless resources of America "from Coca-Cola to Wrigley's chewing gum—were all centrally directed by government agencies."[30]

In fact, Coca-Cola itself was the subject of a curious debate in post-war France. In early 1950, the French National Assembly witnessed the following rather odd exchange that took place between a PCF deputy and the minister of public health:

> *Deputy*: "Monsieur le minister, they are selling a drink on the boulevards of Paris called Coca-Cola."
> *Health Minister*: "I know it."
> *Deputy*: "What's serious, is that you know it and you are doing nothing about it."
> *Health Minister*: "I have, at the moment, no reason to act … ."
> *Deputy*: "This is not simply an economic question, nor is it even simply a question of public health—it's also a political question. We want to know if, for political reasons, you're going to permit them to poison Frenchmen and Frenchwomen."[31]

In the twenty-first century, this dialogue may seem odd. But at the time, Coca-Cola was understood to symbolize complete Americanization—that is, a threat. On the same day this strange exchange took place, the French Parliament, in a nod to anti-American sentiment, authorized the government to ban Coca-Cola if it was found to be harmful. This incident was not simply a Gallic quirk.

For their part, much of the American response was just as extreme. The *New York Enquirer* accused the French of being ingrates for criticizing the country who saved her in two world wars. Another periodical claimed that it was impossible to spread

> ... the doctrines of Marx among people who drink Coca-Cola ... The dark Principles of revolution and a rising proletariat may be expounded over a bottle of vodka ... but it is utterly fantastic to imagine two men stepping up to a soda fountain and ordering a couple of Cokes in which to toast the downfall of their capitalist oppressors.[32]

This is rather silly and would come as a complete shock to anyone who witnessed the Cuban Revolution sweep into Havana in 1959. (A large number of Cuban revolutionaries drank *Cuba Libre*, a drink made up of rum and "Coke.") Obviously, both sides in this debate resorted to rather exaggerated verbiage. Behind all the rhetoric hid a real dispute. That is, should French, or more broadly European, society be remolded into a mirror image of the United States? If a person's view of Coca-Cola was the key measure, Americanization lost in France (at least in the short run), as a 1953 poll reported that 61 percent liked Coke "not at all" versus a mere 17 percent liking the colored sugar-water "well enough" or "a lot."[33]

Behind these seemingly trivial debates lurked far more weighty issues. The entire push for increased consumerism was, from the start, targeted at women. Male leaders on both sides of the Cold War considered female citizens susceptible to being easily bought off. To an extent usually not noticed, the Cold War was fought in the kitchen.[34] Thoughts of shopping, it was hoped, would displace more dangerous thoughts of progress, democracy, or gender equality. To the West, corporations promoted the positive value of an idealized housewife marching into her household task of negotiating mass consumption.[35] In Eastern Europe, women's rights and female involvement in society was maintained, but consumerism was pushed in hopes of avoiding awkward questions about equality or democracy from the common people whom the governments claimed to represent. As the example of Hungary proves, a woman would have a position in Eastern European society, but it would be a second place to the privileged "breadwinner" male.[36] In the capitalist West, men were shown fictional cinematic portraits of powerful Communist women commanding subordinate men.[37] A struggle between the United States and the Soviet Union was being enacted on the big screen, as each side produced films showing their way of life as superior.[38]

Post-war Europe was far more than a mere battleground between the USSR and the United States or even rival classes. Women began to question again their subordinate position in society and the economy.[39] A major theoretical bombshell was lobbed into the comfortable male-dominated world with the publication of *The Second Sex* by Simone de Beauvoir in 1949.[40] Appearing first in French, it sold more than 20,000 copies in its first week; the English edition has since topped a million in sales. This publication's importance was demonstrated by the ever-vigilant Vatican censors quickly placing it on its *List of Prohibited Books*. Whether this ban hurt or helped sales is hard to determine. Widely read and debated, it reopened and expanded discussion of women's oppression. In this volume and in her later work, de Beauvoir disputes the idea that women's struggle should be subordinated to the class struggle. She argues, in her words, that women's struggle appeared "primordial and not at all secondary." Of course, it is necessary to "link the two struggles. But the example of the countries called socialist proves that an economic change in no way entails the decolonization of women."[41] Other scholars have contended that feminist consciousness can survive and grow, even under the most repressive conditions.[42] Throughout the immediate post-war period, legal restrictions against women fell away (for example, equal voting rights were established in France and Italy), while theorists like de Beauvoir helped lay the foundation for modern feminism.[43] Moreover, the increased employment of female workers outside the household appears to have led to the growth of women's consciousness.[44]

Women in many countries became involved in political movements or parties that created a space for female self-activity.[45] In Eastern Europe, women fought to force regimes to live up to their rhetoric. Facing a double burden of working outside the home and trapped in the role of housewife, women demanded the ruling parties at least police the most outrageous acts of male sexism. In the USSR, for example, women demanded that male party members be brought to account for wrongdoing. In one case, a man was expelled from the CPSU on the charge of "unworthy conduct in family life" for, among other things, "the systematic mockery of his wife."[46] This was far from an isolated case, as mainly woman-initiated charges led to a rise in expulsions for "unworthy conduct." In 1954, only 12.41 percent of CPSU expulsions were a result of these personal failings. By 1964, almost a quarter of those party members kicked out had been charged with failings in family or personal life.[47]

After 1945, there was substantial immigration of workers from both economically underdeveloped parts of the continent and beyond. This mass immigration transformed Western Europe. The bulk of these immigrants were, if judged by their position in the productive process, members of the working class. Immigration not only filled the void left by the millions who died in World War II, it also provided a reserve army of workers in nations that otherwise would have faced labor shortages. A number of factors contributed to a schism between indigenous Europeans and the newer immigrant workers. First, immigrants typically worked in less skilled, lower paying jobs and had only infrequent interaction with indigenous workers. There were also differences in language, culture and, often, religion. Despite labor shortages, many resident Europeans feared competition for jobs and reacted to the immigrants with irrational, racist hatred.[48] The irony was, of course, that whenever there were labor shortages, there was less than ever to fear from migrants.

Various surveys conducted in the 1950s clearly show that a great number of workers in the United Kingdom, France and Germany were prejudiced against immigrants. Interestingly, according to one study, French workers were less racially than culturally biased. It found that 62 percent thought there were too many North Africans (mainly Islamic in religious tradition) in France while only 18 percent said there were too many black immigrants (many of whom were Roman Catholic).[49] There have been powerful arguments made that immigration weakened the working class, increased the power of the ruling class and introduced a false consciousness (racism) into the labor movement.[50] Over time, millions of "guest workers," as immigrants were sometimes called, would be transformed into more or less permanent ethnic or cultural minorities in what had once been far more homogenous societies. Like issues of economic and social equality or women's rights, the issue of immigration and the changes it produced would not simply go away. Generations later, these issues still remain.

CHAPTER FOURTEEN

From the Berlin Wall to the Prague Spring: A New Generation of Europeans

On the night of August 12–13, 1961, barbed wire was erected around West Berlin, as what has come to be known as the Berlin Wall was being built, to howls of outrage from the West. This extremely bold move would be judged in mainstream history as a prime example of the vicious and aggressive nature of the Soviets. In point of fact, the USSR only agreed to build this so-called "Anti-Fascist Protection Barrier" after newly elected US President Kennedy indicated the Americans would not oppose this action.[1] As this undermines the orgy of anti-Communist propaganda unleashed over this event, American, at least tacit, agreement with the Wall is not widely known. When *Der Spiegel*, a leading West German news magazine, accused the "Soviet Union and the United States of conspiracy in building the Berlin Wall," US policy makers were livid.[2] Little over a week after the Wall's initial construction, the CIA noted the effect in West Berlin was "a drop off in morale more rapid than had been anticipated." Life-long socialist Willy Brandt was upset about the division of his beloved Berlin. He was also concerned war might be revisiting the heart of Europe. On the other hand, rather than being furious or worried, US leaders, privately, showed annoyance at West Berlin Mayor Willy Brandt for "getting temperamental" and becoming "hysterical."

Why this curious lack of concern or compassion on the part of the United States? There are suggestions that they felt the Soviet's leader Khrushchev needed to be placated so that the possibility of a war over Berlin could be avoided, and any Russian attempt to seize all of the former German capital preempted. In a secret meeting held nine days after the Wall's construction began, former President Eisenhower saw "little change in the Berlin situation" and commented that Khrushchev found himself in a situation from which he couldn't turn back. He also stated this was because there "is enough Oriental in the Soviets that face is important."[3] The cruelty of separating families and neighborhoods seems not to have been an important consideration for the leaders, East or West.

If, for the Western capitalists, the Berlin Wall was the propaganda gift that kept on giving, why did the Soviet Union decide to build it? The answer is far more complex than the Russians simply "hating freedom." Between 1945 and 1961, the East German Republic had lost something like 3,500,000 people out of a population of around 18 million. This caused huge economic problems for the DDR, as they lost highly skilled professionals (trained at state expense) to West Germany and its higher wages. Losses in production were estimated in the billions of Deutschemarks. The SED, ruling party in East Germany, claimed that the Wall was necessary to prevent the infiltration of spies and saboteurs into their nation. This claim has been largely ridiculed in the West, and there is little evidence that this was the most important motive. Still, this was a reality that should not be so lightly dismissed.

Less than six months before the Wall, the CIA discussed six areas of clandestine actions to be considered vis-à-vis East Germany: 1) "action designed to increase East German instability"; 2) "actions designed to symbolize Western determination to remain in Berlin"; 3) "actions designed to inhibit Communist moves by encouraging sections of the Non-Soviet world to preserve a free Berlin and achieve the reunification of Germany" (presumably on the West's terms); 4) "actions designed to counteract Community propaganda"; 5) "actions designed to place the Communists under economic pressure", and 6) "What about insurrection?" To carry out these tasks, they sought to increase the flow of refugees "particularly inducing the flight of those categories of persons possessing skills of critical importance to the regime, such as medical doctors, dentists, engineering and other technical specialists and skilled labor." Such goals might be accomplished by "high-level covert activity action operations and such information activities as 'planting' of news and feature articles in a variety of media appropriate to the target audience."[4] These and other such plans of Western intelligence, which in West Germany's case was led by a former Nazi SS general, must have been known, or at least suspected, by those running the DDR and East Berlin.

How did this affect the average German? Obviously, there was the pain of separation for family members, friends and neighbors. Beyond this, it was a direct blow to the German working class. Before the Wall, West Germans easily traveled into the DDR to purchase cheap, state-subsidized products, allowing them to stretch their wage packet. For East Germans, the possibility of just picking up and moving to the West had given workers in the DDR a degree of power vis-à-vis the East German state. Thus, it was not only the refugees who had benefited from easy access to West

Germany, those Germans who stayed home gained as well.[5] Only days before the Wall, Walter Ulbricht, leader of the SED, complained to the Kremlin, "simply put, the open border forced us to raise living standards faster than our economic capabilities allowed."[6] This had led to a decline in the morale of SED party cadres. Four months late, the CIA saw "the cadres were exhilarated for a time at the success of the sector border closing and the lack of Western response, this enthusiasm was soon dissipated … [when they were told to implement] unrealistic or unpopular regime policies."[7] Still, the Wall was a success in as much as it stopped the economic bleeding of human capital and allowed the DDR to develop their economy, which soon surpassed the rest of the Warsaw Pact, despite the DDR's small size. To the West, it gave a powerful and very concrete propaganda symbol: the "Iron Curtain" was now on display in Berlin. And the two distinct regimes now had more room, if needed, for repressing dissenters. It would be wrong to see the common people as powerless pawns in this Cold War chess game. After all, resistance continued even in the more blatantly repressive DDR. As much as it was distasteful, SED functionaries in East Berlin had to concede the impact of 1960s youth culture and tolerate Western rock n' roll and clothing styles.[8]

A 1960s youth culture developed that was a problem not just for the bureaucrats in East Berlin. The 1950s had been morally conservative and conformist in most aspects of European life. A German feminist activist remembered her childhood as "a time dominated by a horrible moral conformism, against which we naturally rebelled. We wanted to flee from the white Sunday gloves, to run from the way one had to hide fingernails behind the back if they weren't above reproach." She goes on to say how she "fought against the fascist heritage they force on me … soon we came into conflict over a more serious topic: the persecution of the Jews. I identified with the Jews, because I felt myself to be persecuted by my family."[9] Although this may seem a simplistic comparison and strange reaction, it shows the intensity of feeling typical among young rebels.

In the popular mind, this period is bound up with the "sexual revolution." That the 1960s brought great change in sexual mores and practices is without doubt true. However, the rush to sensationalize these changes was done in an a-historical manner and it is often forgotten that the 1920s brought a "sexual revolution" as well.[10] In fact, some scholars have found other "sexual revolutions" earlier in European history as well.[11] All these revolutions were characterized by changes in female attitudes and marked by women seeing themselves as independent masters of their own fate. The ups and downs of female emancipation can be identified with concurrent structural changes like urbanization or a relative weakening of male power by military bloodletting. What is different about the rise of women in the twentieth century is the "diffusion of techniques for contraception and abortion."[12] Without the access to reproductive control, women find themselves handicapped in any struggle for equality or rights.

The post-war period saw the reappearance, not invention, of feminism in a changed historical context. Likewise, there was to be a revival of anti-war movements and the resurgence of anti-systemic struggles painted with broad strokes as a "new left." Beginning in Britain in the 1950s with the Campaign for Nuclear Disarmament (CND), there developed a "ban the bomb" movement against nuclear weapons. From the seemingly modest proposition that it would not be a good thing if the planet and everyone on it was blown up, CND became a focal point of anti-establishment feeling. From 1957 on, CND organized significant protest against the British atomic weapons policy. The immediate post-war years saw a depoliticizing exhaustion resulting from war and the subsequent austerity, not just in the United Kingdom but also throughout Europe. The CND marches and educational work came together with the myriad of crises in 1956: the failed Anglo-Franco-Israeli invasion of the Suez Canal, Khrushchev's denunciation of Stalin, the bitter suppression of the Hungarian revolt by Russian tanks. After Suez, people who had thought their governments were no longer fueled by aggression were shaken, while most Western Communists found it difficult to continue to make excuses for Moscow.

This resulted in the shattering of the old sterile Stalinist-Social Democrat model for many, who sought another way of doing radical politics. Neither the sweet dollar seduction of Washington nor the fairy tales about the Soviet workers' state held the power they once had. CND groups preceded and helped pave the way for New Left formations expanded by a wave of desertions from traditional Communist parties as well as disillusioned socialists of varying stripes. What they had in common was a desire for "some independent socialist body, in which topics of a *wider scope* could be discussed and acted upon."[13] The movement towards banning the bomb became for many the road to reawakened activism. And this reawakening spread far beyond the North Atlantic island nation.

The presence of Third World students in the Federal Republic of Germany brought new radical ideologies that combined with the import of Anglo-American culture to create an anti-authoritarian revolt.[14] In 1966, West Germany's two major parties united in a Grand Coalition headed by Kurt Georg Kiesinger, a former Nazi who had played an active role in the Third Reich's foreign ministry. This helped pave the way for the growth of an extra-parliamentary opposition (APO). The APO criticized Western notions of democracy, anchoring its ideals instead in grass-roots forms of democracy.[15] The SPD had abandoned Marxism even rhetorically in 1959 and now the one-time Socialists were in league with the right-wing Christian Democrats, led by a man who had more than a whiff of Nazism about him. For many Germans, not just students, this appeared to be a continuation of the undemocratic tradition in German politics, if not a step back towards the Nazi past.[16]

The Grand Coalition government proceeded to push new legislation that many thought gave excessive power to the executive. On June 22, 1966, 3,000 students held a sit-in at the Free University of Berlin to protest two important proposals: a restriction on length of study and the increased power of the administration to expel students. Students were likewise upset that another proposal on the limitation of class hours was rejected. But it was not just these specific proposals that were at issue. Rather, it was seen as a matter of rights; that is, the right of those affected to democratically engage in the decision making. Organized by the Socialist German Students Union (SDS), this organization was to be the dawn of a German "new left." Although the SDS had its origins as the youth group of SPD, it had since become the home of radical socialism as the parent group moved to the right. Within a few years after the Social Democratic Party renounced Marxism, they also tossed out the SDS.[17]

In June 1967, a march was organized to protest the visit of the tyrannical Shah of Iran. The planned peaceful dissent was banned and the police violently set upon the demonstrators. After fleeing to a side street to avoid the police violence, 26-year-old Benno Ohnesorg, a first-time protester with a pregnant wife, was shot by an undercover police officer. Benno died before he could receive treatment. The policeman was cleared of all charges. This incident, seen by many as cold-blooded assassination, became the catalytic event for the rise of the new left. Rudi Dutschke, an East German refugee, became the most prominent spokesman for the radical students. Opposed to violence, Dutschke urged the SDS to plan for a "long march through the institutions of power" to create radical change. He was influenced by the writings of Rosa Luxemburg and long political discussions with African and Latin American students. He was as thoughtful as he was committed to radical change.

The young student was also vilified as a monster who wished to destroy society by the Springer media, an empire that controlled 78 percent of West Berlin's newspapers and magazines. Rudi Dutschke was, as the Springer press shouted, "public enemy number one." On April 11, 1968, a young anti-communist shot Dutschke in the head; this sparked off massive protests, particularly focused against the Springer Press empire that was thought to have provoked the attack. Tellingly, it was a politically active intellectual from the field of music, Hans Werner Henze, who provided shelter for Rudi Dutschke following this attempted murder.[18] Although he lived, the former firebrand suffered brain damage and ultimately died some twelve years later from the wounds inflicted during the assassination attempt. As Gretchen, his widow, noted years later, Rudi "was very critical of the Soviet type of communism. He thought that there was a possible kind of communism that could be liberating." He also realized that youth in the 1960s "had to deal with the fact that their parents had supported Hitler ... [and the anti-authoritarian movement wanted to] prevent a new kind of fascism from ever developing again in Germany."[19]

Particularly alarming to the new left was the Grand Coalition's plan to reintroduce "emergency laws" into the West German Basic Law or Constitution. It was not just historians who vividly remembered that a similar set of laws had allowed General von Hindenburg, in his role as president, to create a government independent from elected representatives and then hand power over to Hitler. Amending the Constitution was not a problem, given that the Grand Coalition held a majority in the Parliament. There were worries, however, that many in the old socialist movement would have difficulty accepting something that gave the state so much arbitrary power. APO leaders charged the government with being a monopolistic party-state. They charged the emergency laws as legislation vulnerable to misuse by any future undemocratic oligarchy or dictator. The APO warned that these laws might in the future be the legal basis for suspending basic freedoms guaranteed in the Constitution.[20]

In 1967, a CIA report noted, "Many elements in the SPD—trade unionists in particular—are critical of emergency legislation."[21] When it was up for approval, 80,000 protesters—students, peace activists and militant trade unionists—rallied in the capital on May 11, 1968 to demand its defeat. The SPD leaders, with their smooth reassurances and a few cosmetic changes, undercut any further coordinated protest by workers and students. The US Army, with thousands of remaining occupation troops in Germany, was relieved. In a secret cable to the Department of Defense, army officials reassured Washington that the SPD leaders were confident that the German trade union federation (DGB) would not call a general strike. Still they noted, "Wild cat strikes and work stoppages in Berlin, Frankfurt, Hamburg, Munich and probably Bolchum are likely." As for others, US Army intelligence noted, "[the] SDS is planning demonstrations and strikes in several cities and hopes to coordinate these activities with the workers."[22] Despite this, Washington was assured that there would be no real delay; as anticipated the "emergency law" legislation was passed on May 30, 1968.

To the west, in Amsterdam, there arose a movement that united art, politics and more than a dash of youth culture to produce a unique vision that anticipated some of the softer aspects of the 1960s protests. Starting around May 1965, a collection of young Dutch people created the Provo movement. It was a coming together of "hip" young people and the remnants of the "ban the bomb" movement. These people, who became known as the "Provos," turned towards anarchism and were concerned with such issues as the controversial marriage of the crown princess, the escalation of the Vietnam War and increasing awareness about ecological destruction. Starting with relatively basic acts of street theater, the Provos evolved into a political organization, with a newspaper that had a circulation of 20,000. By June 1966, they even managed to get one of their members elected to the Amsterdam City Council running under the slogan, "Vote Provo for Better Weather."[23] The Provos' outrageous stunts were often followed by violent police crackdowns, all of which generated worldwide publicity.

The Provos' name often got mixed up in things for which they were not actually accountable. For example, when a 2 percent pay cut for construction workers was put forward, the Communist Party of the Netherlands (CPN) and many others called for a protest demonstration. Jan Weggelaar, a 51-year-old construction worker, put on slippers and walked to the nearby protest site. As the crowd grew, the police became more alarmed and ordered everyone to disperse. A riot ensued and Weggelaar was found dead on the street. It is unclear what, or whom, caused his death but it sparked the "battle of Amsterdam." The Provos supported the workers' cause but not the rioting, which the CPN likewise tried to stop. Both the Provos and the Communists were blamed all the same.[24] This was the beginning of the end for Communist and anarchist groups alike. Brief though their lifespan was, the Provos attracted young people from around Europe, and even became a tourist attraction. In a sign of capitalism's ability to co-opt apparently oppositional movements, the Dutch Tourist Board launched a campaign whose tag line was "Meet the Provos!" Although the Provos' movement had rather fizzled out by 1967, thousands of young Europeans floated in and out of Amsterdam because of them, and in the process met up with other angry European youths.[25]

Meanwhile, to the southeast of Amsterdam in the Balkans, a movement was emerging. One London-based writer recalled how he had first visited

Greece around Easter 1967 to attend a peace conference. During the anti-war gathering, wild rumors began to spread around the hall. Someone with family in the Greek armed forces "reported that the Greek military, backed by Washington, was about to launch a coup to pre-empt elections in which they feared the left might do a bit too well." Advised it would be best to leave the "cradle of democracy," the activist caught an early morning plane to London: "That afternoon tanks occupied the streets. Greece remained under the Colonels for the next seven years."[26] Having already killed, exiled, imprisoned, or marginalized the Communists, coup leaders now feared the former prime minister George Papandreou's Center Union. This party was, as the name suggests and the later history of their leaders proves, not exactly far left. The colonels' coup appears to have been timed to pre-empt a monarchist coup that was to be led by generals some short time later. One of the prime motivations for both may well have been fear that a newly elected government might purge the Greek Army.[27]

The events and motivations surrounding the coup of April 21, 1967 in Greece are, frankly, byzantine. At the time, and since, the United States has been thought to be behind this colonels' revolt.[28] Some data, however, suggests that Washington was actually caught by surprise. Some point to the fact that the United States was thinking of buying the Greek elections as a sign that they were not plotting a coup. Leaks to the *Washington Post* and other media outlets about US involvement in the coup may have come about because "a considerable number of people in [the Department of] State probably knew that we were considering something to do with Greece."[29] The argument advanced in this National Security Council memo is that Washington was discussing subverting Greek democracy with money, not suppressing it with force.

There is even evidence that the US may have actually supported the plans of King Constantine, who was not happy with the actions of the lowly colonels. The day of the coup, a CIA cable claimed that the king had asked for US Marines to help him and his generals to retake power. As for the coup leaders, King Constantine had nothing but scorn. The monarch characterized them as "stupid, ultra right-wing bastards, who, having gained control of tanks, have brought disaster to Greece."[30] The Americans took no action against the coup. When the US ambassador was asked why they did nothing, he denied that the US could do anything about it. However, when pressed on the issue of whether there would have been American involvement had the coup been a Communist or leftist action, the ambassador "answered without hesitation. Then, of course, they would have intervened, and would have crushed the coup."[31] The Greek junta would murder and torture thousands during the years 1967–1974. Regardless of the specifics, a hard-line dictatorship took over Greece— the Greek Tourist Board never did promote a "Come see the Torturers" ad campaign.

They promised the regeneration of the "Greece of the Greek Christians," and to that end closed down Parliament and other represen- tative institutions. Not surprisingly, the colonels outlawed strikes, labor unions and the free press, all of which are traditional weapons of the common people. More bizarre were their cultural policies of banning: long hair on men, mini-skirts, the peace symbol, the Beatles, and the reading of Sartre, Mark Twain and Socrates among others. Although they may or may not have had a hand in the installation of this dictatorship, the United States quickly, if quietly, approved. Although one US general enthusias- tically declared the Greek dictatorship was "the best damn Government since Pericles,"[33] by and large, the US was subtler in its support. Public support on the part of the US government had to be delayed for a decent interval. By 1969, National Security heavyweight Henry Kissinger could assure Greece that military aid would be resumed by claiming overriding US security interests as the "public line [to] be taken with members of the Congress and press."[34]

Besides employing outright violence, the Greek dictatorship used an appeasement technique, which was becoming standard throughout the West: sport. The combination of press censorship and the presence of police spies made the previously innocent act of political discussion a dangerous one; Greeks were thus whipped up into a virtual frenzy about sport instead. One observer noted

> ... a passion for soccer especially seemed to have replaced the passion for politics of the previous era, spreading even to the old. Opponents of the regime asserted that this new passion was only an outlet for pent-up aggressiveness which otherwise would have been expressed in the political arena.[35]

In 1974, the government of the "Greece of the Greek Christians" came apart as their botched attempt to unify Cyprus with the mainland led to a fierce Turkish response. It is notable that Turkey was no longer the European backwater of earlier times. By the 1960s, Turkish society had become more urban and had a growing working class, trade unions and strike actions.[36] It was not the only nation that was witnessing rapid social change. Another one on the outskirts of Europe was the British-occupied

Northern Ireland. In Northern Ireland, radicals hoped that the working class divided by religion and tradition could be united in a socialist vision transcending both social democracy and Stalinism. Instead, religious sectarianism won the day, leading to decades of communal violence.[37]

However, the events most remembered from this period of European unrest took place in France, venue for the Revolutions of 1789, 1830, 1848 and the Paris Commune of 1871. What began with student protests spread to become what some claim as the largest general strike in history. Like the rest of the continent, post-war France had changed dramatically in only a few decades. The modernization of French capitalism had led to a rapid, and often chaotic, expansion of higher education, which in turn led to alienation among the growing ranks of students. On March 22, 1968 a group of less than two hundred occupied an administration building at the University of Paris at Nanterre. After the police surrounded the building and the students' demands were published, this tiny group left quietly. Months of struggles followed until the administration ordered the campus to be closed on May 2. Beginning the next day, there were meetings at the Sorbonne campus in central Paris.[38]

When university students and professors united in a protest march, they were attacked by baton-wielding police. The heavy-handed, repressive response enraged not just students but much of the population at large. What had been a rather limited and localized dispute soon spread throughout the country. The 21st Cannes Film Festival ended early as filmmakers withdrew their films in protest and others even occupied the viewing hall. During the Cannes debate, Jean-Luc Godard shouted there "isn't a single film showing the problems of workers or students today." This French "new wave" director went on to argue that there was "no point in showing films here … it's a question of showing solidarity … of the cinema with the students and workers' movements that are happening in France."[39] In and of itself, it was of little importance whether films were shown at Cannes or not, but that filmmakers were hit by the "contagion" is significant.

One activist recalls rushing back from a holiday on the Mediterranean coast upon hearing of the events taking place in Paris's Latin Quarter. Joining a demonstration, he was surprised to see people digging paving stones out of the street. He didn't know if it was a police provocation, but remembers feeling that it was a symbolic gesture to evoke many glorious precedents in French history. The young radical watched as

… chainsaws appeared from no one knows where. Trees were chopped down. Overturned cars were transformed into ramparts, with loopholes and machicolations. The barricade-builders rivaled one another in imagination, as if competing for the most handsome subversive construction, decorating the paving stones with flowerpots, streamers, bits of bric-a-brac.[40]

Certainly, these barricades were useless from a military point of view. And yet, they symbolized a keen desire to link this revolt with the revolutions of the past.

Had this remained a student affair, its impact would have been limited but the actions in Paris were a catalyst to more. The student revolt became a spark setting on fire the French working class, who had pent up frustrations and desires of their own. Typically against the wishes of their Communist/Socialist/Catholic union leaders, millions of workers went on strike. Often overlooked is the role of immigrant workers in these strikes. They were a vital part of the strike movement representing the lowest-paid and worst-treated workers in a plant. Early in the May Days, radicals stressed the importance of internationalism and promoted solidarity between French and foreign workers. Notably during May–June 1968, there were two dozen distinct posters produced, each calling for native and immigrant worker solidarity. When the government announced their plan to deport foreign nationals, students prepared to hold protest rallies.[41]

By late May, the French ruling class was losing its nerve. On May 29, President DeGaulle cancelled a meeting of the Council of Ministers and left Paris. Some government officials burned their papers, thinking the revolution imminent; others made plans for flight and tried to hire private planes. Across the Atlantic, Washington received troubling reports about the French military. US intelligence thought the "attitude of the French armed forces during the present crisis is largely passive and somewhat pessimistic." Further, the American overlords fretted that the French military seemed to "have lost the old habit of independent thinking which endured from Bonaparte to De Gaulle … [if ordered to put down an insurrection] they would probably do so although there might be some difficulties with conscripts." Most troubling, "if pressure from the left were to lead to De Gaulle's departure from the scene they would probably adjust to the new government even if it included Communist participation."[42]

The Americans were not alone in worrying about the French armed forces. This fear that the military lacked the old Bonaparte way of thinking, or that draftees wouldn't fire on workers and students, was also on the mind of the French president. So, a depressed DeGaulle went to the French military forces stationed in Baden-Baden, Germany to consult with the commanding general. Assured of the military's full support, the president of the French Republic returned and soon called new elections. The established leaders of the left political parties and trade unions quickly pulled back. After all, how can you be for democracy and oppose an election? Now, instead of radical change, there was to be an election. The left anticipated, while the right feared, a left-wing landslide. Instead, DeGaulle and the right won the election easily. Had the left won, the loyalty of the army to the bourgeois property and order would have been put to the test. In the event, it was not. The critique of existing society made by rebels was persuasive, but the new left had no counter-plan, while the traditional left had no desire to change structures which gave them a place at the table. "All power to the imagination," shouted many people during May and June 1968. It seemed, however, that the mass of the common people wanted something more concrete than imagination.

As order was restored in Paris and the West's rulers could breathe easily again, the people began to stir in the Soviet Bloc's Czechoslovakia. What has become known to history as the "Prague Spring" was an attempt to transform Czechoslovakia from a bureaucratic, Stalinist country to a democratic socialist nation. Although there were certainly pro-Western rightists looking for an opening, the movement was led by the Communist Party and supported by the bulk of the populace. It was not a revolt for capitalism, as both Washington and Moscow would later claim. Beginning in the mid-1960s, there was increasing uneasiness among many about Czechoslovakia's bureaucratic government policy and its record of economic failures. Some radical socialist critics looked to Yugoslavia and argued that the party should relinquish some of its decision-making power to independent institutions, such as workers' councils and trade unions.

There was even discussion of the re-establishment of a multi-party system for elections to the Czechoslovak National Assembly. Along with intellectuals' protest, there were student demonstrations supported by the party's youth newspaper. When the students accused authorities of police brutality, the trade union newspaper not only agreed with the student complaint but also stressed the "need for establishing regular channels for expressing dissent and obtaining redress of grievances on all important areas (i.e. workers interests)."[43] All of these events were conditioned by the history of pluralism in the country. The citizens by and large considered themselves culturally part of the West, pointing out to tourists that Prague was a hundred miles west of Vienna. The pluralist orientation of Czechs and Slovaks was submerged by first the Nazi occupation and then the Soviets. These traditions were not, however, destroyed.[44] On January 5,

1968, Alexander Dubcek replaced veteran Moscow loyalist Novotny as first secretary of the Communist Party of Czechoslovakia. Soon, he would proclaim, "Socialism with a Human Face."

In a dark foreshadowing to the later Soviet action, none other than Soviet leader Leonid Brezhnev traveled to Prague in early December 1967. The CPSU leader had invited himself to Prague, in the wry words of one CIA analyst, to see "if the Czech political wines were vintage Budapest 1956." Whether true or not, it is significant that a story circulated among party members at that time of Dubcek having told the Russian leader to keep out of Czechoslovak internal matters.[45] By April 1968, the new leaders had increased freedom of speech, the press and travel, along with an economic stress on consumer goods. It was even suggested that there existed the chance of having a multiparty government replace the Communist Party's political monopoly. None of this made Moscow happy. On the other hand, the Dubcek government appeared too wildly popular with the common people. The two largest Western European Communist Parties (CPs), France and Italy, were sympathetic to Prague and fearful of Soviet military intervention. The Belgian Communists, the Finnish party and the rest of Scandinavia all backed "Socialism with a Human Face," as did the Communist Swiss Labor Party and even the traditionally loyal Communist Party of Great Britain. The West German KPD, outlawed in its own country and under the influence of the DDR, sided with Moscow. The Communists in Iceland and the Netherlands were too riddled with party faction fights to formulate a public statement.

Most Western governments were silent for fear of any statements being taken as interference in another nation's internal affairs. In Eastern Europe, the nations of Yugoslavia, Albania and Rumania backed the Dubcek government. The world press was, not surprisingly, all over the place, from far-right ramblings about the danger of a "Czech Trojan horse" to pious wishes in the upmarket mainstream that it would all work out peacefully. The press was largely silent on the role of the United States with one notable exception. *Die Welt*, one of the leading "quality newspapers" in West Germany, claimed that the USSR and the US had a deal defining each nation's European sphere of influence. The paper concluded that the "atomic giants" had agreed on "mutual respect of the status quo." That is, *Die Welt* argued Washington gave the green light to Moscow to do whatever they wanted to do regarding the Prague Spring.[46] Jiri Pelikán, a prominent Czech reform Communist politician, likewise charged that the system of rival blocs was "intended to justify the hegemony of the USA in one half and the USSR in the other, and so to give each the right to punish any country seeking to go its own way."[47]

With or without American blessing, Warsaw Pact armies from the Soviet Union, the DDR, Bulgaria, Poland and Hungary violated Czechoslovakia's borders on the night of August 20–21, 1968. A couple of hundred thousand Warsaw Pact soldiers and two thousand tanks took part in the invasion, which quickly forced Czechoslovak troops to confine themselves to their barracks. The day after the invasion, the 14th Congress of the Czechoslovak Communist Party met secretly in a Prague factory and, under the noses of the Soviets, proclaimed their own legitimacy and the illegality of the invasion. The gathering pledged, "socialism shall grow in our country out of the free striving of workers, peasants and intellectuals; that it shall be a humane socialism consonant with the democratic, progressive traditions of the peoples and minorities of our land."[48]

The newly elected Central Committee of the Communist Party issued a public statement reading in part: "Do not despair. This is not yet the end of all things. To achieve socialism with a human face is still the mission of our nation."[49] To avoid needless bloodshed in a militarily hopeless situation, Dubcek and other leaders directed their people not to resist. There was, however, passive and sly resistance, as road signs were taken down and the invaders often found themselves lost. There were many acts of popular nonviolent resistance, causing the Soviet Union to delay purging the reform Communist leadership. By April 1969, the USSR had the situation under control and Dubcek was expelled from the Communist Party and given a job as a forest ranger. Like elsewhere in Europe, it was the case of a dream deferred, becoming a dream denied.

CHAPTER FIFTEEN

Fighting for Peace in an Atomic Age, 1969–89

"The struggle continues," was more than a mere slogan of the never-say-die radical left. Though wishful thinking was often behind these words, it is nonetheless true that in 1968 the left was still far from achieving all their goals. They continued their movement, taking on class struggles, feminist movements, migration into Europe, concerns about ecological degradation, demands for LGBT rights and any number of other protests. The French flames burned out to join the cold dust of Gaullism, waiting to be swept into the trash heap of history. Heading south, the winds of revolt blew into Italy. During 1967–68, there had been demonstrations and protests in 26 out of 33 universities and in the early spring 1968, over half a million students went on strike. Yet, the student's actions were often isolated from those of the working-class movement and the traditional left. Often influenced by Maoism, students attacked the conservatism of both of the latter. In response, Pier Paolo Pasolini, cultural icon and Communist, wrote a bitter poem complaining that the polemics of the students were historically too late to matter. He went on:

> Now the journalists of all the world (including
> those of the television)
> are licking (as I believe one still says in university)
> your arses. Not me, my friends.
> You have the faces of spoilt rich brats ...
> You are cowardly, uncertain and desperate ... .[1]

Despite these often bitter conflicts, the student explosion did influence many average workers. The Italian republic saw the particular social eruptions during the hot autumn of 1969. One scholar claimed:

> The organization of Italian society was challenged at nearly every level. No single moment in Italy equalled in intensity and in revolutionary

potential the events of May 1968 in France, but the protest movement in Italy was the most profound and long-lasting in Europe. It spread from the schools and universities into the factories and then out again into society as a whole.[2]

There were factory occupations throughout the industrial Italian North. Workers were not only occupying their workplaces, they were also running them. At FIAT, "the production line was run by the Mirafiore plant workers' councils ... instead of Agnelli's management team."[3] Though it did not bring about total social transformation, the gains of that hot autumn were compelling and saw the Italian working class emerge with significant wage increases and greater political leverage.[4] The contrast between traditional left and far left can be seen clearly in the slogans each group boasted. When trade unions proclaimed, "No more rent rises," a more radical group countered with "What do we want? Everything!"[5]

Some radicals were frustrated with the apparent failure of these movements to change Italy. An extremely small number of these people replaced their previous optimism with impatience and turned to physical force to fight the bosses. The most important of these radical assemblies was the *Brigate Rosse* (Red Brigades) who thought that direct, violent action "would destabilize the capitalist structure and make revolution inevitable."[6] The Red Brigades sought not only to provoke a revolution; they also fought against NATO and multinational corporations.

Naturally, this group was soon labeled as "terrorist" by the mainstream, including most of the traditional workers' movement. Terrorists they certainly were, but they were not indiscriminate, choosing their targets carefully and trying to avoid any injury to the innocent. Considered one of the most lethal of such groups in Europe, the Red Brigades conducted an extensive number of attacks on government officials, judges and business leaders. Their most famous operation was the kidnapping in March 1978 and later execution of Aldo Moro, leader of the Christian Democratic Party. Even their enemies had to concede their attacks "have been characterized by precise planning and execution."[7] Still, they did little to advance the cause of the common people as their tactics divided, rather than united, opponents of exploitation and oppression, while giving the rulers credible excuses to attack protest movements.

In the same decade, Europeans witnessed the collapse of three infamous dictatorships in Greece, Spain and Portugal. In the homeland of Socrates, the military dictatorship there faced increasing unrest. In November 1973, students at the Polytechnic protested the lack of freedoms and demanded a return to democracy, while putting forth the slogan "Bread, Education and Liberty." Rather than negotiating with student leaders, the dictatorship sent a tank smashing through the gates of the Athens Polytechnic. This heavy-handed response made martyrs out of the demonstrators and further alienated public opinion, which subsequently engaged in countless protests against the regime. Seeking to play the nationalist card, the government staged a *coup d'état* against the elected president of Cyprus, as the first step toward annexing the island to the Greek mainland. The coup failed and to protect ethnic Turks, the Turkish government responded with invasion. Three days after Turkish troops occupied the north of Cyprus, the colonels' military junta was dismantled and a transition to civilian rule begun. This new democracy had different symbols, rhetoric and a new constitution. Yet, the new democracy began "without any systematic purge of the bureaucracy and the police apparatus; key sections of the state remained in the hands of the old order."[8]

To the west, Spain in the early 1970s anxiously awaited the death (and thus the long rule) of dictator Francisco Franco. The rulers of the Western world fretted that Franco's death might unleash long-repressed popular demands for real democracy and social justice. Of special concern was the rebirth of a radical trade unionism in a country where there existed underground Communist, socialist and even anarchist workers' organizations.[9] The CIA hoped that "Spain is on the verge of transition to a far more complex form of authoritarian rule."[10] Western governments worried that in the long term, any opening-up of the Spanish system would give rise to escalating political demands and renewed class struggle. They desired to guide into power a type of neo-Francoist parliamentary system in order to marginalize any real possibility for radical change. Fearing democracy in Spain meant "the Communists are on the march," US President Ford said, "I think we should do whatever we need to in Spain."[11] After Franco finally died in November 1975, Spain's transition mirrored that of Greece, in that it left the old order in control of much of the state apparatus. A constitutional monarchy replaced General Franco's dictatorship and a freely elected Parliament was chosen. Despite a few coup attempts, the old Francoists decided to play by the new rules of the game ... as long as nothing too radical was done.

The so-called "Carnation Revolution" of 1974 in Portugal proved to be far more potentially radical and complex than the transitions of either Greece or Spain. Portugal was a nation with little history of democracy; it had been ruled by an authoritarian dictatorship since 1932. On April 24, 1974, a group of younger officers secretly organized as the Armed

Forces Movement (AFM) overthrew the dictatorship by means of a *coup d'état*. This let loose a huge wave of popular protest, as the long-repressed Portuguese population took to the streets. The depth of radicalization that existed in 1974 had four main features: 1) the revolutionary process was the result of the army's defeat by African peasant rebels in Portugal's colonies of Guinea-Bissau, Angola and Mozambique; 2) the military debacle was accompanied by an economic crisis that hit Portugal in 1973; 3) unlike other revolts, the workers' movement emerged as the central protagonist, and 4) the workers' movement was notably recent, and concentration in Lisbon's industrial belt, with the lack of official union structures, gave the rank and file more space to develop democratic institutions.[12] These characteristics made the events in the little Iberian nation of great concern to the rich and powerful throughout the West.

Nor was this some sudden, wholly unexpected development for Portugal. For fifteen years from the early 1960s until the revolution, thousands of young men had deserted from the military. One summed up the predominant feeling when he asked, "Why do we have to kill African people, peasants like us?"[13] Portugal's ruling class was not unaware of the power of the African rebellions and the resulting growth of anti-war sentiment—they simply ignored these facts. As early as 1961, even the American CIA was amazed that Lisbon didn't understand their fundamentally losing hand in their African colonies. They went on to predict that

> ... the situation in Portuguese Africa will worsen ... [the military establishment] would be severely strained by any such combination of revolts, and might soon lose control of all but the principal towns and communication lines in Angola and all but the port areas in Guinea.[14]

In addition, the economic distress that preyed upon the average citizen of Portugal was far from a state secret.

With the start of the 1974 revolution, various interests sought to control and channel events in a manner least threatening to capitalism and the established order. Among those trying to ensure that things did not "get out of hand" in Portugal was, of course, the American government. On October 16, 1974, a CIA report was presented to Henry Kissinger, the US president's national security advisor, entitled, "Proposed Covert Action in Portugal." The report argued the need for "a stronger Socialist Party" and the formation of an effective centrist party to "provide noncommitted AFM officers with an attractive alternative" to the Portuguese Communist Party (PCP) or other radical groups. To accomplish these aims, the CIA suggested giving "advice, guidance and funding" while "finding a specific centrist candidate to support." President Ford responded, "Let's do it."[15] Meanwhile, among the bulk of the Portuguese public, radicalization was increasing, to the left rather than the right. When in 1975, the situation appeared to worsen—that is, for Western capital—the US administration directed money to favored media outlets in Portugal, with Kissinger noting "that is what we did in Chile."[16]

By January 1975, the question, "Who needs bosses?" was being asked by common people throughout the nation. By July, the following poster was posted at a factory entrance: "Work is not a commodity, it's a right. We want to work to live and not live to work. For the capitalist, the worker is a machine." This was followed by factory occupations; 24 in the last trimester of 1974 and 83, 55 and 14 respectively in the trimesters of 1975.[17] Neither the traditional ruling class nor their foreign overlords were cheered by these direct actions, which also took place among peasants in the countryside. In a conversation on August 12, 1975, Henry Kissinger, by that time the US secretary of state, drew together key advisors to discuss what to do about Portugal. The situation was serious, and Kissinger commented, "I am not so much against a coup as such, shocking as it may sound to some of my colleagues." Immediately, the US ambassador to Portugal responded, "No, I am also not against a coup if it worked." A few minutes later, Kissinger chastised the ambassador by saying, "I want it confirmed that we are not running a seminar here of theological students. Your Mission must know that. All of you must know that we are clearly in a revolutionary situation where there are no rewards for losing moderately." Later still, the secretary of state admonished his group:

> We need to act in Portugal. I am reminded of Chile at an earlier time … You must take some risks … I want it understood that what we want in Portugal cannot be done without risks. I'll back you if you get caught taking risks. I even back up incompetents if what they are doing succeeds.[18]

It was not only foreign heads of state who were prepared to drown the Carnation Revolution in blood if need be. During the revolution, a West German investigative journalist traveled to Portugal, claiming to be an operative from far-rightists high up in his government. This ruse enabled him to find a rat's nest of far-right organizations, with threads leading as high as Portugal's ranking primate archbishop, waiting to physically destroy the left. Bragging about the arms they had received from the CIA and prior German support, one would-be assassin said, "We've already got lists of dangerous left-wingers who'll be killed when we've won."[19] Strangely, another told his German "contact" that the head of PCP was the only politician he had respect for, "He's brave and sticks to his ideas. I'd kill him if I could but I still respect him."[20] It never came to that Chilean-style solution, however.

On November 25, 1975, the coup came, not from the US, but from left-wing military units. Paratroopers seized a number of airbases along with the national television and radio stations. This incursion was quickly defeated and the leftist solders were arrested in a rightist counter-coup. Although they initially supported the left-wing solders, the PCP quickly adopted a passive stance and went so far as to issue a leaflet calling on workers to remain calm. The result was the beginning of the end of the Portuguese revolution. As a scholarly study concluded, "the revolution was defeated with the coup of 25 November 1975 when the only force with national power—the trade union federation Intersindical dominated by the PCP—failed to resist."[21] Shakespeare once remarked that tide and time wait for no one, it seems this applies equally to the Portuguese revolution.

Despite their small and big differences, most all of the movements thus far described had one thing in common. That is, the leadership was male dominated. Take for example, the May–June movement in France. Although women were a vital part of that movement, the credit (and blame) went to men like Daniel Cohn-Bendit. Currently a Green Party leader in Germany, Cohn-Bendit has been credibly accused of sexist behavior throughout his political career. Entering into French parliamentary politics after 1968, he is said to have mounted a sexist campaign against far left opponent Arlette Laguiller, claiming she was nothing but a puppet for men behind the scenes.[22] If the CIA can be believed (admittedly a rather big "if"), Cohn-Bendit was considered a traitor by much of the German left because after becoming wealthy from books and films, he "reneged on promises to turn his money over to the 'cause.'"[23] The problem of sexism was much more than just the behavior of certain individuals. It was systemic and its roots went far back in European history.

As one feminist activist noted, we "only know ourselves in societies in which masculine power and masculine culture dominate, and can only aspire to an alternative in a revolutionary movement which is male defined."[24] But many women were no longer willing to be just camp followers; 1968, and the years that followed, spawned vigorous feminist activity. Sheila Rowbotham, British feminist historian, describes her experiences when she was brought on to the staff in December 1968 with the "underground" newspaper *Black*

Dwarf. Rowbotham was put in charge of women's coverage and shortly thereafter the staff of *Black Dwarf* decided to do a special issue on women's issues. Rowbotham immersed herself in the task, lining up feminist authors and "furiously writing" herself. The quality of the content was excellent and unlike so much of post-1968 writing has mainly stood the test of time. When she saw the layout for the "1969 Year of the Militant Woman?" issue, her heart sank. The male designer had decided on a pink cover with "a cartoon dolly bird looking out from a 'V' sign, holding a hammer and sickle. Below this image he had drawn a woman in a boiler suit in comic-book style, her pocket buttons substituting for protruding nipples."[25]

One could hardly read the feminist articles in the issue as it was covered in nude photos of everyone from Marilyn Monroe to Yoko Ono. Although the editor pulled some of the most offensive photos and ads, Rowbotham missed a particularly nasty ad the designer had snuck in, an example of the dark and seedy side of the underground press and the movement in general. The ad read, "DWARF DESIGNER SEEKS GIRL: Head girl type to make tea, organize paper, me. Free food, smoke, space. Suit American negress. Phone ... ."[26] To his credit, Tariq Ali, the main editor of *Black Dwarf,* saw that the designer parted company with the newspaper the next day. All the same, incidents like this assured that even the calmest feminists often boiled with rage at their male "comrades." These male sexist behaviors would suggest that there may be something to the claim that porn was "Britain's most significant contribution to the sixties scene [as part of] a popular movement supported by legions of male masturbators who bought soft-core porn."[27]

The growth of the women's liberation movement was more than merely an Anglo-American phenomenon. Yet, one might be forgiven for thinking this if they read most of the English-language books on the subject. It is also a mistake to adopt a model "that assumed steady liberalization and the gradual overcoming of obstacles to sexual freedom."[28] Women's liberation history has been comprised (and continues to be) more of a series of battles, advances and retreats. There are periods of renewed sexual conservatism that gives a foundation to anti-feminist and anti-gay sentiments. Further, women's liberation is an international movement that neither began nor ended in the twentieth century. For centuries preceding and on into the twenty-first century, women have fought in various ways for their rights and to achieve equality.[29] In France, demands for female rights were heard during the 1789 Revolution and have come to the forefront repeatedly ever since. It has been argued that unlike the Anglo-Saxon world, France had an "uninterrupted tradition of class consciousness among working-class men

and women [so] feminist consciousness was born second to class consciousness and thus that there continues to be very real class consciousness within
the movement itself."[30]

French feminists have often worked within existing political structures
more than those in Britain or even Germany. Although French women have
asserted women's issues successfully within larger organizations, activists
always had to navigate that gray area between having influence and being
co-opted. When in the 1970s, the French Communist Party declared itself
"the women's liberation party," was this a feminist success or a ploy by
the PCF to win female recruits?[31] In Italy, women from all backgrounds
concerned themselves with reproductive issues. Into the 1970s, abortion
was outlawed and considered a serious crime "against the race." Yet, in
1978, a liberal abortion law was passed after the tireless work of a wide
range of women, including Roman Catholic nuns.[32]

The situation among German women was complicated by the fact that
there were two Germanys, not counting German-speaking Austria. Both
West and East Germany shared a rich history of feminist struggle, yet the
former was influenced by the American empire across the Atlantic, while
the latter lived in the dark shadow of the USSR. In the spring of 1968,
Helke Sander spoke to West German radical students and hammered home
"the injustice of patriarchy, women's purely token presence in situations
of power, the political implications of personal life, the rights and needs
of mothers."[33] It was assumed in the West that women's liberation was not
possible under the shadow of the Berlin Wall. It is true the hidebound rulers
of the German Democratic Republic (DDR) could scarcely be accused of
feminism. Nonetheless, the logic of their society and the struggle of East
German women allowed the DDR to lead the West Germans in an area
that one would have thought would not even be a contest. Look at female
participation in the work force as of 1988. In the DDR, 78.1 percent of
women worked and earned 83.2 percent of what men did, while in the West
German economy only 55 percent of women worked, earning only 70
percent of the male wage.

As concerns motherhood, the East German woman also had an advantage
since she was given six weeks of leave before birth and twenty weeks
afterward. During this time, she was paid her full wages followed by a paid
parental leave at 70–90 percent of wages until her child reached the age of
one. In the BRD, mothers got six weeks of maternity leave before and eight
weeks after birth at average pay. After that, 80.2 percent of children in the
DDR were in free day care until age three and 89.1 percent of older children
(up to till age 10) were in after-school care. By contrast, only 3 percent of

children under the age of three were in public day care in West Germany. Women in East Germany were entitled to 40 paid leave days per year to care for sick children, while their Western sisters had a mere 5 paid days of child illness leave. German women who chose to terminate their pregnancy were committing a crime in both East and West, although the DDR had a larger number of exceptions in 1950.[34] In 1972, however, the East German Volkskammer legalized abortion for the first twelve weeks of pregnancy. The BRD followed suit in 1974, only to have the law struck down by their Constitutional Court the following year. When in 1976, abortion was made legal in the BRD, the procedure was limited to medical necessity, rape, or serious psychological problems, but then only if approved by two doctors with counseling and a three-day waiting period.[35]

The question of gay rights also has an interesting history. In the post-war era of deep concern over the declining birth rate, it is hardly surprising that both Germanys saw homosexuality as a threat to society.[36] However in 1950, the DDR reverted to the much milder anti-gay law of the Weimar Republic, while the West German state continued to adhere to the more repressive Nazi-era version. In 1968, it was the East Germans who first decriminalized "homosexual acts between consenting adults ... a full year before this happened in West Germany."[37] Jürgen Lemke, one of the best-known gay figures in the DDR, has even claimed that he felt more secure as a gay person in East Germany than he has since unification.[38] There is, however, a problem in too uncritical celebration of social movements.

There is always the danger that identity politics will allow the substance of a people's movement to be appropriated or deflected by an individual who merely looks the part. Surely, few feminists had the United Kingdom's Margaret Thatcher in mind when they demanded women in leadership roles. Naturally, she was widely hailed by the dumb, the numb, or the cynical because Thatcher was the first female prime minister in Britain. As Glenda Jackson, Labour MP, pointed out, Maggie was female but not what most of the workers or poor would consider a woman. By that, Jackson meant that Thatcher was biologically female but acted with the cold-bloodedness associated with the worst type of male leaders. Interestingly, when Thatcher died, there were numerous spontaneous demonstrations where people drank and chanted "Maggie, Maggie, Maggie, Dead, Dead, Dead." Her death may have been a wise career move, as she had little more to look forward to except increased hostility to her legacy but the damage she did to trade unions, workers and the poor while alive is most remarkable. When she was first elected prime minister, the US president was warned that she was still a "dogmatic lady" and it "will take patience to deal with

Mrs. Thatcher's hard-driving nature and her tendency to hector."[39] But the US leaders quickly warmed to the "Iron Lady," so much so that in 1983, despite huge leads in the polls, the CIA worried about her re-election. They even put together a secret briefing paper entitled: "U.K. Election Prospects—What if Thatcher Loses?"[40] She did not lose, however.

Instead, a year after war over the Falkland Islands, the British government allowed delivery of "sensitive electronic warfare equipment to the Argentine Navy," which had ordered the equipment prior to the conflict. Further, despite "widely recognized human rights violations … [Thatcher's government] lifted its embargo on military sales to Chile … [Chile] ranks as the largest buyer of British arms in Latin America." According to US intelligence, the UK's philosophy, as regards arms sales, became to "satisfy the customer."[41] If this desire to satisfy the customer was the motive for much of Britain's foreign policy, so it was at home. Domestically though, the individuals who qualified as the "customers" to be "satisfied" were not the average citizens or residents—they were the barons of finance. Much as feudal barons were once placated at the expense of serfs, the common people of the United Kingdom were now ever more expendable to the demands of capital.

The greatest struggle against this policy was the Miners' Strike of 1984–85. Trade unions in the coal fields had long been a pain in the side of British capitalism. To destroy this stubborn bastion of resistance, the Conservative Party government hit upon a radical solution—that is, effectively eliminate the British coal industry. Naturally, this objective was never publicly declared nor was it implemented all at once. Instead after 1981, a series of pit closures and wage controls were put forth. The government reasoned that if the miners did nothing, then the coal industry could be reduced to oblivion gradually over a period of time. If they fought back, the miners would be crushed. The National Union of Mineworkers (NUM) chose to fight; this involved 135,000 workers striking for nearly a year, resulting in 26 million working days "lost."[42] In earlier times, a show of militancy such as this may have secured at least a partial victory. By 1984, however, it was cheaper to import foreign coal than dig it out of British soil, so there was little incentive for Thatcher and her corporate backers to compromise.

Senior Conservative leaders inside and outside of Parliament had quietly prepared for a final conflict with the NUM since before the 1979 Thatcher victory. Their goal was to destroy the NUM, speed up pit closures and prepare for the privatization of the very few remaining profitable mines.[43] Since coal mines were to be abandoned in some areas but not others, the "effect was to fragment not unite."[44] Powerful differences separated mining communities in terms of not just economics but also factors such as involvement of women in strike support, sympathetic local authorities and the weight of political tradition."[45] The NUM was attacked in the tabloid press, which described the NUM as rolling in Moscow gold, while Polish coal was being imported to break the strike. No tactic was too low nor lie too vile for the "defenders of civilization," if it furthered the destruction of the trade union.[46]

As the Thatcher government prepared for the 1984–85 strike with almost military precision, and determined there would be no compromise or negotiated settlement, the Labour Party support was tepid at best. The parliamentary leaders of the proletariat feared that NUM leader Arthur Scargill was too radical and might cost Labour votes. Always principled the Labour Party is, their typical principle being getting into office. It was a hard-fought and complex battle, but in the end the NUM was ruthlessly destroyed in order to promote the "free market" and management's right to manage. It is good to remember the involvement of groups like "Women Against Pit Closures," which was an autonomous movement supporting the NUM. They showed that even if women were excluded from work in the coalfields—a fact that limited their impact within the NUM—they could all the same, make an important contribution.[47]

But it would be a grave to mistake to think that the Lords of Finance were always against unions. At the same historical moment when the murder of trade unionism was being plotted in much of the Western world, trade unions were vigorously supported in Poland. The CIA supported legitimate workers' grievances within Stalinist Poland to maximize discomfort and pressure on the Soviet Bloc. On September 29, 1981, the *Wall Street Journal*—normally not considered a friend of unions or the common people—published an editorial in support of Poland's *Solidarność* (Solidarity) union movement. The paper rather short-temperedly rejected CIA involvement, while noting the AFL-CIO was providing hundreds of thousands of dollars in support. This money came from, and was often delivered through, CIA front organizations.[48] This was not done to support "free labor," but rather because it was useful to gain influence in growing protest movements and precluded a resistance to the Polish government that might take an anti-capitalist direction.[49]

Later, in a *Time* magazine cover story, the same Carl Bernstein who gained fame for exposing the Watergate scandal, detailed how Pope John Paul II worked with the CIA, the US government and other Western agencies to transform Solidarity from a grass-roots people's movement into an instrument of anti-Soviet policy.[50] This is not to say that most union members had any idea of who was actually bankrolling their organization. This operation was uniquely useful for the West because it was difficult for most leftists and trade unionists to criticize a workers' movement against oppression—although the steady supply of cheap Polish coal into the UK during the miners' strike made some people wonder. Later, a congressman on the House Intelligence Committee would brag, "We provided the supplies and technical assistance in terms of clandestine newspapers, broadcasting, propaganda, money, organizational help and advice."[51]

At the end of the day, the covert operations and intelligence evaluations were unable to really influence or even understand one of the greatest developments of the twentieth century: the collapse of the Soviet Union. The day after Christmas in 1991, the Soviet Union that had been a dream for so many and the nightmare for many more was formally dissolved. When Mikhail Gorbachev was chosen as general secretary in 1985, there was little thought that his rule would end with the destruction of the nation he led. After a period of stagnation that had seized up all aspects of Soviet society like a noose tightly pulled around the neck, the new leader was seen as a reformer who would breathe new life into the Soviet Union. To revive the economy, Gorbachev understood the need for drastic reforms of the social and political structure. He sought more openness, restructuring of outdated procedures, and fought for new thinking. What he got was rabid nationalism pulling the multi-ethnic empire apart and the persistent inability to improve the living standards of the common people. As *Komsomolskaya Pravda* wrote in a sympathetic farewell, "He didn't know how to make sausage, but he did know how to give freedom."[52]

Left critic Boris Kagarlitsky argued that by the "late 1980s, we had a huge country with an inefficient super-centralised (and not particularly planned) economy and a bloated, hypertrophic bureaucracy that was dreaming of acquiring property as well as power."[53] The Soviet Union had long ago ceased to be socialist in any sense that Marx or Lenin would have recognized. By late in the twentieth century, the Soviets were battling with the demons of nationalism, often caused in part by their own contribution to nation building.[54] Lenin had sought to calm these demons through generosity, a policy long abandoned for Stalin's policy of repression. At the end, they came back with a vengeance, playing a major part in the USSR's dissolution. The economy had been distorted by a vain attempt to match US defense spending, particularly as regards nuclear weapons. Members of the privileged strata beheld a chance to line their pockets and become a new bourgeoisie. The old party bureaucrats, long cynical about public proclamations concerning a socialist future, gave in to unrestrained greed and sought to privatize state assets.[55] The result was a market economy of sorts that was closer in form to a confidence trick played on the populace by the new elite.[56] This has been termed by some as "market Stalinism." A joke circulating at the time in Russia said "socialism in one country" had been replaced by "apocalypse in one country."[57]

Perhaps this was inevitable in a top-down society that was undemocratic with an economy plagued by scarcity, resulting itself from the lack of democracy and transparency in the planning process. There had been a social contract between the Soviet Union, their allies and the common people. The workers would surrender political freedoms in return for guaranteed employment, stable prices and ever-rising levels of consumption.[58] Of course, there were clear, distinct social classes in the Soviet Union and her Eastern European allies. It is hardly a shock that these classes often found themselves in competition, if not outright warfare, over the allocation of resources.[59] Whether the clearly non-socialist Soviet system could have been reformed is a question safely left for specialists and later historical study.[60] All the same, the collapse altered the course of not just Russia's history but that of other societies as well. For average Europeans, the end of the USSR was sometimes for the best, often for the worse, and almost always a bit of both.

CHAPTER SIXTEEN

Europe Falls into the
Twenty-First Century

The Berlin Wall came crashing down, albeit while DDR border guards stood around waiting for orders that never came; the evil Soviet Empire had collapsed into the recycling bin of history. The euphoria of those dancing on the Wall was real—and often enhanced by impressive quantities of drink or something special to smoke. It was, as some said, "the end of history," where all was right in this best of all possible worlds. The captive Europeans had liberated themselves. No more secret police spying on innocent, ordinary citizens. Freedom combined with unheard-of levels of individual consumption. If it was capitalism, it was to be capitalism with a human face. What could go wrong after that?

Fast-forward a quarter of a century. A poll taken in January 2015, finds that 82 percent of respondents in the old East Germany report that life was better before unification. Quizzed on this counter-intuitive outlook, they said there was "more sense of community, more facilities, money wasn't the dominant thing, cultural life was better and they weren't treated, as they are now, like second-class citizens."[1] Many Europeans were shocked when the Snowden exposé showed that the Americans spied on everyone all the time.[2] It was like the Russian KGB or German Stasi with space age technology. Wasn't state spying one of the major faults of the old systems? One study even asked, "Do Communists have better sex?" The answer, at least if the DDR is considered a representative sample for Communists, is yes.[3] This research was even made into a documentary film.[4] Of course, save for a handful of die-hard Stalinists, no one truly longs for a repressive state and the denial of freedom, nor do they long for the return of the other horrors of the old system.

The problem appears to be that with the fall of the Berlin Wall, people expected to gain freedom and social security. What they got was "actually existing capitalism." The philosopher Slavoj Žižek tells of a rumor floating about Germany after the fall of Gorbachev and the USSR. The story, which may or may not have happened, says that Gorbachev went to Berlin to visit Willy Brandt, long-time leader of the German Social Democrats. When Gorbachev rang his doorbell, Brandt refused to answer. Not because he believed in Soviet-style rule, but because the collapse of the Soviets endangered his life work as a social reformer. As Žižek comments:

> Brandt knew that the capitalist system is ready to make considerable concessions to the workers and the poor only if there is a serious threat of an alternative, of a different mode of production ... the moment the alternative vanishes, one can proceed to dismantle the welfare state.[5]

The Soviet collapse dismantled not only the welfare state but also entire nation-states. Czechoslovakia broke into two separate nations, while Yugoslavia splintered into numerous small entities.[6] Whether the first may be considered a farce is debatable; that the second was a tragedy is not. After World War I, various southern Slavs with different histories and religions had been united in a multicultural country. Partitioned by the Nazis during World War II, Yugoslavia was reborn under the Communist strongman Tito who brought together Slovenia, Croatia, Bosnia, Serbia, Montenegro and Macedonia, along with the self-governing provinces of Kosovo and Vojvodina. The slogan of Tito's Yugoslavia was "Brotherhood and Unity." After Tito's death, nationalism began to resurface and by 1991 Yugoslavia began to break apart with the encouragement of various Western interests. In the civil wars that followed, atrocities that had not occurred on European soil since 1945 became commonplace. In Bosnia-Herzegovia alone, roughly 200,000 people were murdered in the period 1992–95. Finally, NATO intervened, thus ending the civil war, and the various nationalist butchers went to ground or migrated to the West.

Tito's Yugoslavia had hardly been a utopia, socialist or otherwise. What it had been was a stable, peaceful nation that refused to take sides during the Cold War and allowed citizens to travel abroad. A Yugoslav woman told a British journalist of her longings for the old system. She related, "My father is Serb and my mother is Croat. My best friend is Muslim. My nearest neighbors are Muslims, and next to them are Serbs. Why should I fight these people? Like most of my friends, I only wish the Communists were back!"[7] These seem understandable sentiments in the context of a vicious and bloody civil war. In all the Soviet Bloc nations, people found that most of what was said by the government about "actually existing socialism" was a pack of lies. However, what had been said about capitalism was true.

In Bulgaria, almost half the population was at risk for poverty by 2011, according to the European Commission, while 44 percent had experienced "severe material deprivation".[8] Anelia, a Bulgarian woman, remembers all "those years, I was forced to write about unemployment and exploitation and imperialism and neocolonialism and apartheid and military dictatorships ... I was a good writer. I could write passionately. But I didn't believe a word of it." As of 2014, this woman who speaks four languages fluently and has years of professional experience cannot find work. Daily she sends out emails to try and get a job interview. She worries about how she will pay her bills or support herself. "I thought it was all lies." Anelia shook her head, "Can you imagine that all that time I was actually writing the truth?"[9]

Even in more prosperous Germany, unification meant a harder life for average women. Of all the groups hit by West Germany's abortion of the DDR, that is, the destruction of East German Society, women were some of those most negatively affected. Before in the old DDR, working mothers easily reconciled family and professional lives, unlike their sisters in the West. As numerous studies indicate, reunification led to a sharp rise in female unemployment in the East and resulted in drastic changes in their way of life and future plans, as well as a loss of self-confidence."[10] East German workers (male and female alike) were humiliated by their new West German bosses who doubted their qualifications and sneered at the work habits of the East Germans. Women had it even harder, as full female employment was an Eastern, not Western, tradition. As the *New York Times* admitted with the collapse of the old system, "women in the former Communist East seemed to be the big losers."[11]

Yet, East German women were far from passive in this situation and one sociologist has commented that the "East Germany model of gender equality collapsed with the wall, but a quarter of a century later it still shapes the way mothers brought up under it see themselves and their role in society."[12] This has resulted in the ironic situation in which women from the West see East German women as pace setters. Ms. Domscheit-Berg, a female former opponent of the old DDR government, still maintains that it was a bad system. Yet, she also admits "But on women, the East was ahead. We are still far from where we were 20 years ago, but at least we are moving in the right direction."[13] Before, women in East Germany had unheard-of economic independence "because they could depend on solid and reliable social welfare. That is an important prerequisite for equal rights, perhaps even the essential one."[14] One could easily be forgiven for thinking that these examples concern only older people with difficulty in adjusting to the new.

Still, there is a wealth of evidence suggesting that young people are not all ecstatic about capitalism and market either. Polish-born Agata Pyzik, living in London since 2010, appears to be leading the life of a successful writer, publishing in the *Guardian* and *New Statesman* among others—just the sort of successful, English-speaking "new European" that should sing the praises of the market society. Still, she finds much that is wrong (even evil) in the post-Soviet world built by the Western bourgeoisie and their loyal governmental employees. Take, for example, the place of women in the nations of the ex-Bloc, now remolded by the Western profit motive:

> What strikes you is the seediness, the astonishing amounts of peep-shows, sex-shops and various strip and "Gentlemen's Clubs", and the more one goes east the more sleazy it gets ... in a hotel, on the shelf there's lots of flyers, totally assuming you're there to use Eastern girls' charm. The sex industry that mushroomed in the East is only one side of its capitalist transition.[15]

Even decades after the collapse of the Soviet Union, most Westerners continue to harbor stereotypical prejudices about East Europeans and doubtlessly the reverse is also true. The gap is illustrated by a story told by Russian Marxist Boris Kagarlitsky. He was having an intellectual argument, that he found rather boring, with some young Swedish revolutionaries. After the scheduled lecture/discussion was over, the Swedes wanted to drink bottles of beer in the park. However, upon reaching the park, the Swedish radicals were horrified that they had forgotten a bottle opener. Kagarlitsky proceeded to open the bottles using the table as he explained that there are at least a half a dozen other ways. As the Russian noted, it seemed that the idea of not using the "proper" tool was hard for the Westerners to wrap their brains around.[16] The Eastern intellectual has criticized the fundamentally flawed stereotypes that seem to color most Western discussion of the ex-Soviet Bloc. For example, to most Westerners, the "whole of Russian society is seen as just one reactionary mass with a slave psychology."[17] This was never true and is becoming less true as the countries of the former Warsaw Pact nations change.

In fact, 2012 saw intense popular protest, not only in Russia but also Rumania, Bulgaria and Slovenia. It has been argued that the common people are only now "acting out the clumsily put together capitalist democracy of the early 1990s." This rising class struggle gets passed over with a few media mutterings about the "excluded" falling for "populism." Despite all the evidence of increased class divisions and conflicts, "nobody dares to call it class war."[18] By early 2014, cities were aflame in the Bosnian Federation as protesters demanded jobs, the chance of a decent life and the end of corruption. Interestingly, a photo from one of the demonstrations showed protesters waving Bosnian, Serbian and Croatian flags side by side. This action expresses the desire of many dissidents to ignore ethnic differences. As one Slovenian intellectual said:

> The people of Bosnia finally understand who their true enemy is: not other ethnic groups but their own nationalist elites pretending to protect them from the others. It is as if the old and much abused Titoist motto of "brotherhood and unity" of Yugoslav nations has now become relevant.[19]

The decades after the Soviet collapse in the West saw the continued rise of green parties. Focused on the environment and campaigning as warriors for peace and ecological salvation, these groups differ somewhat throughout the continent. Most grew up in the shadow of European Social Democracy and hailed from the so-called "1968 generation" of new leftists. If the 1968ers began to the left of classic Social Democratic or socialist parties, they soon found themselves outflanked on the left by the offspring of European Communism. In Germany, former Communists and left-wing socialists united in *Die Linke* (The Left) while France saw the birth of the *Front de Gauche* (Left Front) and the European Parliament would see a Nordic Green Left faction unite many far leftist members.

As European liberalism collapsed, often striking their colors and hopping aboard the larger ship of Christian Democracy captained by big business, the Greens took over the abandoned position of "defender of civil liberties."[20] By 1998, Green politician Joschka Fischer was Germany's foreign minister while his party was forced to renounce its traditional pacifist position.[21] The German Greens, and other green movements as well, repeatedly found themselves having more in common with conservatives than any left group, when it came to preserving traditional culture and even foreign policy.[22] Often forgotten is that there exists a reactionary ecological trend apparent in far-right groups like the Danish People's Party or even the National Front in France.[23] Ecological concerns were even an important part of the Nazi movement before and during World War II.[24]

If those in the West had it better than their co-workers to the East, it did not mean that all was well. Employers used undocumented workers in addition to their usual tricks to cut into living standards. This is a difficult area for the scholar to examine, as there is no such thing as a single "black market." The underground economy consists of a myriad of different layers ranging from illegal economic activity (for example, drug trafficking) to informal labor (for example, legal work done for cash without reporting to governmental agencies). Even within an occupation, conditions may vary widely. For example, legal and unionized Dutch sex workers, whose union is part of the national trade union federation,[25] enjoy a fair degree of agency, safety and autonomy, yet work in a field in which many of their non-unionized colleagues are illegally exploited, if not enslaved. There is a wealth of data suggesting that globalization has led to a boom in sweatshops that exploit workers by flaunting both local laws and international treaties.

An investigative reporter posing as an "illegal" Turkish worker was shocked to find out how the most basic laws were almost openly ignored. Pretending he could only speak a few words of German, he repeated the word "new" in response to questions about his training and background. He was taken on regardless. He explains, "That was it. That's how easy it is to be employed in one of the most modern steel mills in Europe. No documents, no one even asks for my name; at first, my nationality doesn't seem of any interest to anyone."[26] The treatment of foreign workers is worse than terrible. As the undercover journalist notes, "We're treated like domestic animals or beasts of burden."[27] He reports that they were sent into an area with signs warning, *"Breathing apparatus must be worn!"* Yet, not even gloves let alone special safety equipment was ever provided."[28] Later, the journalist, still in disguise, was sent along with actual immigrant workers into a nuclear power plant leaking radiation. They were neither given protective clothing nor informed of the risks.[29]

According to the data released by the International Monetary Fund (IMF) in April 2011, the relative (and typically real) wages of workers have fallen in what the IMF terms "advanced economies" (AE). For the year 2010, the IMF found that wage increases failed to keep up with rising prices as hourly earnings were up only 1.2 percent in the former and 6.5 percent in the latter. Meanwhile, the AE group showed a productivity increase of 5.5 percent. Therefore, unit labor costs fell by −4.0 percent in the advanced economies. Put more plainly, workers were paid less for more work.[30] Further, there has been a wholesale assault on workers' rights. This is true both for workers organized in trade unions and those who lack union protection. Looking at the percentage of workers in trade unions can be misleading, as some nations with a small number of dues-paying trade union members have significant union influence, such as in France. Still, the numbers are indicative of recent trends. In France, union membership fell from 8.1 percent (1999) to 7.7 percent (2012). In Germany, the decline was from 25.3 percent (1999) to 17.9 percent (2012) as the United Kingdom witnessed a drop from 30.1 percent (1999) to 25.8 percent (2012).[31] Why this decline? One noted scholar contends that both old-style trade unionism and old-style workers' parties "can no longer cope with the challenges offered by the contemporary world. Globalization and neoliberal challenges require new policies and practices they apparently cannot offer."[32]

After the 2008 economic meltdown, the situation worsened even for native-born workers with proper papers. A European Union study of quality of life published in 2015 gives some general facts. It found that 37.6 percent of Europeans reported low satisfaction with their material living conditions. Unsurprisingly, the study found that being "in employment is also a source of satisfaction. The lowest level of financial satisfaction was reported by the unemployed ... [and] the self-employed appeared less satisfied with their financial situation than employees."[33] By 2013, poverty affected over 83 million people in the European Union countries and "almost 30% of the EU population reported that their household was not able to face unexpected expenses and approximately 12% of them expressed great difficulties in making ends meet." Of course, matters were much worse in some parts of Europe than others with low levels of satisfaction the norm in Greece (65.9 percent), Portugal (67 percent), Croatia (64.5 percent) and Bulgaria (78.5% percent).[35] This is the result of the victory of an ideology that may be fairly summed up by an American joke that goes: how many economists does it take to change a light bulb? Answer: if the light bulb needs changing, the market will do it. In other words, let business prosper—by hook, crook, or government subsidy—even if the common people suffer as a result.

Statistics cannot convey the human cost of these economic developments. They can't show the heartache of those trying to keep body and soul together with temporary or part-time work. Nor can statistics describe the demeaning insecurity of people pushed to the edge of their patience while attempting to hold on to some shred of dignity. In 2009, a French journalist went to a city where she was unknown and spent a year working odd jobs and living with those living near the bottom of the social pyramid.[36] Far from naive, she was still shocked at how badly they were treated and what being part of the working poor did to people's confidence and hope for the future.

The journalist describes a typical event. She becomes friendly with Marilou, a woman who cleans a supermarket from 6:30 a.m. until 8:30 a.m., then offices from 6:45 p.m. until 8:00 p.m. One day, Marylou's supervisor calls her in and says, "You're making calls on your mobile phone during working hours, you're talking to your colleagues. We're going to let you go."[37] The journalist outlines many similar situations in which workers are consistently berated and made to feel stupid. One woman is dressed-down by a manager who says, "I'm not sure you're capable of understanding, so don't try and teach people things they don't need to learn. It's going to be the way I say, full stop." A co-worker consoled her by pointing out the "other day, he told me, 'Don't be such a total idiot.'"[38] Many have given up on the political process. When a group of workers are told there is an election, no one takes it seriously. As one woman argues, "We get taken in every time ... we're always wrong, even when we win."[39] This has usually been the fate of those in the lower levels of the common people.

Still, it would be wrong to see only the negative in the story of Europe's common people. Those whose ancestors were unfree, illiterate peasants, bound to the land, are far better off today. In the twenty-first century, commoners live longer, healthier lives with a degree of personal autonomy unheard of in centuries past. They have far more control over their destiny than did Europeans hundreds of years ago. This is no inevitable development but rather the fruits of the struggles waged for democracy, equality and solidarity. One only need look at certain other countries, like Saudi Arabia where they still execute people for "witchcraft," to see that there were alternative, and negative, outcomes possible. Even a comparison with the United States proves that neither (near) universal health care nor decent public transportation are inescapable byproducts of industrialization.

If the average European worker or farmer lives a significantly better life than others around the planet, it is in large measure because they have fought. None of the advantages that so many enjoy today were gifts from an enlightened ruling class. Every reform, every concession by those with wealth and power came as a result of the self-activity of average Europeans.

Often the commoners have lost, at least in the short run. There have been periods of reaction and brutal repression but when people fight they have the possibility of making great advances. When they sink into apathy or despair, nothing changes. At the end of the day, the common people of Europe might weave a colorful, textured and nuanced tapestry based on the ideals of justice, solidarity and peace. On the other hand, the European future could turn out to be little more than a brutalist etching by the International Monetary Fund—based on an idea by Ayn Rand. Only time will tell. Only one thing is certain. Without a vision of a better world and the will to struggle for it, the people are lost.

Notes

Introduction

1. An extreme example is Holocaust deniers like the former Northwestern University Professor Arthur Butz, *The Hoax of the Twentieth Century*, Newport Beach, CA: Noontide Press, 1977.

2. Ian S. Lustick, "History, historiography, and political science: multiple historical records and the problem of selection bias," *The American Political Science Review*, 90(3), September, 1996: 605–18.

3. Tristram Hunt, "History is where the great battles of public life are now being fought," *Observer*, May 11, 2013.

4. Lisa Rosenbaum, "The Whole Ball Game," *New England Journal of Medicine*, March 7, 2013: 959.

5. *The Literary Gazette*, No. 345, August 30, 1823: 545.

6. Pamela J. Annas and Robert C. Rosen (eds.), *Literature and Society*, New York: Prentice Hall, 2000: 643.

7. William Ander Smith, "Henry Adams, Alexander Hamilton and the American people as a 'Great Beast'", *New England Quarterly*, 48(2), June, 1975: 216–30.

8. Mary Beard, *Woman as a Force in History*, New York: Macmillan, 1946.

9. Sheila Rowbotham, *Hidden from History, 300 Years of Women's Oppression and the Fight Against it*, London: Pluto Press, 1975.

10. Whether it should be "west" or "West" is an involved discussion. For sake of simplicity, it is rendered "West" with a capital W as is traditional in most cases.

11. Judith M. Bennett, "Feminism and history," *Gender & History*, 1(3) Autumn, 1989.

12. There are significant and important discussions about the relative importance of these three biases, with some arguing that class is fundamental while others opt for gender or race. It is a worthwhile discussion but outside the main focus of this book.

13. For a more detailed discussion, see Hugh Thomas, *The Slave Trade: The History of the Atlantic Slave Trade, 1440–1870*, London: Picador, 1997.

14. F. Scott Fitzgerald, *The Great Gatsby*, London: Wordsworth Editions, 1993: 11.

15. Niall Ferguson, *Civilization: The West and Rest*, London: Allen Lane, 2011.

16. Tyrone Beason, "Niall Ferguson's 'Civilization': They're gaining on us," *Seattle Times*, November 27, 2011.

17. This is, of course, the contention of Marx and Engels. See, for example, their *Communist Manifesto*.

18. See the classic work, Shulamith Firestone, *The Dialectic of Sex*, New York: Farrar, Straus & Giroux, 1970.

19. Natalie Angier, "Do races differ? Not really, DNA shows," *New York Times*, August 22, 2000.

20. David Hackett Fischer, *Historians' Fallacies: Toward a Logic of Historical Thought*, New York: Harper Torchbooks, 1970.

21. Edward Hallett Carr, *What is History?*, New York: Vintage Books, 1961: 149.

22. Eric Hobsbawm, "In defense of history. It is fashionable to say 'my truth is as valid as yours.' But it's not true," *Guardian*, January 14, 2005.

23. George Rudé, *The Crowd in History; A Study of Popular Disturbances in France and England, 1730–1848*, London: Serif, 2005.

24. Douglas Johnson, "Obituary: Roland Mousnier," *Independent*, February 13, 1993.

25. After pages of impressive evidence and stimulating reasoning, this is basically his conclusion in Roland Mournier, *Peasant Uprisings in 17th Century France, Russia & China*, New York: Harper, 1972.

26. "Harvard Professor Niall Ferguson apologizes for saying theories of John Maynard Keynes are wrong because he was gay and childless," *Daily Mail*, May 4, 2013.

27. In the preface to his *History of the Russian Revolution*, Leon Trotsky argued, "The serious and critical reader will not want a treacherous impartiality, which offers him a cup of conciliation with a well-settled poison of reactionary hate at the bottom, but a scientific conscientiousness, which for its sympathies and antipathies—open and undisguised—seeks support in an honest study of the facts, a determination of their real connections, an exposure of the causal laws of their movement.

28. Adam Nicolson, *God's Secretaries: The Making of the King James Bible*, New York: Harper, 2003.

29. Binjamin W. Segel, *A Lie and a Libel: The History of the Protocols of the Elders of Zion*, Lincoln, NE: University of Nebraska Press, 1996.

30. Neil Baldwin, *Henry Ford and the Jews: The Mass Production of Hate*, New York Public Affairs Press, 2002.

31. Gary S. Messinger, *British Propaganda and the State in the First World War*, Manchester: Manchester University Press, 1992: 41.

32. Christopher Hill, "Puritanism, capitalism and the scientific revolution," *Past & Present*, 29, December, 1964: 90.

Chapter One
"The King's in His Castle ... All's Right with the World": The Collapse of the Middle Ages

1. We speak here only of the *Western* Roman Empire, the Eastern portion continued and then transformed itself into the Byzantine Empire and survived until the middle of the fifteenth century.

2. Like most everything else, historians disagree as to what exactly the term "feudalism" means or should mean. The current author accepts the broader definition of feudalism to include not only the warrior elite but all three estates of society. See Marc Bloc, *Feudal Society*, two volumes, Chicago, IL: University of Chicago Press, 1961.

3. Women were not allowed to become Pope, cardinals, bishops, or even village priests in the Roman Catholic Church.

4. Eltjo Buringh and Jan Luiten van Zanden, "Chartering the 'Rise of the West': Manuscripts and printed books in Europe, a long-term perspective from the sixth through eighteenth centuries," *The Journal of Economic History*, 69(2), June 2009: 417.

5. Robert Fossier, *The Ax and the Oath: Ordinary Life in the Middle Ages*, Princeton, NJ and Oxford: Princeton University Press, 2010: 231.

6. Ibid., 276.

7. For more on the earlier Catholic Church, see Peter Arris, *Empires of Faith: The Fall of Rome to the rise of Islam*, New York: Oxford University Press, 2012, and Peter Brown, *Through the Eye of a Needle: Wealth, the Fall of Rome and the Making of Christianity in the West, 350–550 AD*, Princeton, NJ: Princeton University Press, 2012.

8. Fossier, *The Ax and the Oath*, 91.

9. Roisin Cossar, "Clerical 'concubines' in northern Italy during the fourteenth century," *Journal of Women's History*, 23(1), 2011: 110.

10. Ibid., 112–13.

11. Ibid., 115.

12. Ibid., 125.

13. For imaginative, if speculative, comments on Martin Luther's relation to sexuality, one could do worse than the classic study, Erik H. Erikson, *Young Man Luther: A Study in Psychoanalysis and History*, New York: W.W. Norton & Co., 1993.

14. Mark Pegg, "On Cathars, Albigenses, and good men of Languedoc," *Journal of Medieval History*, 27(2), 2001.

15. John Clare Moore, *Pope Innocent III (1160/61–1216): To Root up and to Plant*, Boston, MA and Leiden: Brill, 2003: 180.

16. Diarmaid MacCullough, "Dualism in doubt," *Times Literary Supplement*, July 6, 2012: 3–4.

17. R.I. Moore, *The War on Heresy*, Cambridge, MA: Harvard University Press, 2012.

18. See Bloc, *Feudal Society*.

19. Adam Smith, *An Inquiry into the Nature and Causes of the Wealth of Nations*, New York: P.F. Collier & Son, 1909: 548.

20. Fossier, *The Ax and the Oath*, 41.

21. Ibid., 42.

22. Ibid., 47.

23. Chris Gatling, "Genghis Khan, witches and cults," *Current World Archaeology*, No. 53, 2012: 62.

24. Jörg Wettlaufer, "The *jus primae noctis* as a male power display: A review of historic sources with evolutionary interpretation," *Evolution and Human Behavior*, 21(2), 2000: 111–23.

25. Jeffrey L. Singman, *Daily Life in Medieval Europe*, Westport, CT: Greenwood Press, 1999: 54–5.

26. Fossier, *The Ax and the Oath*, 61.

27. Gundula Mülder and Michael P. Richards, "Fast or feast: reconstructing diet in later medieval England by stable isotope analysis," *Journal of Archaeological Science* 32, 2005: 41.

28. Morris Bishop, *The Middle Ages*, New York: Mariner Books, 2001: 216.

29. Ulf Nyrén, *Games Laws in Sweden*, PhD dissertation, University of Gothenburg, Sweden, 2012.

30. Perry Anderson, *Lineages of the Absolutist State*, London: Verso, 1979: 429.

31. Ibid., 431.

32. Marth E. McGinty, *Fulcher of Chartres: Chronicle of the First Crusade*, London: Oxford University Press, 1941.

33. To read what the Arab people made of the Crusades, see Amin Maalouf, *The Crusades through Arab Eyes*, New York: Schocken, 1989.

34. Oliver J. Thatcher and Edgar Holmes McNeal (eds.), *A Source Book for Medieval History*, New York: Scribner's, 1905: 513–17.

35. Mary Erler and Maryanne Kowaleski, *Gendering the Master Narrative: Women and Power in the Middle Ages*, Ithaca, NY: Cornell University Press, 2003. Also see Emilie Amt, *Women's Lives in Medieval Europe: A Sourcebook*, London: Routledge, 2010.

36. Speros Vryonis, *Byzantium and Europe*, New York: Harcourt, Brace & World, 1967: 152.

37. David Crouch, *The English Aristocracy 1070–1272: a Social Transformation*, New Haven, CT: Yale University Press, 2011.

38. Richard Preston, *Men in Arms: A History of Warfare and its Interrelationships with Western Society*, New York: Holt, Rinehart and Winston, 1991.

39. Biographies of Joan of Arc are a bit of an industry, with her being pictured as everything from a saint, to a fascist, to a leader of the working class. One reasonable introduction, translated from French, is Régine Pernoud, *Joan of Arc: Her Story*, London: Palgrave Macmillan, 1999.

40. Nicholas Wright, *Knights and Peasants: The Hundred Years War in the French Countryside*, London: Boydell Press, 2000.

41. David Herlihy and Samuel K. Cohn, Jr., *The Black Death and the Transformation of the West*, Cambridge, MA.: Harvard University Press, 1997.

42. Simon A.C. Penn and Christopher Dyer, "Wages and earnings in late medieval England: Evidence from the enforcement of the Labour Laws," *Economic History Review*, 43(3) 1990: 356–7.

43. Samuel K. Cohn, Jr., *Lust for Liberty: The Politics of Social Revolt in Medieval Europe, 1200–1425*, Cambridge, MA.: Harvard University Press, 2006: 14.

44. Ibid., 97.

45. Ibid., 239.

46. Eric J. Goldberg, "Popular revolt, dynastic politics and aristocratic factionalism in the early Middle Ages: the Saxon Steelinga reconsidered," *Speculum*, 70(3) July 1995: 467–501.

47. For a fruitful discussion of this, see Sylvia Resnikow, "The cultural history of a democratic proverb," *Journal of English and German Philology*, 36 (1037): 391–405.

48. Sylvia Federico, "The imaginary society: Women in 1381," *Journal of British Studies*, 40(2) April, 2001: 159–83.

49. See: Rodney Hilton, *Bondsmen Made Free*, London: Routledge, 2003, and Michel Mollat and Philippe Wolff, *The Popular Revolutions of the Late Middle Ages*, London: George Allen & Unwin, 1973.

50. William Beik, *Urban Protest in Seventeenth Century France*, Cambridge: Cambridge University Press, 1997.

51. Charles C. Mann, *1493: Uncovering the New World Columbus Created*, New York: Vintage, 2012.

52. Bloch, *Feudal Society*, Volume I, 71.

53. Bloc, *Feudal Society*, Volume II, 421.

54. Paul Freedman, "The German and Catalan peasant revolts," *American Historical Review*, 98(1), February 1993: 42–3.

55. For a classic Marxist outline of this process, see Friedrich Engels, "The decline of feudalism and the rise of the bourgeoisie," *Monthly Review*, April 1957: 445–54.

56. For a fascinating introduction to the problems associated with understanding the end of feudalism, see Ellen Meiksins Wood, *Liberty and Property*, London: Verso, 2012: 7–9.

Chapter Two
"The Other Reformation":
Martin Luther, Religious Dogma and the Common People

1. Karl Kautsky, *Communism in Central Europe in the Time of the Reformation*, London: T. Fisher Unwin, 1894: 27.

2. Ibid., 59.

3. Ibid., 65.

4. More research is needed on this point but this is Kautsky's contention, ibid., 75. For a further discussion of this topic from the far left, see Norah Carlin, "Medieval workers and the permanent revolution," *International Socialism*, 2(1), July 1978: 43–54.

5. Matthew 10:34. See also Luke 22:35–38. *The New Testament*, Nashville, TN: The Gideons International, 1985: 18, 158.

6. Kautsky, *Communism in Central Europe*, 72.

7. To look into the mind of Luther, a useful start is Martin Luther, *Martin Luther: Selections from His Writings*, New York, Anchor Books, 1958.

8. See John Calvin, *John Calvin: Selections from His Writings*, New York: HarperCollins, 2006.

9. Geoffrey Dipple, *Just as in the Time of the Apostles: Uses of History in the Radical Reformation*, Kitchener: Pandora Press, 2005.

10. Mark 10:25. See also Matthew 19:24 and Luke 18:25. *The New Testament*, 37, 84, 148.

11. Acts 4:32, ibid., 223.

12. Acts 4:35, ibid., 223.

13. Bard Thompson, *Humanists and Reformers*, Grand Rapids, MI: B. Eerdmans Publishing Co., 1996, 43.

14. Elizabeth L. Eisenstein, *The Printing Press as an Agent of Change*, Cambridge and New York: Cambridge University Press, 1979.

15. Claus-Peter Clasen, "Medieval heresies in the Reformation," *Church History*, 32(4) December 1963: 392.

16. Ibid., 392.

17. For background on the loose confederation of petty German states, see Joachim Whaley, *Germany and the Holy Roman Empire, Vol. I: Maximilian I to the Peace of Westphalia, 1493–1648*, Oxford and New York: Oxford University Press, 2011.

18. Friedrich Engels, *The Peasant War in Germany*, in Marx and Engels, *Collected Works*, Vol. 10, New York: International Publishers, 1978.

19. James M. Stayer, *The German Peasants' War and Anabaptist Community of Goods*, Montreal: McGill-Queen's University Press, 1991.

20. Sometimes also spelled Münzer. For an insight into his thought, see Thomas Müntzer, *The Collected Works of Thomas Müntzer*, London: T. & T. Clark Ltd., 1994.

21. Peter Matheson, "Review essay: Recent German research on Thomas Müntzer," *The Mennonite Quarterly Review*, (86), January 2012: 97–109.

22. Thomas Müntzer, *Sermon to the Princes*, London: Verso, 2010, 90–91.

23. Roland H. Bainton, *Here I Stand: A Life of Martin Luther*, Nashville, TN: Pierce & Smith Co., 1978: 211–12.

24. Engels, *The Peasant War in Germany*, 451.

25. C. Arnold Snyder and Linda A. Huebert Hecht (eds.), *Profiles of Anabaptist Women: Sixteenth-Century Reforming Pioneers*, Waterloo, Ontario: Wilfred Laurier University Press, 1996.

26. Cornelius J. Dyck, *An Introduction to Mennonite History*, Scottdale, PA: Herald Press, 1967: 45.

27. Martin Luther, *On the Jews and Their Lies* (1543), in *Collected Works*, Vol. 47, Minneapolis, MN: Augsburg Fortress, 1971. This attack is so violent that one could be forgiven if they thought it was a twentieth-century Nazi booklet and not from the pen of the great leader of the Reformation.

28. E.G. Rupp and Benjamin Drewery, *Martin Luther, Documents of Modern History*, London: Edward Arnold, 1970, 126.

29. Charles H. George, *Five Hundred Years of Revolution: European Radicals from Hus to Lenin*, Chicago: Charles H. Kerr, 1998, 60.

30. Thomas F. Sea, "The economic impact of the German Peasants' War—The question of reparations," *Sixteenth Century Journal*, VIII(3) 1977: 80.

31. Ibid., 77.

32. Ibid., 86.

33. Ibid., 90.

34. Roland Bainton, *Studies on the Reformation*, Boston, MA: Beacon Press, 1963.

35. Robert Friedman, "Anabaptist," in *The Mennonite Encyclopedia*, Vol. I. Scottdale, PA.: Mennonite Publishing House, 1955: 113–14.

36. John Calvin, *Treatises Against the Anabaptists and Against the Libertines*, Grand Rapids, MI: Baker Academic Press, 2001.

37. At over 1,500 pages, the classic work on the entirety of the Radical Reformation remains George H. Williams, *The Radical Reformation*. 3rd revised edn., Kirksville, MO: Sixteenth Century Publishers, 1992.

38. For more detail on the Swedish Reformation, consult L.A. Anjou, *The History of the Reformation in Sweden*, Ann Arbor, MI.: University of Michigan Press, 2006.

39. Kirsi Stierna, *Women and the Reformation*, New York: Wiley-Blackwell, 2008.

40. Alexandor Sandor Unghvary, *The Hungarian Protestant Reformation in the Sixteenth Century under the Ottoman Impact: Essays and Profiles*, Lewistown, NY: Edwin Mellen Press, 1989.

41. Paul Fox, *Reformation in Poland: Some Social and Economic Aspects*, London: Greenwood Press, 1971.

42. Thomas McCrie, *The Reformation in Spain*, Rapidan, VA.: Harland Publications, 1998.

43. A title the English monarchies continue to use into the present.

44. Maynard Smith, *Henry VIII and the Reformation*, New York: Russel & Russel, 1962, 47–54.

45. C.H. and Katherine George, *The Protestant Mind of the English Revolution, 1576–1640*, London: Oxford University Press, 1961. This classic work debunks the whole Weberian "Spirit of Capitalism" argument and is highly recommended.

46. Eamon Duffy, Saints, *Sacrilege and Sedition: Religion and Conflict in the Tudor Reformation*, New York: Continuum, 2012.

47. H.R. Trevor-Roper, *The European Witch-Craze of the Sixteenth and Seventeenth Century and Other Essays*, New York: Harper, 1969: 107–15.

48. For an excellent collection of documents concerning this issue, see Alan C. Kors and Edward Peters, eds., *Witchcraft in Europe, 1100–1700: A Documentary History*, Philadelphia: University of Pennsylvania Press, 1972.

49. Anne L. Barstow, *Witchcraze: A New History of the European Witch Hunts*, New York: Harper, 1995.

50. Nachman Ben-Yehuda, "The European witch craze of the 14th to 17th centuries: A sociologist's perspective," *American Journal of Sociology*, 86(1), July 1980: 11.

51. Dale Hoak, "The great European witch-hunts: A historical perspective," *American Journal of Sociology*, 88(6), May 1983: 1271.

52. Ibid., 1273.

53. Barbara Ehrenreich and Deirdre English, *Witches, Midwives and Nurses: A History of Women Healers*, New York: Feminist Press of CUNY, 2010.

54. Lisa Vollendorf, "Good sex, bad sex: Women and intimacy in early modern Spain," *Hispania*, 87(1), March 2004: 10.

55. Caroline Bingham, "Seventeenth-century attitudes toward deviant sex," *The Journal of Interdisciplinary History*, 1(3), Spring, 1971: 448.

56. Vern L. Bullough, "Heresy, witchcraft and sexuality," *Journal of Homosexuality*, 1, 1974: 183–201.

57. Hoak, "The great European witch-hunts," 1273.

Chapter Three
The World Turned Upside Down: The Crisis of the Seventeenth Century and the English Revolution, 1640–49

1. H.R. Trevor-Roper, "The general crisis of the 17th century," *Past & Present*, 16, November 1959: 31–32.
2. E.J. Hobsbawm, "The general crisis of the European economy in the 17th century," *Past & Present*, 5, May 1954: 33.
3. Ibid., 35.
4. Caroline Arcini, "A plague on all your houses," *Current World Archaeology*, 4(10), April/May 2011: 26–30.
5. Hobsbawm, "The general crisis," 41.
6. Ibid., 48.
7. Ibid., 46.
8. Ibid., 54.
9. Jan de Vries, "The economic crisis of the seventeenth century after fifty years," *Journal of Interdisciplinary History*, 40(2), Autumn 2009: 151–94.
10. Jonathan Israel, *The Dutch Republic: Its Rise, Greatness and Fall*, New York: Oxford University Press, 1998, 115.
11. The Anabaptists had been leaders of the Dutch Reformation from 1530 until 1560 when decades of persecution and defeat had driven them underground or into inactivity. See ibid., 85.
12. Rudolf M. Dekker, "Women in revolt: Popular protest and its social basis in Holland in the seventeenth and eighteenth centuries," *Theory and Society*, 16(3), May 1987: 339.
13. Ibid., 340.
14. Ibid., 342.
15. Ibid., 343.
16. Immanuel Wallerstein, *The Modern World-System II: Mercantilism and the Consolidation of the European World Economy, 1600–1750*, Berkeley: University of California Press, 2011.
17. For a detailed history, see Peter H. Wilson, *The Thirty Years War: Europe's Tragedy*, Cambridge, MA.: Harvard University Press, 2009.
18. Lynette M. Deem, "Swiss Peasants' War of 1653," in Immanuel Ness (ed.), *International Encyclopedia of Revolution and Protest*, London: Blackwell, 2009.
19. Karen Barkey, "Rebellious alliances: The state and peasant revolt in seventeenth century France and the Ottoman Empire," *American Sociological Review*, 56(6), December 1991: 699–715.
20. In fact, urban disorder was more important and widespread in medieval England than often thought. See Samuel K. Cohn, Jr., *Popular Protest in Late Medieval English Towns*, Cambridge: Cambridge University Press, 2012.
21. C.H. George, for example, argued that the English Revolution "has determined a great deal of the course of world history in the past three hundred years. The bourgeois triumph ... [decided] ... the geography and the timing of the Industrial

Revolution." See Charles H. George, *Five Hundred Years of Revolution: European Radicals from Hus to Lenin*, Chicago, IL: Charles H. Kerr, 1998: 69.

22. Ibid., 72.

23. Christopher Hill, "Parliament and people in seventeenth century England," *Past & Present*, 92, August 1981: 115.

24. Ibid., 124.

25. Thomas Penn, *Winter King: Henry VII and the Dawn of Tudor England*, New York: Simon & Schuster, 2011.

26. C.H. George, "Puritanism as history and historiography," *Past & Present*, 41, December 1968: 82.

27. George, *Five Hundred Years of Revolution*, 90.

28. James Holstun, *Ehud's Dagger: Class Struggle in the English Revolution*, London: Verso, 2000: xiii.

29. Thomas Corns, Ann Hughes and David Loewenstein (eds.), *The Complete Works of Gerrard Winstanley*, 2 vols., Oxford: Oxford University Press, 2009.

30. George, *500 Years of Revolution*, 100.

31. Ibid., 108.

32. Robert C. Allen, "The great divergence in European wages and prices from the Middle Ages to the First World War," *Explorations in Economic History*, 38, 2001: 415.

33. Ibid., 431.

34. Ibid., 432.

Chapter Four
The Rise of the Third Estate: The French People Revolt

1. The evidence suggests that either this conversation did not take place, or Zhou Enlai mistakenly thought he was being asked about Maoist parties in early 1970s France.

2. There seem to be countless editions but one good one is Charles Dickens, *A Tale of Two Cities*, London: Penguin, 2003.

3. According to a 2010 article in a British newspaper, *A Tale of Two Cities* has sold over two hundred million copies making it one of, if not the, best-selling novel in history: David Mitchell, "On historical fiction," *The Telegraph*, May 8, 2010.

4. Casey Harison, "The French Revolution on film: American and French perspectives," *The History Teacher*, 38(3), May 2005: 299.

5. Mick LaSalle, "Rock 'n' roll queen just wants little fun before the Revolution," *San Francisco Chronicle*, October 20, 2006.

6. See, for example, Marcellus, "Reflections on the French Revolution," *The Belfast Monthly Magazine*, 9(53), December 31, 1812: 434–6.

7. Edmund Burke, *Reflections on the Revolution in France*, London: Penguin, 1986.

8. Among these slave owners was Thomas Jefferson. See Paul Finkelman, "Thomas Jefferson and antislavery: The myth goes on," *The Virginia Magazine of History and Biography*, 102(2), April 1994: 193–228.

9. Finkelman, "Thomas Jefferson and antislavery," 206.
10. Philip Gourevich, "Once more unto the breach, the other winner of France's election," *Harper's Magazine*, July 2012: 53.
11. William Beik, *Urban Protest in Seventeenth-Century France: The Culture of Retribution*, Cambridge: Cambridge University Press, 1997.
12. Robert C. Allen, "The great divergence in European wages and prices from the Middle Ages to the First World War," *Explorations in Economic History*, 38, 2001: 427.
13. Ibid., 428.
14. Ibid.
15. William B. Wilcox, "An historian looks at social change," in A.S. Eisenstadt (ed.), *The Craft of American History*, New York: Harper, 1966: 25.
16. George Rudé, *The Crowd in the French Revolution*, New York: Oxford University Press, 1967: 59.
17. Ibid., 55–7.
18. Ibid., 57–8.
19. George Rudé, "Wages and popular movements during the French Revolution," *The Economic History Review*, 6(3), 1954: 247.
20. Ibid.
21. Ibid., 249.
22. Richard Munthe Brace, "The problem of bread and the French Revolution at Bordeaux," *The American Historical Review*, 51(4), July 1946: 650.
23. Mitchell Abidor (ed. and trans.), *The Great Anger*, Pacifica, CA: MIA, 2009: 52.
24. Rudé, "Wages and popular movements", 251–2.
25. Karren Offen, "The new sexual politics of French revolutionary historiography," *French Historical Studies*, 16(4), Autumn 1990: 919.
26 Jane Abray, "Feminism in the French Revolution," *The American Historical Review*, 80(1), February 1975: 47.
27. Ibid., 48.
28. Ibid., 62.
29. David Andress, *Massacre at the Champ de Mars: Popular Dissent and Political Culture in the French Revolution*, Suffolk, UK: The Royal Historical Society, 2000.
30. David Coward, "The march of the women," *Times Literary Supplement*, May 10, 2013: 12.
31. Robert R. Palmer, "Popular democracy in the French Revolution: Review article," *French Historical Studies*, 1(4), Autumn 1960: 452.
32. Clifford D. Conner, *Jean-Paul Marat: Tribune of the French Revolution*, London: Pluto Press, 2012.
33. Lisa DiCapo, "Women workers, state-sponsored work, and the right to subsistence during the French Revolution," *The Journal of Modern History*, 71(3), September 1999: 519.
34. Sophie Wahnich, *In Defense of the Terror: Liberty or Death in the French Revolution*, London: Verso, 2012: 65.
35. Morris Slavin, *Herbertistes to the Guillotine: Anatomy of a "Conspiracy" in Revolutionary France*, Baton Rouge: Louisiana State University Press, 1994.

36. Louis R. Gottschalk, "Communism during the French Revolution, 1789–1793," *Political Science Quarterly*, 40(3), 1925: 450.
37. Palmer, "Popular democracy in the French Revolution," 469.
38. George Lefebvre, *The French Revolution from 1793–1799*, New York: Columbia University Press, 1964.
39. DiCapo, "Women workers, state-sponsored work," 547.
40. Dorinda Outram, "Revolution, domesticity and feminism: Women in France after 1789," *The Historical Journal*, 32(4), December, 1989: 972.
41. Charles H. George, *Five Hundred Years of Revolution: European Radicals from Hus to Lenin*, Chicago, IL: Charles H. Kerr, 1998: 179.
42. Isser Woloch, "In the aftermath of the French Revolution," *The History Teacher*, 28(1), November, 1994: 9.
43. Michael Broers, *Napoleon: Soldier of Destiny*, London: Faber & Faber, 2014.

Chapter Five
Becoming an Appendage to the Machine: The Revolution in Production

1. There is some dispute as to when this term came into general use. While the expression was used very early on, some credit Friedrich Engels for popularizing the term in his 1845 book, *The Condition of the Working Class in England*. For more on this discussion, see Anna Bezanson, ""The early use of the term Industrial Revolution," *The Quarterly Journal of Economics*, 36(2), February 1922: 343–9.
2. Peter N. Stearns, *The Industrial Revolution in World History*, Boulder, CO: Westview Press, 1993: 5.
3. E.P. Thompson, "Time, work-discipline and industrial capitalism," *Past & Present*, 38, December 1967: 56–97.
4. Sidney Pollard, "Factory discipline in the Industrial Revolution," *The Economic History Review*, 16(2), 1963: 255.
5. E.J. Hobsbawm, "The standard of living during the Industrial Revolution: A discussion," *The Economic History Review*, 16(1), 1963: 131.
6. Frederick Engels, "The attitude of the bourgeoisie toward the proletariat," in Karl Marx and Frederick Engels: *Collected Works*, Vol. 4, New York: International Publishers, 1975: 571.
7. Adam Smith, *An Inquiry into the Nature and Causes of the Wealth of Nations*, Dublin: N. Kelly, 1801: 67.
8. Hobsbawm, "The Standard of Living," 119–34.
9. Gregory Clark, "Shelter from the storm: Housing and the Industrial Revolution, 1550–1909," *The Journal of Economic History*, 62(2), June 2002: 489.
10. Wanda Minge-Kalman, "The Industrial Revolution and the European family: The institutionalization of 'childhood' as a market for family labor," *Comparative Studies in Society and History*, 20(3), July 1978: 456.
11. Wesley, John. "Sermon 140, On Public Diversions," *Sermons of John Wesley*: http://wesley.nnu.edu/john-wesley/the-sermons-of-john-wesley-1872-edition/sermon-140-on-public-diversions–.

12. A.E. Dinge, "Drink and working-class living standards in Britain, 1870–1914," *The Economic History Review*, 25(4), November 1972: 621.

13. Anne E.C. McCants, "Poor consumers as global consumers: The diffusion of tea and coffee drinking in the eighteenth century," *The Economic History Review*, 61(51), August 2008: 172–200.

14. Steven Topik, "Coffee as a social drug," *Cultural Critique*, 71, Winter 2009: 81.

15. Geert Bekaert, "Calorie consumption in industrializing Belgium," *The Journal of Economic History*, 51(3), September 1991: 651–2.

16. Ibid., 653.

17. C. Lis and H. Soly, "Food consumption in Antwerp between 1807 and 1859: A contribution to the standard of living debate," *The Economic History Review*, 30(3), August 1977: 465.

18 Ibid., 466–8.

19. Ibid., 481.

20. Janet Siskind, "An axe to grind: Class relations and silicosis in a 19th-century factory," *Medical Anthropology Quarterly*, 2(3), September 1988: 199–214.

21. Anne Parrella, "Industrialization and murder: Northern France, 1815–1904," *The Journal of Interdisciplinary History*, 22(4), Spring 1992: 653.

22. Jane Humphries, *Childhood and Child Labour in the British Industrial Revolution*, Cambridge: Cambridge University Press, 2010: 10.

23. Ibid., 200.

24. Ibid., 370.

25. Minge-Kalman, "The Industrial Revolution and the European family," 462.

26. Stephen Nicholas and Richard H. Stecker, "Heights and living standards of English workers during the early years of industrialization, 1770–1815," *Journal of Economic History*, 51(4), December 1991: 955.

27. Stephen Nicholas and Deborah Oxley, "The living standards of women during the Industrial Revolution, 1795–1820," *The Economic History Review*, 46(4), November 1993: 739.

28. Ibid., 746.

29. E.J. Hobsbawm, *Industry and Empire*, London: Weidenfeld & Nicholson, 1968.

30. P.A. [Philip Abrams], "The origins of the Industrial Revolution," *Past & Present*, 17, April, 1960: 76.

31. Lars G. Sandberg, "The case of the impoverished sophisticate: Human capital and Swedish economic growth before World War I," *The Journal of Economic History*, 39(1), March 1979: 225–41.

32. John Chapman, "The chronology of English enclosure," *The Economic History Review*, 37(4), November 1984: 557–9.

33. E.P. Thomson, *The Making of the English Working Class*, New York: Pantheon Books, 1964: 218.

34. David Eltis and Stanley L. Engerman, "The importance of slavery and the slave trade to industrializing Britain," *The Journal of Economic History*, 60(1), March 2000: 141.

35. Eric Williams, *Capitalism and Slavery*, London: Russel & Russel, 1961: 36.

36. Joseph E. Inikor, "Slavery and the development of industrial capitalism in England," *The Journal of Interdisciplinary History*, 17(4), Spring, 1987: 793.

37. Jens Möller, "Towards Agrarian Capitalism: The Case of Southern Sweden during the 19th Century," *Geografiska Annaler*, 72(213), 1990: 60.

38. Desmond Reilly, "Salts, Acids and Alkalis in the 19th Century. A Comparison between Advances in France, England and Germany," *ISIS*, 42(4), December, 1951: 293.

39. Michael Andrew Zmolek, *Rethinking the Industrial Revolution: Five Centuries of Transition From Agrarian to Industrial Capitalism in England*, Leiden: Brill, 2013: 839.

40. Frank E. Manuel, "The Luddite movement in France," *The Journal of Modern History*, 10(2), January 1938: 197.

41. Abdul Qaiyum Lodhi and Charles Tilly, "Urbanization, crime and collective violence in 19th-century France," *American Journal of Sociology*, 79(2), September 1973: 296–318.

42. Karl Marx and Frederick Engels, *Collected Works*, Vol. 3, London: Lawrence & Wishart, 1975: 202, original emphasis.

43. "Christina von Hodenburg, "Weaving survival in the tapestry of village life: Strategies and status in the Silesian weaver revolt of 1844," in Jan Kok (ed.), *Rebellious Families: Household Strategies and Collective Action in the Nineteenth and Twentieth Centuries*, New York: Berghahn Books, 2002: 53.

Chapter Six
From the Revolutions of 1848–49 to
the First Peoples Democracy: Paris Commune

1. David H. Pinkney, "The crowd in the French Revolution of 1830," *The American Historical Review*, 70(1), October 1964: 2.

2. Ibid., 3.

3. Ibid., 6.

4. Ibid., 17.

5. Pricilla Robertson, *Revolutions of 1848: A Social History*, Princeton, NJ: Princeton University Press, 1952.

6. Eric Hobsbawm, *The Age of Capital, 1848–1875*, New York: Barnes & Noble Books, 1996: 15. See also Mark Traugott, "The Crowd in the French Revolution of February, 1848," *The American Historical Review*, 93(3), June 1988: 638–52.

7. Hobsbawm, *The Age of Capital*: 15.

8. Whitney Walton, "Writing the 1848 Revolution: Politics, gender, and feminism in the works of French women of letters," *French Historical Studies*, 18(4), Autumn 1994: 1001–24.

9. Judith A. DeGroat, "The public nature of women's work: Definitions and debates during the Revolution of 1848," *French Historical Studies*, 20(1), Winter 1997: 33–5.

10. Elizabeth Fox-Genovese, "Culture and consciousness in the intellectual history of European women," *Signs*, 12(3), Spring 1987: 541–2.

11. Malcolm I. Thomas and Jennifer Grimmet, *Women in Protest, 1800–1850*, New York: St. Martin's Press, 1982.

12. Wolfram Siemann, *The German Revolution of 1848–49*, London: Macmillan Press, 1998: 187.

13. For more on this major thinker, see William A. Pelz, *Karl Marx: A World to Win*, New York and London: Pearson Longman Publishers, 2012.

14. Robertson, *Revolutions of 1848*, 73.

15. Hobsbawm, *The Age of Capital*, 25–6.

16. Siemann, *The German Revolution*, 223.

17. Robertson, *Revolutions of 1848*, 412.

18. See William A. Pelz, "Giuseppe Garibaldi, socialism and the International Workingmen's Association," *la parola del Popolo*, XXXII(160), Maggio–Giungo 1982.

19. Frederick Engels, "Garibaldi in Calabria," in Marx & Engels, *Collected Works*, Vol. 17, New York: International Publishers, 1981: 478.

20. Institute of Marxism-Leninism, *Documents of the First International, 1864–1866, Vol. I*, London: Lawrence & Wishart, 1962: 99. (These volumes are mainly the minutes of the London-based General Council of the IWMA.)

21. Institute of Marxism-Leninism, *Documents, Vol. I*, 186.

22. Ibid., 193.

23. Institute of Marxism-Leninism, *Documents of the First International, 1866–1868, Vol. II*, London: Lawrence & Wishart, 1963: 63.

24. Institute of Marxism-Leninism, *Documents, Vol. I*, 166–7.

25. Institute of Marxism-Leninism, *Documents of the First International, 1868–1870, Vol. III*, London: Lawrence & Wishart, 1964, 173.

26. Institute of Marxism-Leninism, *Documents of the First International, 1871–1872, Vol. V*, London: Lawrence & Wishart, 1965, 149–50.

27. Institute of Marxism-Leninism, *Documents, Vol. V*, 298.

28. Institute of Marxism-Leninism, *Documents, Vol. I*, 288.

29. Ibid., 205.

30. Ibid., 213.

31. Institute of Marxism-Leninism, *Documents, Vol. IV*, 32.

32. Ibid., 49, 323–9.

33. Ibid., 81.

34. Institute of Marxism-Leninism, *Documents, Vol. II*, 239.

35. David Morgan, "A law unto herself," *Socialist History Society Newsletter*, 3(2), November 2013: 3.

36. Institute of Marxism-Leninism, *Documents, Vol. V*, 119, 270, 306–7, 439–49, 463–76.

37. Institute of Marxism-Leninism, *Documents, Vol. II*, 213–14.

38. Institute of Marxism-Leninism, *The Hague Congress of the First International, September 2–7, 1872—Minutes and Documents*, Moscow: Progress Publishers, 1976: 99 (hereafter referred to as *Hague Congress—Minutes*).

39. This is Marx's argument, ibid., 98.

40. Institute of Marxism-Leninism, *Documents, Vol. II*, 103.

41. See Pelz, "Giuseppe Garibaldi, socialism and the International Workingmen's Association."

42. Institute of Marxism-Leninism, *Documents, Vol. IV*, 454.

43. Ibid., 96.

44. Emile Zola, *Germinal*, New York: Oxford University Press, 1998: 142.

45. Institute of Marxism-Leninism, *Documents, Vol. II*, 265–70.

46. Ibid., 139.

47. Institute of Marxism-Leninism, *Documents, Vol. III*, 68.

48. Ibid., 116.

49. Institute of Marxism-Leninism, *Documents, Vol. IV*, 158.

50. Ibid., 242.

51. Institute of Marxism-Leninism, *Documents, Vol. V*, 89.

52. Henry Collins, "Review of *Papers of the General Council of the International Workingmen's Association*," *The Economic History Review*, 19(3), 1966: 689.

53. Institute of Marxism-Leninism, *Documents, Vol. V*, 197.

54. John W. Boyle, "Ireland and the First International," *Journal of British Studies*, 11(2), May 1970: 62.

55. Roger Morgan, *The German Social Democrats and the First International, 1864–1872*, Cambridge: Cambridge University Press, 230.

56. Julian P.W. Archer, *The First International in France, 1864–1872: Its Origins, Theories and Impact*, Lanham, MD.: University Press of America, 1997.

57. J.J. Giele, *The First International in the Netherlands. An Investigation into the Origins of the Dutch Labour Movement from 1868 to 1876*, Nymegen: SUN, 1973.

58. Henry Collins and Chimen Abramsky, *Karl Marx and British Labour Movement: Years of the First International*, New York: St. Martin's Press, 1965.

59. Institute of Marxism-Leninism, *Documents, Vol. V*, 96.

60. Edward Acton, "Short notes," *The English Historical Review*, 95(377), October 1980: 931.

61. Institute of Marxism-Leninism, *Documents, Vol. V*, 460–61.

62. Ibid., 118.

63. Institute of Marxism-Leninism, *Hague Congress—Minutes*, 74.

64. Institute of Marxism-Leninism, *Documents, Vol. V*, 68.

65. Ibid., 156.

66. For one example, see "The International," *Chicago Tribune*, August 6, 1871: 2.

67. Otto Pflanze, "Bismarck and German nationalism," *The American Historical Review*, 60(3), April 1955: 566.

68. Frederick Engels, "The role of force in history," in Marx and Engels, *Collected Works*, Vol. 26, New York: International Publishers, 1990: 458–9.

69. George, *Five Hundred Years of Revolution*, 201.

70. Donny Gluckstein, *The Paris Commune: A Revolution in Democracy*, Chicago, IL: Haymarket Books, 2011: 167.

71. For more detail, see the eyewitness accounts of March 18, 1871 in Stewart Edwards (ed.), *The Communards of Paris, 1871*, Ithaca, NY: Cornell University Press, 1973: 56–66.

72. Gluckstein, *The Paris Commune*, 179.

73. For many original resources on the Paris Commune, one would do well to visit the McCormick Library of special collections at Northwestern University. It is home to one of the best collection of original material on the Commune outside of France. The collection includes over 1,200 photos and images that can be found on the library website.

74. Bertolt Brecht, *Collected Plays*, Col. 8, London: Methuen, 2003: 63.

75. The uprising in Paris seems to have even inspired Maoists in China or so they claimed in an article marking the 101st anniversary of the Commune: Lu Kuo-Cheng, "The 'Internationale' spurs us on," *Peking Review*, 11, March 7, 1972: 6–8.

76. Edwards, *The Communards*, 112–21.

77. Ibid., 122–39.

78. Edith Thomas, *The Women Incendiaries*, New York: George Braziller, 1966: 165–88.

79. "Letter from Elisabeth Dmitrieff, 24 April 1871," in Stewart Edwards (ed.), *The Communards of Paris, 1871*, Ithaca, NY: Cornell University Press, 1973: 133–4.

80. Edith Thomas, *Louise Michel*, Montreal: Black Rose Books, 1980. Also see Louise Michel, *Red Virgin: Memories of Louis Michael*, Tuscaloosa: University of Alabama Press, 1981.

81. Eugene Schulkind, "Socialist women during the 1871 Paris Commune," *Past & Present*, 106(1), February 1985: 124–63.

82. Carolyn J. Eichner, *Surmounting the Barricades: Women in the Paris Commune*, Bloomington: Indiana University Press, 2004.

83. Thomas, *The Women Incendiaries*, 224.

84. Gluckstein, *The Paris Commune*, 159.

85. Ibid., 162–3.

86. Robert Gildea, *The Past in French History*, New Haven, CT: Yale University Press, 1994: 44.

87. Colette E. Wilson, *Paris and the Commune, 1871–78: The Politics of Forgetting*, Manchester: Manchester University Press, 2007.

Chapter Seven
The Rise of the Working Classes: Trade Unions and Socialism, 1871–1914

1. John Merriman, *Massacre: The Life and Death of the Paris Commune*, New York: Basic Books, 2014.

2. Jürgen Kuczynski, *The Rise of the Working Class*, New York: McGraw-Hill, 1975.

3. F.F. Ridley, *Revolutionary Syndicalism in France: The Direct Action of its Time*, Cambridge: Cambridge University Press, 2008.

4. Margot Finn, *After Chartism: Class and Nation in English Radical Politics 1848–1874*, Cambridge: Cambridge University Press, 1993.

5. Wolfgang J. Mommsen, *Development of Trade Unionism in Great Britain and Germany, 1880–1914*, London: Unwin Hyman, 1985.

6. Richard W. Reichard, *From Petition to the Strike: A History of Strikes in Germany, 1869–1914*, New York: Peter Lang, 1991.

7. Radicals were far less likely to share such anti-female prejudice, as shown by the immense success of *Woman Under Socialism* written by August Bebel in 1883, which went through 50 German and 15 foreign-language editions by 1914.

8. Dick Geary (ed.), *Labour and Socialist Movements in Europe before 1914*, London: Bloomsbury, 1989.

9. For background on this movement, see Richard W. Reichard, *Crippled from Birth: German Social Democracy, 1844–1870*, Ames: Iowa State University Press, 1969.

10. William A. Pelz (ed.). *Wilhelm Liebknecht and German Social Democracy: A Documentary History*, Chicago, IL: Haymarket Books, 2016.

11. Gerhard A. Ritter, "Workers' culture in imperial Germany: Problems and points of departure for research," *Journal of Contemporary History*, 13, 1978: 165–89.

12. Hans-Josef Steinberg, "Workers' libraries in Germany before 1914," *History Workshop Journal*, 1(1), 1976: 166–80.

13. The classic survey of these developments in Britain is Henry Pelling, *The Origins of the Labour Party*, New York: St. Martin's Press, 1954.

14. David Kirby, "'The Workers Cause': Rank-and-File Attitudes and Opinions in the Finnish Social Democratic Party 1905–1918," *Past & Present*, 111, May, 1986: 139–64.

15. Roger Moore, *The Emergence of the Labour Party*, Atlantic Highlands, NJ: Humanities Press, 1978.

16. The classic account and in many ways still the best introduction is James Joll, *The Second International, 1889–1914*, New York: Harper & Row, 1966.

17. Daniel Guerin, *Anarchism From Theory to Practice*, New York: Monthly Review Press, 1970.

18. Vernon L. Lidke, *The Outlawed Party: Social Democracy in Germany, 1878–1890*, Princeton, NJ: Princeton University Press, 1966.

19. Vernon L. Lidke, *The Alternative Culture: Socialist Labor in Imperial Germany*, New York: Oxford University Press, 1985.

20. Note, for example: Mark Tragott (ed.) *The French Worker: Autobiographies from the Early Industrial Era*, Berkeley, CA.: University of California Press, 1993; Alfred Kelly (ed.), *The German Worker: Working-Class Autobiographies from the Age of Industrialization* , Berkeley, Ca.: University of California Press, 1987, and; Mary Jo Maynes, *Taking the Hard Road: Life Course in French and German Workers' Autobiographies in the Era of Industrialization*, Chapel Hill, N.C.: University of North Carolina Press, 1995.

21. Peter Nettl, "The German Social Democratic Party 1890–1914 as a Political Model," *Past & Present*, 30, April 1965: 65–95.

22. Arthur Deakin, "The International Ttrade Uunion Mmovement," *International Affairs*, 26(2), April, 1950: 167.

23. "International Ttrade-Uunion Sstatistics," *Monthly Review of the U.S. Bureau of Labor Statistics*, 2(5), May, 1916: 82–83.

24. Richard J. Evans, *Proletarians and Politics: Socialism, Protest and the Working Class in Germany Before the First World War*, London: Palgrave Macmillan, 1991.

25. Adelheid Popp, *The Autobiography of a Working Woman*, Chicago, IL: F.G. Browne & Co., 1913.

Chapter Eight
Protest and Mutiny Confront Mass Slaughter: Europeans in World War I

1. Christopher Clark, *The Sleepwalkers: How Europe Went to War in 1914*, New York: HarperCollins, 2013.

2. Note the slightly mocking tone of Rob Hughes, "Tale of 1914 Christmas Day Truce Is Inspiring, Though Hard to Believe," *New York Times*, December 23, 2014.

3. Dave Sherry, *Empire and Revolution: A Socialist History of the First World War*, London: Bookmarks, 2014: 54.

4. Harvey Goldberg, *The Life of Jean Jaurès*, Madison: University of Wisconsin Press, 1968: 461.

5. Jeffrey Verhey, *The Spirit of 1914: Militarism, Myth and Mobilization in Germany*, Cambridge: Cambridge University Press, 2003: 55.

6. Clark, *The Sleepwalkers*, 183.

7. Ralf Hoffrogge, *Working-Class Politics in the German Revolution: Richard Müller, the Revolutionary Shop Stewards and the Origins of the Council Movement*, Leiden: Brill, 2015: 25.

8. Nicoletta F. Gullace, "Sexual violence and family honor: British propaganda and international law during the First World War," *The American Historical Review*, 102(3), June 1997: 723–5.

9. Gullace, "Sexual Violence," 717.

10. Ben Jackson, "Review of *MI5 in the Great War*," *London Review of Books*, 37(2), January 22, 2015: 24.

11. Clark, *The Sleepwalkers*, 553.

12. Wilson was fond of this statement and used it in many speeches. See, for example, *The Nation*, 111, 1920: 371.

13. Eric Hobsbawm, *The Age of Empire, 1875–1914*, New York: Vintage Books, 1987: 318.

14. Clark, *The Sleepwalkers*, 337.

15. Sherry, *Empire and Revolution*, 23.

16. W.E. Burghardt DuBois, "The African Roots of War," *The Atlantic Monthly*, 115 (5), May 1915: 707–14.

17. Richard Rathbone, "World War I and Africa," *The Journal of African History*, 19(1), 1978: 4.

18. Martin Gilbert, *A History of the Twentieth Century*, Vol. I: 1900–1933, New York: William Morrow, 1997.

19. David Stevenson, *Armaments and the Coming of the War, Europe 1904–1914*, New York: Clarendon Press, 1996, and David Herrmann, *The Arming of Europe and the Making of the First World War*, Princeton, NJ: Princeton University Press, 1996.

20. Adam Hochschild, *To End All Wars: A Story of Loyalty and Rebellion, 1914–1918*, New York: Mariner Books, 2011: 70.

21. Ibid., 71.

22. Brook Millman, "HMG and the war against dissent, 1914–18," *Journal of Contemporary History*, 40(3), 2005: 439.

23. Susan Kingsley Kent, "The politics of sexual difference: World War I and the demise of British feminism," *Journal of British Studies*, 27(3), 1988: 253.

24. "A letter from the trenches," *The Advocate of Peace*, 77(10), November 1915: 252.

25. A.E. Ashworth, "The sociology of trench warfare 1914–18," *The British Journal of Sociology*, 19(4), December, 1968: 408.

26. Ibid., 421.

27. Malcolm Brown and Shirley Seaton, *Christmas Truce: The Western Front December 1914*, London: Pan Books, 1994: xxi.

28. *Military Issue*, Holiday 2014, Minneapolis: 1–2.

29. Brown and Seaton, *Christmas Truce*, 163.

30. Ibid., 196–206.

31. Marc Ferro et al., *Meetings in No Man's Land, Christmas 1914 and Fraternization in the Great War*, London: Constable & Robinson, 2007: 212.

32. Gloden Dalas and Douglas Gill, *The Unknown Army: Mutinies in the British Army in World War I*, London: Verso, 1985.

33. Ferro et al., *Meetings in No Man's Land*, 8.

34. Eric J. Leed, "Class and disillusionment in World War I," *Journal of Modern History*, 50(4), December 1978: 682.

35. Ibid., 681.

36. E.J. Leed, *No Man's Land: Combat and Identity in World War I*, Cambridge: Cambridge University Press, 1979. For more on the psychological damage on the men who fought it, see Michéle Barrett, *Casualty Figures: How Five Men Survived the First World War*, London: Verso, 2007.

37. Henri Barbusse, *Under Fire*, New York: Penguin Books, 2004: 317.

38. Louis Barthas, *Poilus: The World War I Notebooks of Corporal Louis Barthas, Barrelmaker, 1914–1918*, trans. Edward M. Strauss, New Haven, CT: Yale University Press, 2014: 48.

39. Julius Koettgen, *A German Deserter's War Experience: Fighting for the Kaiser in the First World War*, Barnsley, UK: Pen & Sword Military, 2013: 69.

40. William Hermanns, *The Holocaust: From a Survivor of Verdun*, New York: Harper & Row Publishers, 1972: 61.

41. Barthas, *Poilus*, 80.

42. Annette Becker, *1914–1918: Understanding the Great War*, London: Profile Books: 25–6.

43. Paul Fox, "Confronting postwar shame in Weimar Germany: Trauma, heroism and the war art of Otto Dix," *Oxford Art Journal*, 29(2), 2006: 247–67.

44. Ibid., 250.

45. Craig Gibson, *Behind the Front, British Soldiers and French civilians, 1914–1918*, Cambridge: Cambridge University Press, 2014.

46. For more on this fatally declining empire, see Eugene Rogan, *The Fall of the Ottomans: The Great War in the Middle East, 1914–1920*, New York: Basic Books, 2015.

47. Deborah Thom, *Nice Girls and Rude Girls: Women Workers in World War I*, London: I.B. Tauris Publishers, 1998.

48. Ibid., 122–43.

49. Note the significance of food shortages in the Austro-Hungarian Empire: Maureen Healy, *Vienna and the Fall of the Habsburg Empire: Total War and Everyday Life in World War I*, Cambridge: Cambridge University Press, 2004. For Germany, see C. Paul Vincent, *The Politics of Hunger: Allied Blockade of Germany, 1915–1919*, Athens: Ohio University Press, 1985.

50. Avner Offer, "The working classes, British naval plans and the coming of the Great War," *Past & Present*, 107, May 1985: 226.

51. Marion C. Siney, "Britisoh official histories of the blockade of the Central Powers during the First World War," *The American Historical Review*, 68(2), January 1963: 400–401.

52. Tilak R. Sareen, *Secret Documents on Singapore Mutiny 1915*, New Delhi: Mounto Publishing House, 1995. Also, see Harish K. Puri, "Revolutionary organization: A study of the Ghadar movement," *Social Scientist*, 9(2/3), September–October 1980: 53–66.

53. Don Dignan, *The Indian Revolutionary Problem in British Diplomacy, 1914–1919*, New Delhi: Allied Publishers, 1983.

54. Donal Nevin, *James Connolly, A Full Life: A Biography of Ireland's Renowned Trade Unionist and Leader of the 1916 Easter Rising*, Dublin: Gill & Macmillan, 2014.

55. Akinjide Osuntokun, "Disaffection and revolts in Nigeria during the First World War, 1914–1918," *Canadian Journal of African Studies*, 5(2), Spring 1971: 171–92.

56. C.M. Andrew and A.S. Kanya-Forstner, "France, Africa, and the First World War," *The Journal of African History*, 19(1), 1978: 23.

57. John Horne, "Immigrant workers in France during World War I," *French Historical Studies*, 14(1), Spring 1985: 57–88.

58. Andrew and Kanya-Forstner, "France, Africa, and the First World War," 15.

59. Princess Eveyln Blücher, *An English Wife in Berlin*, New York: E.P. Dutton & Company, 1920, 39.

60. Ibid., 93.

61. Siegfried Sassoon, *Memoirs of an Infantry Officer*, New York: Penguin Books, 2013: 229.

62. Ibid., 245.

63. Dalas and Gill, *The Unknown Army*, 20.

64. Blücher, *An English Wife in Berlin*, 95.

65. Barthas, *Poilus*, 134–5.

66. Ferro, *Meetings in No Man's Land*, 212–31.

67. Richard M. Watt, *Dare Call it Treason: The True Story of the French Army Mutinies of 1917*, New York: Dorset Press, 2001.

68. Rick Smith, "France commemorates a dark chapter in World War I history," *The New York Times*, April 15, 2007.

69. Barthas, *Poilus*, 310.

70. Ibid., 328.

71. Pétain stated at the time that he believed in social hierarchy while "rejecting the false idea of the natural equality of men": Mark Mazower, *Dark Continent: Europe's Twentieth Century*, New York: Vintage, 2000: 73.

72. G.J. Meyer, *A World Undone: The Story of the Great War, 1914 to 1918*, New York: Random House, 2007: 540.

73. Alexander Watson, *Ring of Steel: Germany and Austria-Hungary in World War I*, New York: Basic Books, 2014: 330.

74. Watson, *Ring of Steel*, 332.

75. Blücher, *An English Wife in Berlin*, 158.

76. Vincent, *The Politics of Hunger*, 170.

77. Watson, *Ring of Steel*, 373–4.

78. John Mueller, "Changing attitudes towards war: The impact of the First World War," *British Journal of Political Science*, 21(1), January 1991: 11.

Chapter Nine
War Leads to Revolution: Russia (1917), Central Europe (1918–19)

1. Albert Resis, "*Das Kapital* Comes to Russia," *Slavic Review*, 29(2), June 1970: 221.

2. Ronald Grigor Suny, "Violence and class consciousness in the Russian working class," *Slavic Review*, 41(3), Autumn 1983: 440.

3. Victor Serge, *Year One of the Russian Revolution*, New York: Holt, Reinhart and Winston, 1972: Chapter 1.

4. This is the date in the Western calendar. In Russia, it was still February since the czar's regime still used a different calendar from other European nations.

5. Roger Pethybridge, "Political repercussions of the supply problem in the Russian Revolution of 1917," *Russian Review*, 29(4), October 1970: 382.

6. For a detailed treatment of this as well as other events of the 1917 revolutions by a radical participant, see Leon Trotsky, *History of the Russian Revolution*, Chicago, IL: Haymarket Books, 2007.

7. Melissa K. Stockdale, "'My death for the Motherland is happiness': Women, patriotism, and soldiering in Russia's Great War, 1914–1917," *The American Historical Review*, 109(1), February 2004: 88.

8. Ibid.: 88–116.

9. William G. Rosenberg, "Workers' control on the railroads and some suggestions concerning social aspects of labor politics in the Russian Revolution," *The Journal of Modern History*, 49(2), June 1972: D1181–D1219.

10. Pethybridge, "Political Repercussions," 389.

11. Ibid., 384.

12. Alfred Erich Senn, "The myth of German money during the First World War," *Soviet Studies*, 28(1), January 1976: 90.

13. John L. Snell, "Benedict XV, Wilson, Michaelis, and German socialism," *Catholic Historical Review*, 37, July 1951: 151–78.

14. Rex A. Wade, "Argonauts of peace: The Soviet delegation to Western Europe in the summer of 1917," *Slavic Review*, 26(3), September 1967: 467.

15. Paul Avrich, "The anarchists in the Russian Revolution," *Russian Review*, 26(4), October 1967: 343.

16. Pethybridge, "Political Repercussions," 399.

17. Ziva Galiliy Garcia, "Workers, industrialists, and Mensheviks: Labor relations and the question of power in the early stages of the Russian Revolution," *Russian Review*, 44(3), July 1985: 268.

18. Ronald Grigor Suny, "Toward a social history of the October Revolution," *The American Historical Review*, 88(1), February 1983: 34–5.

19. Alexander Rabinovich, *The Bolsheviks Come to Power: The Revolution of 1917 in Petrograd*, Chicago, IL: Haymarket Books, 2009.

20. For an eyewitness report by someone won over to the Bolshevik cause, see John Reed, *Ten Days that Shook the World*, New York: International Publishers, 1919.

21. Suny, "Toward a Social History," 52.

22. Marc Ferro, *October 1917: A Social History of the Russian Revolution*, London: Routledge & Kegan Paul, 1980.

23. Barbara Evans Clements, "Working-class and peasant women in the Russian Revolution, 1917–1923," *Signs*, 8(2), Winter 1982: 215–35.

24. Isaac Deutscher, "The French Revolution and the Russian Revolution: Some suggestive analogies," *World Politics*, 4(3), April 1952: 381.

25. John L. Snell, "The Russian Revolution and the German Social Democratic Party in 1917," *American Slavic and East European Review*, 15(3), October 1956: 339–50.

26. Alexander Watson, *Ring of Steel: Germany and Austria-Hungary in World War I*, New York: Basic Books, 2014: 495–6.

27. Ralf Hoffrogge, *Working-Class Politics in the German Revolution: Richard Müller, the Revolutionary Shop Stewards and the Origins of the Council Movement*, Leiden: Brill, 2015: 49.

28. Ibid., 49–50.

29. Gaetano Salvemini, "Economic conditions in Italy, 1919–1922," *The Journal of Modern History*, 23(1), March 1951: 29.

30. Daniel Horn, *The German Naval Mutinies of World War I*, New Brunswick, NJ: Rutgers University Press, 1969: 138–68.

31. Icarus (Ernst Scheider), *The Wilhelmshaven Revolt: A Chapter of the Revolutionary Movement in the German Navy 1918–1919*, Honley Nr. Huddensfield, York: Simian Press, 1975: 17.

32. David Woodward, *The Collapse of Power: Mutiny in the High Sea Fleet*, London: Arthur Barker, 1973.

33. Horn, *German Naval Mutinies*, 309.

34. Icarus (Ernst Scheider), *The Wilhelmshaven Revolt*, 14.

35. Richard A. Comfort, "The political role of the free unions and the failure of council government in Hamburg, November 1918 to March 1919," *International Review of Social History*, 9(1), 1964: 47–64.

36. Allen Mitchell, *Revolution in Bavaria 1918–1919: The Eisner Regime and the Soviet Republic*, Princeton, NJ: Princeton University Press, 1965.

37. D.K. Buse, "Ebert and the German crisis 1917–1920," *Central European History*, (5)3, 1972: 234–55.

38. Hans Peter Hanssen, *Diary of a Dying Empire*, Bloomington: Indiana University Press, 1955: 342–4.

39. Watson, *Ring of Steel*, 559.

40. It has long been proven that this revolt was not some sort of premeditated Communist plot. See Eric Waldman, *The Spartacist Uprising of 1919*, Milwaukee, WI: Marquette University Press, 1958.

41. Robert G.L. White, *Vanguard of Nazism: the Free Corps Movement in Postwar Germany, 1918–1923*, New York: W.W. Norton & Company, 1969.

42. A similar story played out in Munich, see Mitchel, *Revolution in Bavaria 1918–1919*.

43. J.P. Nettl, *Rosa Luxemburg*, New York: Schocken Books, 1989.

44. Princess Eveyln Blücher, *An English Wife in Berlin*, New York: E.P. Dutton & Company, 1920: 325.

45. Pierre Broué, *The German Revolution, 1917–1923*, Chicago, IL: Haymarket Books, 2006.

46. Paul Porter, "The writers' revolution: Munich 1918–19," *Journal of Contemporary History*, 3(4), October 1968: 145.

47. Rosa Levine-Meyer, *Leviné: The Life of a Revolutionary*, Farnsborough, England: Saxon House, 1973: 217.

48. Porter, "The Writers' Revolution," 151.

50. Ibid.

51. Helmut Gruber, *Red Vienna: Experiment in Working-Class Culture, 1919–1934*, New York: Oxford University Press, 1991.

52. Peter A. Toma, "The Slovak Soviet Republic of 1919," *American Slavic and East European Review*, 17(2), April 1958: 210.

53. Ibid., 212.

54. William Brustein, "The 'Red Menace' and the rise of Italian fascism," *American Sociological Review*, 56(5), October 1991: 654.

55. John M. Foot, "'White Bolsheviks'? The Catholic Left and the Socialists in Italy, 1919–1920," *The Historical Journal*, 40(2), June 1997: 415–33.

56. Paolo Spriano, *The Occupation of the Factories: Italy, 1920*, London: Pluto Press, 1975.

57. Roberto Franzosi, "Mobilization and counter-mobilization processes: From the 'Red Years' (1919–20) to the 'Black Year' (1921–1922) in Italy," *Theory and Society*, 26(2/3), April–June 1997: 275–304.

58. Salvemini, "Economic conditions," 37.

59. W. Bruce Lincoln, *Red Victory: A History of the Russian Civil War, 1918–1921*, New York: Da Capo Press, 1999.

60. Clifford Kinvig, *Churchill's Crusade: The British Invasion of Russia, 1918–1920*, London: Continuum, 2007.

61. Winston Churchill, *Churchill Speaks, 1897–1963*, London: Chelsea House, 1980: 372.

62. Winston S. Churchill, "Zionism versus Bolshevism," *Illustrated Sunday Herald*, February 8, 1920: 5.

63. David S. Foglesong, *American's Secret War Against Bolshevism: U.S. Intervention in the Russian Civil War, 1917–1920*, Chapel Hill: University of North Carolina Press, 1995: 95.

64. Ibid., 226.

65. Arno W. F. Kolz, "British economic interests in Siberia during the Russian Civil War, 1918–1920," *The Journal of Modern History*, 48(3), September 1976: 490–91.

66. Ibid., 491.

67. Robert Gerwarth, "The Central European counter-revolution: Paramilitary violence in Germany, Austria and Hungary after the Great War," *Past & Present*, 200, August 2008: 175–209.

68. Peter N. Stearns, *Revolutionary Syndicalism and French Labor: A Cause without Rebels*, New Brunswick, NJ: Rutgers University Press, 1971.

69. Louis Barthas, *Poilus: The World War I Notebooks of Corporal Louis Barthas, Barrelmaker, 1914–1918*, trans. Edward M. Strauss, New Haven, CT: Yale University Press, 2014: 383.

Chapter Ten
Economic Collapse and the Rise of Fascism, 1920–33

1. Eugene Rogan, *The Fall of the Ottomans: The Great War in the Middle East, 1914–1920*, New York: Basic Books, 2015.

2. Andrew Mango, *Atatürk: the Biography of the founder of Modern Turkey*, New York: Overlook Press, 2002.

3. Note that this was significantly before women had these rights in either France or Italy.

4. In this regard, it is noteworthy that not just Nazis and nationalists but even the German Communist Party denounced the Treaty of Versailles.

5. Charles S. Maier, "The truth about the treaties?," *The Journal of Modern History*, 51(1), March 1979: 56–67.

6. Steven B. Webb, *Hyperinflation and Stabilization in Weimar Germany*, New York: Oxford University Press, 1989.

7. Pierre Broué, *The German Revolution, 1917–1923*, Chicago, IL: Haymarket Books, 2006: 709–11.

8. Richard A. Comfort, *Revolutionary Hamburg: Labor Politics in the early Weimar Republic*, London: Oxford University Press, 1967.

9. Larissa Reissner, *Hamburg at the Barricades and Other Writings on Weimar Germany*, London: Pluto Press, 1977.

10. Robert F. Wheeler, "German labor and the Comintern: A problem of generations?" *Journal of Social History*, 7(31), Spring 1974: 304–21.

11. Jürgen Kuczynski, *Labour Conditions in Western Europe, 1820 to 1935*, New York: International Publishers, 1937: 23.

12. Ibid., 73.

13. Ibid., 95.

14. Ibid., 99.

15. Ibid., 104.

16. J. Ronald Shearer, "Shelter from the storm: Politics, production and the housing crisis in the Ruhr coal fields," *Journal of Contemporary History*, 34(1), January 1999: 25.

17. Ibid., 40.

18 Colin Storer, *A Short History of the Weimar Republic*, London: I.B. Tauris, 2013: 54.

19 Christopher Clark, *Iron Kingdom: The Rise and Downfall of Prussia, 1600–1947*, Cambridge, MA.: Belknap Press, 2006: 252–3.

20. Ibid., 465–6.

21. Robert Gerwarth and John Horne, "Vectors of violence: Paramilitarism in Europe after the Great War, 1917–1923," *The Journal of Modern History*, 83(3), September 2011: 497.

22. Ibid., 498.

23. Piero Melograni, "The cult of the Duce in Mussolini's Italy," *Journal of Contemporary History*, 11(4), October 1976: 225.

24. Joseph Rothschild, "The military background of Pilsudski's coup d'état," *Slavic Review*, 21(2), June 1962: 241–60.

25. Joseph Rothschild, "The ideological, political and economic background of Pilsudski's coup d'état of 1926," *Political Science Quarterly*, 78(2), June 1963: 236–7.

26. Neal Pease, "Poland and the Holy See, 1918–1939," *Slavic Review*, 50(3), Autumn 1991: 524.

27. Ibid., 528.

28. Jonathan Zorch, "The enigma of the Gajda Affair in Czechoslovak politics in 1926," *Slavic Review*, 35(4), December 1976: 683.

29. Ibid., 696.

30. Jon V. Kofas, *Authoritarianism in Greece: the Metaxas Regime*, New York: Columbia University Press, 1983.

31. Lito Apostolakou, "'Greek' workers or Communist 'others': The contending identities of organized labour in Greece, c. 1914–1936," *Journal of Contemporary History*, 32(3), July 1977: 422.

32. Ibid., 424.

33. Keith Jeffrey, "The British Army and internal security 1919–1939," *The Historical Journal*, 24(2), 1981: 377.

34. Ibid., 379.

35. Ralph H. Desmarais, "The British government's strikebreaking organization and Black Friday," *Journal of Contemporary History*, 6(2), 1971: 112.

36. Ibid., 113.
37. William Gallagher, *Revolt on the Clyde: An Autobiography*, London: Lawrence & Wishart, 1936.
38. Desmarais, "The British government's strikebreaking," 115.
39. "Women's role in War of Independence revealed," *Irish Examiner*, March 11, 2013.
40. D.H. Robertson, "A Narrative of the General Strike of 1926," *The Economic Journal*, 36(143), September 1926: 375–93. A more recent account is Anne Perkins, *A Very British Strike: 3 May–12 May 1926*, London: Pan Publishing, 2007.
41. Lindsey German and John Rees, *A People's History of London*, London: Verso, 2012: 193.
42. Tony Cliff and Donny Gluckstein, *Marxism and Trade Union Struggle: General Strike of 1926*, London: Bookmarks, 1986. For a critique of the role of the Communist Party of Great Britain, see James Hinton and Richard Hyman, *Trade Unions and Revolutions: The Early Industrial Politics of the Communist Party*, London: Pluto Press, 1975.
43. John Foster, "British imperialism and the labour aristocracy," in Jeffrey Skelley (ed.), *The General Strike 1926*, London: Lawrence & Wishart, 1976: 17–33.
44. Sue Bruley, *The Women and Men of 1926: A Gender and Social History of the General Strike and Miners' Lockout in South Wales*, Cardiff: University of Wales Press, 2010: 26.
45. Hester Barron, *The 1926 Miners' Lockout: Meanings of Community in the Durham Coalfield*, New York: Oxford University Press, 2009.
46. Sue Bruley, "The politics of food: Gender, family, community and collective feeding in South Wales in the General Strike and miners' lockout of 1926," *20th Century British History*, 18(1), 2007: 54–77.
47. Bruley, *The Women and Men of 1926*, 108.
48. Jan Myrdal, *Confessions of a Disloyal European*, Minneapolis: University of Minnesota Press, 1990.
49. Timothy A. Tilton, "A Swedish road to socialism: Ernst Wigforss and the ideological foundations of Swedish social democracy," *The American Political Science Review*, 73(2), June, 1979: 508.
50. Richard F. Tomasson, ""The extraordinary success of the Swedish social democrats," *The Journal of Politics*, 31(3), August 1969: 772–98.
51. On the situation of women, see Alexandra Kollontai, *The Autobiography of a Sexually Emancipated Communist Woman*, New York: Schocken Books, 1975.
52. Moshe Lewin, *Lenin's Last Struggle*, New York: Pantheon Books, 1968.
53. Leon Trotsky, *The Revolution Betrayed*, New York: Pathfinder Press, 1973.
54. Sheila Fitzpatrick, "The Bolsheviks' dilemma: Class, culture, and politics in the early Soviet years," *Slavic Review*, 47(4), Winter 1988: 604.
55. Ibid., 610.
56. Ibid., 601.
57. Sheila Fitzpatrick, "Stalin and the making of a new elite, 1928–1939," *Slavic Review*, 38(3), September 1979: 385.

58. Alexandra Kollantai, *Selected Writings*, New York: W.W. Norton & Company, 1980.

59. Kurt Tucholsky, *Berlin! Berlin! Dispatches from the Weimar Republic*, New York: Berlinica, 2013: 179.

60. Tim Mason, "National socialism and the working class, 1925–May, 1933," *New German Critique*, 11, Spring 1977: 91.

61. Ibid., 56.

62. Sherwin Simmons, "'Hand to the friend, fist to the foe': The struggle of signs in the Weimar Republic," *Journal of Design History*, 13(4), 2000: 319–39.

63. Mason, "National socialism," 50–51.

64. Wolfgang Leonhard, *Betrayal: The Hitler-Stalin Pact of 1939*, New York: St. Martin's Press, 1989: 187.

65. Storer, *A Short History*, 197.

66. David Abraham, *The Collapse of the Weimar Republic*, Princeton, NJ: Princeton University Press, 1981: 11. In reward for his left-wing contribution to the debate about fascism, Abraham was hounded from Princeton and later replaced on the faculty by a right-wing historian who basically claims the Holocaust happened because Germans are inherently racist.

Chapter Eleven
Against Fascist Terror, War and Genocide, 1933–45

1. Brian Jenkins, "The *six février* 1934 and the 'survival' of the French Republic," *French History*, 20, 2000: 333–51.

2. Some things never change.

3. Andrzej Olechnowicz, "Liberal anti-fascism in the 1930s: The case of Sir Ernest Barker," *Albion: A Quarterly Journal Concerned with British Studies*, 36(4), Winter 2004: 643.

4. Arnie Bernstein, *Swastika Nation: Fritz Kuhn and the Rise and Fall of the German-American Bund*, New York: St. Martin's Press, 2013.

5. Leon Trotsky, *Whither France?*, New York: Pioneer Publishers, 1968.

6. Arthur Mitzman, "The French working class and the Blum government (1936–1937)," *International Review of Social History*, 9, 1964: 363–90.

7. Christopher Moore, "Socialist realism and the music of the Popular Front," *The Journal of Musicology*, 25(4), Fall 2008: 475.

8. Ibid., 502.

9. Helmut Gruber, "Willi Münzenberg's German Communist propaganda empire, 1921–1933," *The Journal of Modern History*, 38(3), September 1966: 278–97.

10. David J. Buch and Hana Worthen, "Ideology in movement and a movement in ideology: The *Deutsche Tanzfestspiele* 1934 (9–16 December, Berlin)," *Theatre Journal*, 59(2), May 2007: 215–39.

11. Edward Ousselin, "Film and the Popular Front: 'La Bella Equipe' and 'Le Crime de M. Lange'," *The French Review*, 79(5), April 2006: 954.

12. Jonathan Buchsbaum, "Toward victory: Left film in France, 1930–35," *Cinema Journal*, 25(3), Spring 1986: 22.
13. Ibid. 35–6.
14. Michael Seidman, "The birth of the weekend and the revolts against work: The workers of the Paris region during the Popular Front (1936–38)," *French Historical Studies*, 12(2), Autumn 1981: 274.
15. Gary Cross, "Vacations for all: The leisure question in the era of the Popular Front," *Journal of Contemporary History*, 24(4), October 1989: 609.
16. Ibid., 610.
17. Ibid., 612.
18. Robert F. Wheeler, "Organized sport and organized labour: The Workers' Sports Movement," *Journal of Contemporary History*, 13(2), April 1978: 193.
19. David A. Steinberg, "The Workers' Sport Internationals 1920–28," *Journal of Contemporary History*, 13(2), April 1978: 233.
20. Wheeler, "Organized sport," 201.
21. Arnd Kruger and William J. Murray (eds.), *The Nazi Olympics: Sports, Politics and Appeasement in the 1930s*, Chicago: University of Illinois Press, 2003.
22. Richard D. Mandell, *The Nazi Olympics*, New York: Macmillan Company, 1971.
23. Michael Mackenzie, "From Athens to Berlin: The 1936 Olympics and Leni Riefenstahl's *Olympia*," *Critical Inquiry*, 29(2), Winter 2003: 302–36.
24. Wheeler, "Organized sport," 202.
25. Joan Tumblety, "The Soccer World Cup of 1938: Politics, spectacles and *la Culture Physique* in interwar France," *French Historical Studies*, 31(1), Winter 2008: 77–116.
26. Douglas Little, "Red scare, 1936: Anti-Bolshevism and the origins of British non-intervention in the Spanish Civil War," *Journal of Contemporary History*, 23(2), April 1988: 296–7.
27. Gabriel Jackson, "The Spanish Popular Front, 1934–7," *Journal of Contemporary History*, 5(3), 1970: 21.
28. Ibid., 25–6.
29. Bruce Lincoln, "Revolutionary exhumations in Spain, July 1936," *Comparative Studies in Society and History*, 27(2), April 1985: 246.
30. Ibid., 260.
31. Pelai Pagès i Blanch, *War and Revolution in Catalonia, 1936–1939*, Chicago, IL: Haymarket Books, 2014: 29.
32. Temma E. Kaplan, "Spanish anarchism and women's liberation," *Journal of Contemporary History*, 6(2), 1971: 101.
33. Mercedes Vilanova, "Anarchism, political participation, and illiteracy in Barcelona between 1934 and 1936," *American Historical Review*, 97(1), February 1992: 96–120.
34. Kaplan, "Spanish anarchism," 109–10.
35. Pagès i Blanch, *War and Revolution*, 124–5.
36. Jackson, "The Spanish Popular Front," 34.
37. Little, "Red scare," 299.
38. Ibid., 301.

39. Ibid., 307.
40. Arnold Krammer, "Germans against Hitler: The Thaelmann Brigade," *Journal of Contemporary History*, 4(2), April 1969: 65–6.
41. Josie McLellan, "'I wanted to be a little Lenin': Ideology and the German International Brigade volunteers," *Journal of Contemporary History*, 41(2), April 2006: 293.
42. Ibid., 303.
43. Paul Preston, *The Spanish Holocaust: Inquisition and Extermination in Twentieth-Century Spain*, New York: W. W. Norton & Company, 2012: 471.
44. Ibid., 207.
45. Ibid., 205–6.
46. Ibid., xix.
47. Ibid., 204.
48. Krammer, "Germans against Hitler", 81.
49. Roy Medvedev, *Let History Judge: The Origins and Consequences of Stalinism*, New York: Columbia University Press, 1989.
50. Hiroaki Kuromiya, "Stalin and his era," *The Historical Journal*, 50(3), September 2007: 713.
51. Ibid., 714.
52. Michael Geyer and Sheila Fitzpatrick (eds.), *Beyond Totalitarianism: Stalinism and Nazism Compared*, Cambridge: Cambridge University Press, 2009.
53. Wolfgang Leonhard, *Betrayal: The Hitler-Stalin Pact of 1939*, New York: St. Martin's Press, 1989: 62–3.
54. Medvedev, *Let History Judge*, 444.
55. Leonhard, *Betrayal*, 112–20.
56. Ibid., 123.
57. Ibid., 133.
58. Bertoldt Brecht, *Selected Poems*, New York: Harvest Book, 1947: 129.
59. An excellent introduction is Chris Bambery, *The Second World War: A Marxist History*, London: Pluto Press, 2014.
60. One did not have to practice Judaism, or could even be a practicing Christian, and still be murdered as Jewish.
61. Raul Hilberg, *The Destruction of the European Jews*, London: Holmes & Meier, 1985.
62. Sybil Milton, "Gypsies and the Holocaust," *The History Teacher*, 24(4), August 1991: 375–87.
63. Richard Plant, *The Pink Triangle: The Nazi War Against Homosexuals*, New York: Holt, 1988.
64. Günter Morsch and Astrid Ley (eds.), *Sachenhausen Concentration Camp, 1936–1945: Events and Developments*, English-language edn., Berlin: Metropol Verlag, 2013.
65. Donny Gluckstein, *A People's History of the Second World War: Resistance versus Empire*, London: Pluto Press, 2012.
66. Tim Mason, *Social Policy in the Third Reich: The Working Class and the 'National Community', 1918–1939*, New York: Bloomsbury, 1993.

67. Hans Mommsen, "The German resistance against Hitler and the restoration of politics," *The Journal of Modern History*, 64, Supplement: Resistance Against the Third Reich, December 1992: S119.

68. Marjan Schwegman, "Women in resistance organisations in the Netherlands," in Paul Thompson and Natasha Burchardt (eds.), *Our Common History: The Transformation of Europe*, London: Pluto Press, 1982: 303.

69. Ada Gobetti, *Partisan Diary: A Woman's Life in the Italian Resistance*, Oxford: Oxford University Press, 2014: 7.

70. Anna Maria Bruzzone, "Women in the Italian Resistance," in Paul Thompson and Natasha Burchardt (eds.), *Our Common History*: 280.

71. Yvan Craipeau, *Swimming against the Tide: Trotskyists in German Occupied France*, London: Merlin Press, 2013: 138–9.

72. Gluckstein, *A People's History*, chapters 3 and 4.

73. Nathan Stoltzfus, *Resistance of the Heart: Intermarriage and the Rosenstrasse Protest in Nazi Germany*, New York: W.W. Norton, 1996.

74. Edwin Black, *IBM and the Holocaust: The Strategic Alliance Between Nazi Germany and America's Most Powerful Corporation*, New York: Random House, 2001.

75. A.C. Grayling, *Among the Dead Cities: The History and Moral Legacy of the WWII Bombing of Civilians in German and Japan*, New York: Walker & Company, 2006.

76. Kenneth P. Werrell, "The strategic bombing of Germany in World War II: Costs and accomplishments," *The Journal of American History*, 73(3), December 1986: 709.

77. Kenneth Hewitt, "Plan Annihilation: Area bombing and the fate of urban places," *Annals of the Association of American Geographers*, 73(2), June 1983: 263.

78. Panikos Panayi, "Exploitation, criminality, resistance: The everyday life of foreign workers and prisoners of war in the German Town of Osnabrck, 1939–49," *Journal of Contemporary History*, 40(3), July 2005: 493–4.

79. Richard Overy, *The Bombers and the Bombed: Allied Air War over Europe, 1940–1945*, New York: Viking Press, 2014.

80. Craipeau, *Swimming against the Tide*, 288.

81. Gabriel A. Almond and Wolfgang Krauss, "The size and composition of the anti-Nazi opposition in Germany," *PS: Political Science and Politics*, 32(3), September 1999: 563–9.

Chapter Twelve
A New Europe, 1945–48?

1. Albert Resis, "The Churchill-Stalin secret 'percentages' agreement on the Balkans, Moscow, October, 1944," *The American Historical Review*, 83(2), April 1978: 374–5.

2. Ibid., 387.

3. Roger Moorhouse, *Berlin at War*, New York: Basic Books, 2010: 376–80.

4. James Mark, "Remembering rape: Divided social memory and the Red Army in Hungary 1944–1945," *Past & Present*, 188, August 2005: 133.

5. Ibid., 159.

6. Perry Biddiscombe, "Dangerous liaisons: The anti-fraternization movement in the U.S. occupation zones of Germany and Austria," *Journal of Social History*, 34(3), Spring 2001: 611–47.

7. Klaus Wiegrefe, "Postwar rape: Were Americans as bad as the Soviets?": http://www.spiegel.de/international/germany/book-claims-us-soldiers-raped-190-000-german-women-post-wwii-a-1021298.html.

8. Christopher Simpson, *Blowback: America's Recruitment of Nazis and its Effects on the Cold War*, London: Weidenfeld and Nicolson, 1988.

9. *Forging an Intelligence Partnership: CIA and the Origins of the BND, 1949–56* (2006) in *U.S. Intelligence on Europe*, Leiden and Boston, MA: Brill, 2015: http://primarysources.brillonline.com/browse/us-intelligence-on-europe.

10. Chris Harman, *Bureaucracy and Revolution in Eastern Europe*, London: Pluto Press, 1974.

11. OSS, Monthly Report of Steering Division, SI/Germany, August 2, 1945 in *U.S. Intelligence on Europe*, Leiden and Boston, MA: Brill, 2015: http://primarysources.brillonline.com/browse/us-intelligence-on-europe.

12. Monthly Evaluation Report, September 12, 1946 in *U.S. Intelligence on Europe*, Leiden and Boston, MA: Brill, 2015: http://primarysources.brillonline.com/browse/us-intelligence-on-europe.

13. II, Broadway organization, etc. December 4, 1945 in *U.S. Intelligence on Europe*, Leiden and Boston, MA: Brill, 2015: http://primarysources.brillonline.com/browse/us-intelligence-on-europe.

14. Richard Fletcher, "How CIA money took the teeth out of British socialism," in Philip Agee and Lois Wolf (eds.), *Dirty Work: The CIA in Western Europe*, New York: Dorset Press, 1978: 189.

15. Hugh Wilford, *The CIA, the British Left and the Cold War*, London: Frank Cass, 2003.

16. White House, "Memorandum of conference with former President Eisenhower," August 21, 1961 in *U.S. Intelligence on Europe*, Leiden and Boston, MA: Brill, 2015: http://primarysources.brillonline.com/browse/us-intelligence-on-europe.

17. Geoff Eley, "Legacies of antifascism: Constructing democracy in postwar Europe," *New German Critique*, 67, Winter 1996: 79.

18. G. Franco Romagnoli, *The Bicycle Runner: A Memoir of Love, Loyalty and the Italian Resistance*, New York: St. Martin's Press, 2009: 127.

19. Leonard Krieger, "The inter-regnum in Germany, March–August 1945," *Political Science Quarterly*, 64(4), December 1949: 513.

20. Ibid., 514.

21. OSS, Monthly Report of Steering Division, SI/Germany, August 2, 1945 in *U.S. Intelligence on Europe*, Leiden and Boston, MA: Brill, 2015: http://primarysources.brillonline.com/browse/us-intelligence-on-europe.

22. Ingrid Strobl, *Partisans: Women in the Armed Resistance to Fascism and German Occupation (1936–1945)*, Oakland, CA: AK Press, 2008.

23. Eley, "Legacies of antifascism", 100.

24. SPAIN, No. 5 of CIA Report, 21 November 1946 in *U.S. Intelligence on Europe*, Leiden and Boston, MA: Brill, 2015: http://primarysources.brillonline.com/browse/us-intelligence-on-europe.

25. CIA, "Possible Emergency Demands for US Military Aid," December 9, 1949 in *U.S. Intelligence on Europe*, Leiden and Boston, MA: Brill, 2015: http://primarysources.brillonline.com/browse/us-intelligence-on-europe.

26 M. Mufakharul Islam, "The great Bengal famine and the question of FAD yet again," *Modern Asian Studies*, 41(2), March 2007: 421.

27. Madhusree Mukerjee, *Churchill's Secret War: The British Empire and the Ravaging of India during World War II*, New York: Basic Books, 2011.

28. Nisid Hajari, *Midnight's Furies: The Deadly Legacy of India's Partition*, New York: Houghton Mifflin Harcourt, 2015.

29. Paul R. Brass, "The partition of India and retributive genocide in the Punjab, 1946–47: Means, methods, and purposes," *Journal of Genocide Research*, 5(1), 2003: 71–101.

30. CIA, " Review of the world situation as it relates to the security of the United States," September 16, 1947 in *U.S. Intelligence on Europe*, Leiden and Boston, MA: Brill, 2015: http://primarysources.brillonline.com/browse/us-intelligence-on-europe.

31. Alain-Gerard Marsot, "The crucial year: Indochina 1946," *Journal of Contemporary History*, 19(2), April 1984: 337–9.

32. R.E.M. Irving, *The First Indochina War: French and American Policy*, London: Croom Helm, 1975.

33. John Stockwell, *In Search of Enemies: A CIA Story*: New York: W.W. Norton & Company, 1978: 201.

34. Georges N. Nzongola, "The bourgeoisie and revolution in the Congo," *Journal of Modern African Studies*, 8(4), December 1970: 530.

35. Thomas Kanza, *Conflict in the Congo: The Rise and Fall of Lumumba*, Baltimore, MD: Penguin Books, 1972.

36. J. Edgar Hoover, French activities, October 15, 1946 in *U.S. Intelligence on Europe*, Leiden and Boston, MA: Brill, 2015: http://primarysources.brillonline.com/browse/us-intelligence-on-europe.

37. CIA, Memorandum for the President, November 26, 1946 in *U.S. Intelligence on Europe*, Leiden and Boston, MA: Brill, 2015: http://primarysources.brillonline.com/browse/us-intelligence-on-europe.

38. Geoffrey Swain, "The Cominform: Tito's International?," *The Historical Journal*, 35(3), September 1992: 660.

39. Rossana Rossanda, *The Comrade from Milan*, London: Verso, 2010: 105.

40. Telegram from Rome Embassy to State Department, December 12, 1947 in *U.S. Intelligence on Europe*, Leiden and Boston, MA: Brill, 2015: http://primarysources.brillonline.com/browse/us-intelligence-on-europe.

41. CIA, "Consequences of Communist accession to power in Italy by legal means," March 5, 1948 in *U.S. Intelligence on Europe*, Leiden and Boston, MA: Brill, 2015: http://primarysources.brillonline.com/browse/us-intelligence-on-europe.

42. Trevor Barnes, "The secret Cold War: The C.I.A. and American foreign policy in Europe, 1946–1956" [Part II], *The Historical Journal*, 25(32), September 1982: 662.

43. Rossanda, *The Comrade from Milan*, 115.

44. Trevor Barnes, "The secret Cold War: The C.I.A. and American foreign policy in Europe, 1946–1956" [Part I], *The Historical Journal*, 24(2), June 1981: 413.

45. CIA, "Remarks by CGT leaders concerning the coming revolution in France," December 22, 1948 in *U.S. Intelligence on Europe*, Leiden and Boston, MA: Brill, 2015: http://primarysources.brillonline.com/browse/us-intelligence-on-europe.

46. Geert Van Goethem and Robert Anthony Waters, Jr. (eds.), *American Labor's Global Ambassadors: The International History of the AFL-CIO during the Cold War*, London: Palgrave Macmillan, 2013.

47. Peter Weiler, *British Labour and the Cold War*, Redwoods, CA: Stanford University Press, 1988.

48. Rossanda, *The Comrade from Milan*, 136.

49. Ian Birchall, *Workers Against the Monolith: Communist Parties since 1943*, London: Pluto Press, 1974.

50. Geoffrey Swain, *Tito: A Biography*, London: I.B. Tauris, 2010.

51. CIA, "Review of the world situation," July 14, 1948 in *U.S. Intelligence on Europe*, Leiden and Boston, MA: Brill, 2015: http://primarysources.brillonline.com/browse/us-intelligence-on-europe.

52. Swain, "The Cominform," 652–3.

53. Strobl, *Partisans*, 51.

54. Ibid., 57.

55. Vesna Drapac, "Women, resistance and the politics of daily life in Hitler's Europe: The case of Yugoslavia in comparative perspective," *Aspasia*, 3(1), 2009: 55–78.

56. Nanette Funk et al., "Dossier on women in Eastern Europe," *Social Text*, 27, 1990: 119.

57. Svetozar Vukmanovic, *Struggle for the Balkans*, London: Merlin Press: 296–8.

58. Duncan Wilson, "Self-management in Yugoslavia," *International Affairs*, 54(2), April 1978: 253–63.

59. Alan Whitehorn, "Yugoslav workers' self-management: A blueprint for industrial democracy?," *Canadian Slavonic Papers*, 20(3), September 1978: 421–8.

60. Patricia A. Taylor, Bruker D. Granjean and Niko Tos, "Work satisfaction under Yugoslav self-management: On participation, authority and ownership," *Social Forces*, 65(4), June 1987: 1033.

61. CIA, "Review of the world situation," July 14, 1948 in *U.S. Intelligence on Europe*, Leiden and Boston, MA: Brill, 2015: http://primarysources.brillonline.com/browse/us-intelligence-on-europe.

62. Andre Gerolymatos, *Red Acropolis, Black Terror: The Greek Civil War and the Origins of Soviet-American Rivalry*, New York: Basic Books, 2004: 47–9.

63. Donny Gluckstein, *A People's History of the Second World War: Resistance versus Empire*, London: Pluto Press, 2012: 51.

64. CIA, "The Greek situation," February 7, 1947 in *U.S. Intelligence on Europe*, Leiden and Boston, MA: Brill, 2015: http://primarysources.brillonline.com/browse/us-intelligence-on-europe.

65. Eleni Fourtouni, *Greek Women in Resistance*, Chicago, IL: Lakeview Press, 1986.

66. Strobl, *Partisans*, 15.

67. Dominique Eudes, *The Kapetanios: Partisans and Civil War In Greece*, New York: Monthly Review Press: 75–6.

68. Mark C. Jones, "Misunderstood and forgotten: The Greek naval mutiny of April 1944," *Journal of Modern Greek Studies*, 20(2), October 2002: 367–97.

69. CIA, "Possible consequences of Communist control of Greece in the absence of US counteraction," February 9, 1948 in *U.S. Intelligence on Europe*, Leiden and Boston, MA: Brill, 2015: http://primarysources.brillonline.com/browse/us-intelligence-on-europe.

70. CIA, "Continuing instability in Greece," January 19, 1949 in *U.S. Intelligence on Europe*, Leiden and Boston, MA: Brill, 2015: http://primarysources.brillonline.com/browse/us-intelligence-on-europe.

71. Eudes, *The Kapetanios*, 354.

Chapter Thirteen
Europeans in the Cold War: Between Moscow and Washington

1. Gabriel Gorodetsky, "The origins of the Cold War: Stalin, Churchill and the formation of the Grand Alliance," *Russian Review*, 47(2), April 1988: 145–70.

2. R. Harrison Wagner, "The decision to divide Germany and the origins of the Cold War," *International Studies Quarterly*, 24(2), June 1980: 155–90.

3. Thomas G. Paterson, "The abortive American loan to Russia and the origins of the Cold War, 1943–1946," *The Journal of American History*, 56(1), June 1969: 70.

4. Ibid., 91–2.

5. Michael Cox, "From the Truman Doctrine to the second superpower detente: The rise and fall of the Cold War," *Journal of Peace Research*, 27(1), 1990: 25–41.

6. Dianne Kirby, "Divinely sanctioned: The Anglo-American Cold War alliance and the defense of Western civilization and Christianity, 1945–48, *Journal of Contemporary History*, 35(3), July 2000: 385–412.

7. CIA, "CIA Berlin analysis of uprising in East Germany," July 8, 1953 in *U.S. Intelligence on Europe*, Leiden and Boston, MA: Brill, 2015 http://primarysources.brillonline.com/browse/us-intelligence-on-europe.

8. CIA NSC Briefing, "East Germany," July 8, 1953 in *U.S. Intelligence on Europe*, Leiden and Boston, MA: Brill, 2015: http://primarysources.brillonline.com/browse/us-intelligence-on-europe.

9. Renate Hürtgen, "Strikes in East Germany (1949–1989)," in Antonio Simoes do Paco, Raquel Varela and Sjaak van der Velden (eds.), *Strikes and Social Conflict: Towards a Global History*, Lisbon: International Association Strikes and Social Conflict, 2012: 447.

10. For a nuanced view of these events by a critical but left-wing East German author, see Stefan Heym, *5 Days in June: A Novel*, Buffalo, NY: Prometheus Books, 1978.

11. Stephen Kinzer, *The Brothers: John Foster Dulles, Allen Dulles and Their Secret Cold War*, New York: Henry Holt and Company, 2013: 140–42.

12. Bertolt Brecht, *Poems 1913–1953*, London: Methuen, 1976: 440.

13. CIA, "Current Intelligence Bulletin," November 13, 1956 in *U.S. Intelligence on Europe*, Leiden and Boston, MA: Brill, 2015: http://primarysources.brillonline.com/browse/us-intelligence-on-europe.

14. Rossana Rossanda, *The Comrade from Milan*, London: Verso, 2010: 155.

15. Kinzer, *The Brothers*, 213.

16. CIA Memorandum, "Radio Free Europe," February 19, 1957 in *U.S. Intelligence on Europe*, Leiden and Boston, MA: Brill, 2015: http://primarysources.brillonline.com/browse/us-intelligence-on-europe.

17. While it is, of course, impossible to feel another's oppression, a visit to the Museum of Political Exiles in Athens give a clear picture of the level of repression in post-Civil War Greece.

18. Department of State, "Increasing threats to the regimes in Spain and Portugal," in *U.S. Intelligence on Europe*, Leiden and Boston, MA: Brill, 2015: http://primarysources.brillonline.com/browse/us-intelligence-on-europe.

19. CIA, "The political future of Spain," December 5, 1947 in *U.S. Intelligence on Europe*, Leiden and Boston, MA: Brill, 2015: http://primarysources.brillonline.com/browse/us-intelligence-on-europe.

20. CIA, "Unrest in Spain," May 1, 1956 in *U.S. Intelligence on Europe*, Leiden and Boston, MA: Brill, 2015: http://primarysources.brillonline.com/browse/us-intelligence-on-europe.

21. Kinzer, *The Brothers*, 89–90.

22. Allen W. Dulles, Deputy Director CIA, "Analysis of the power of the Communist Parties of France and Italy and of measures to counter them," September 15, 1951 in *U.S. Intelligence on Europe*, Leiden and Boston, MA: Brill, 2015: http://primarysources.brillonline.com/browse/us-intelligence-on-europe.

23. Ibid.

24. Ibid.

25. Stephen A. Marglin and Juliet B. Schor (eds.), *The Golden Age of Capitalism: Reinterpreting the Postwar Experience*, New York: Oxford University Press, 1990.

26. E.H. Phelps Brown, "Levels and movements of industrial productivity and real wages internationally compared, 1860–1970," *The Economic Journal*, 83(329), March 1973: 67.

27. Greg Castillo, "Domesticating the Cold War: Household consumption in Marshal Plan Germany," *Journal of Contemporary History*, 40(2), April 2005: 284.

28. Sheryl Kroen, "A political history of the consumer," *The Historical Journal*, 47(3), September 2004: 728–36.

29. Ibid., 732.

30. Reinhold Wagnleitner, *Coca-Colonization and the Cold War*, Chapel Hill: University of North Carolina Press, 1994: 51.

31. Richard F. Kuisel, "Coca-Cola and the Cold War: The French face Americanization, 1948–1953," *French Historical Studies*, 17(1), Spring 1991: 96.
32. Ibid., 110.
33. Ibid., 115.
34. Susan E. Reid, "Cold War in the kitchen: Gender and the de-Stalinization of consumer taste in the Soviet Union under Khrushchev," *Slavic Review*, 61(2), Summer 2002: 211–53.
35. Castillo, "Domesticating the Cold War", 280.
36. Mark Pittaway, *From the Vanguard to the Margins: Workers in Hungary, 1939 to the Present*, Chicago, IL: Haymarket Books, 2015: 124–7.
37. Michael Kackman, *Citizen Spy: Television, Espionage and Cold War Culture*, Minneapolis: University of Minnesota Press, 2005: 32.
38. Tony Shaw and Denise J. Youngblood, *Cinematic Cold War: The American and Soviet Struggle for Hearts and Minds*, Lawrence: University of Kansas Press, 2014.
39. Of course, this is far from the first time women have risen up, nor is de Beauvoir the first feminist author. See, for example: Katherine Connelly, *Sylvia Pankhurst: Suffragette, Socialist and Scourge of Empire*, London: Pluto Press, 2013.
40. Simone de Beauvoir, *The Second Sex*, New York: Alfred A. Knopf, 1953.
41. Margaret A. Simons, Jessica Benjamin and Simone de Beauvoir, "Simone de Beauvoir: An interview," *Feminist Studies*, 5(2), Summer 1979: 333.
42. Aurora G. Morcillo, *True Catholic Womanhood: Gender Ideology in Franco's Spain*, DeKalb: Northern Illinois University Press, 2000.
43. Ann Taylor Allen, *Women in Twentieth-Century Europe*, New York: Palgrave Macmillan, 2008, Chapter 5.
44. Lee Ann Banaszak and Eric Plutzer, "The social basis of feminism in the European Community," *The Public Opinion Quarterly*, 57(1), Spring 1993: 29–53.
45. Wendy A. Pojmann, *Italian Women and International Cold War Politics, 1944–1968*, New York: Fordham University Press, 2013.
46. Edward D. Cohn, "Sex and the married communist: Family troubles, marital infidelity and party discipline in the postwar USSR, 1945–64," *Russian Review*, 68(3), July 2009: 429.
47. Ibid., 448.
48. Stephen Castes and Godula Kosack, *Immigrant Workers and Class Structure in Western Europe*, London: Oxford University Press, 1973: 175.
49. Ibid., 432–3.
50. Ibid., 480–81.

Chapter Fourteen
From Berlin Wall to Prague Spring—A New Generation of Europeans

1. Frederick Kempe, *Berlin 1961*, New York: Penguin Books, 2011: 247.
2. CIA, "West Germany: The role and influence of the media," April 1984 in *U.S. Intelligence on Europe*, Leiden and Boston, MA: Brill, 2015: http://primarysources.brillonline.com/browse/us-intelligence-on-europe.

3. White House, "Memorandum of conference with former President Eisenhower," August 21, 1961 in *U.S. Intelligence on Europe*, Leiden and Boston, MA: Brill, 2015: http://primarysources.brillonline.com/browse/us-intelligence-on-europe.

4. CIA, "Clandestine action in support of the U.S. Berlin policy," March 23, 1961 in *U.S. Intelligence on Europe*, Leiden and Boston, MA: Brill, 2015: http://primarysources.brillonline.com/browse/us-intelligence-on-europe.

5. Corey Ross, "Before the Wall: East Germans, communist authority, and the mass exodus to the West," *The Historical Journal*, 45(2), June 2002: 459–80.

6. Corey Ross, "East Germans and the Berlin Wall: Popular opinion and social change before and after the border closure of August 1961," *Journal of Contemporary History*, 39(1), January 2004: 25.

7. CIA, "Unrest in East Germany," December 4, 1961 in *U.S. Intelligence on Europe*, Leiden and Boston, MA: Brill, 2015: http://primarysources.brillonline.com/browse/us-intelligence-on-europe.

8. Ross, "East Germans," 42.

9. Dagmar Herzog, "Pleasure, sex, and politics belong together: Post-Holocaust memory and the sexual revolution in West Germany," *Critical Inquiry*, 24(2), Winter 1998: 442.

10. John Levi Martin, "Structuring the sexual revolution," *Theory and Society*, 25(1), February 1996: 105.

11. Edward Shorter, "Female emancipation, birth control, and fertility in European history," *The American Historical Review*, 78(3), June 1973: 605–40.

12. Ibid., 612.

13. Henry J. Steck, "The re-emergence of ideological politics in Great Britain: The Campaign for Nuclear Disarmament," *The Western Political Quarterly*, 18(1), March 1965: 100, original emphasis.

14. Tim Brown, *West Germany in the Global Sixties: The Anti-Authoritarian Revolt*, Cambridge: Cambridge University Press, 2013.

15. Kurt L. Shell, "Extraparliamentary opposition in post-war Germany," *Comparative Politics*, 2(4), July 1970: 653.

16. Michael A. Schmidtke, "Cultural revolution or cultural shock? Student radicalism and 1968 in Germany," *South Central Review*, 16(4), 17(1), Winter 1999–Spring 2000: 79.

17. Ibid., 80.

18. Wes Blomster, "Commentary," *Perspectives of New Music*, 16(2), Spring/Summer 1978: 25.

19. Deutsche Welle, "Interview: Remembering student-movement firebrand Rudi Dutschke," *DW.COM*, 24 December 2009.

20. Rob Burns and Wilfred Van Der Will, *Protest and Democracy in West Germany: Extra-Parliamentary Opposition and the Democratic Agenda*, New York: St. Martin's Press, 1988.

21. CIA, "Bonn's policies under the Kiesinger government," March 30, 1967 in *U.S. Intelligence on Europe*, Leiden and Boston, MA: Brill, 2015: http://primarysources.brillonline.com/browse/us-intelligence-on-europe.

22. US Army Cable, May 24, 1968 in *U.S. Intelligence on Europe*, Leiden and Boston, MA: Brill, 2015: http://primarysources.brillonline.com/browse/us-intelligence-on-europe.

23. Richard Kempton, *Provo: Amsterdam's Anarchist Revolt*, New York: Autonomedia, 2007: 81.

24. Ibid., 92–104.

25. Richard Ivan Jobs, "Youth movements: Travel, protest and Europe in 1968," *The American Historical Review*, 114(2), April 2009: 382–3.

26. Tariq Ali, "Diary," *London Review of Books*, July 30, 2015: 38.

27. Stephen G. Xydis, "Coups and countercoups in Greece, 1967–1973 (with postscript)," *Political Science Quarterly*, 89(3), Autumn 1974: 510.

28. William Blum, *Killing Hope: U.S. Military and CIA Interventions since World War II*, Monroe, ME: Common Courage Press, 1995: 215–21.

29. National Security Council (NSC), Memorandum, May 15, 1967 in *U.S. Intelligence on Europe*, Leiden and Boston, MA: Brill, 2015: http://primarysources.brillonline.com/browse/us-intelligence-on-europe.

30. CIA, Cable to White House Situation Room, April 21, 1967 in *U.S. Intelligence on Europe*, Leiden and Boston, MA: Brill, 2015: http://primarysources.brillonline.com/browse/us-intelligence-on-europe.

31. Andreas Papendreou, *Democracy at Gunpoint: The Greek Front*, New York: Doubleday, 1970: 294.

33. Ibid.

34. National Security Council (NSC), "US policy toward Greece—Military assistance," November 14, 1969 in *U.S. Intelligence on Europe*, Leiden and Boston, MA: Brill, 2015: http://primarysources.brillonline.com/browse/us-intelligence-on-europe.

35. Xydis, "Coups and countercoups", 529.

36. Ronnie Margulies and Ergin Yildizoglu, "Trade unions and Turkey's working class," *MERIP Reports*, 121, February 1984: 15–20, 31.

37. Simon Prince, "The global revolt of 1968 and Northern Ireland," *The Historical Journal*, 49(3), September 2006: 875.

38. For a day-to-day account of the events, see Daniel Singer, *Prelude to Revolution: France in May 1968*, Chicago, IL: Haymarket Books, 2013, Chapter 3.

39. Richard Brody, *Everything is Cinema: The Working Life of Jean-Luc Godard*, New York: Metropolitan Books, 2008: 331.

40. Daniel Bensaïd, *An Impatient Life: A Memoir*, London: Verso, 2013: 60.

41. Jobs, "Youth movements", 395.

42. US Air Force, Cable to Department of Defense, June 3, 1968 in *U.S. Intelligence on Europe*, Leiden and Boston, MA: Brill, 2015: http://primarysources.brillonline.com/browse/us-intelligence-on-europe.

43. CIA, "Czechoslovakia: A new direction," January 12, 1968 in *U.S. Intelligence on Europe*, Leiden and Boston, MA: Brill, 2015: http://primarysources.brillonline.com/browse/us-intelligence-on-europe.

44. David W. Paul, "The repluralization of Czechoslovak politics in the 1960s," *Slavic Review*, 33(4), December 1974: 723–5.

45. CIA, "Czechoslovakia: A New Direction."
46. Department of State, "Western European attitudes toward the Czechoslovak crisis," July 24, 1968 in *U.S. Intelligence on Europe*, Leiden and Boston, MA: Brill, 2015: http://primarysources.brillonline.com/browse/us-intelligence-on-europe.
47. Jiri Pelikán (ed.), *The Secret Vysocany Congress: Proceedings and Documents of the Extraordinary Congress of the Communist Party of Czechoslovakia, 23 August 1968*, London: Allen Lane, 1971: 300.
48. Ibid., 270.
49. Ibid., 272.

Chapter Fifteen
Fighting for Peace in an Atomic Age, 1969–89

1. Nicholas Cullinan, "From Vietnam to Fiat-Nam: The politics of *arte povera*," October, 124, Spring 2008: 19.
2. Paul Ginsborg, *A History of Contemporary Italy: Society and Politics, 1943–1988*, New York: St. Martin's Press, 2003: 298.
3. Rosanna Rossanda, *The Comrade from Milan*, London: Verso, 2010: 326.
4. Valdo Spini, "The New Left in Italy," *Journal of Contemporary History*, 7(1/2), January–April 1972: 67.
5. Ginsborg, *A History of Contemporary Italy*, 316.
6. Cullinan, "From Vietnam to Fiat-Nam", 26.
7. White House, "Terrorist group profiles", November 1988 in *U.S. Intelligence on Europe*, Leiden and Boston, MA: Brill, 2015: http://primarysources.brillonline.com/browse/us-intelligence-on-europe.
8. George Kassimeris, "Junta by another name? The 1974 *Metapolitefsi* and the Greek extra-parliamentary left," *Journal of Contemporary History*, 40(4), October 2005: 745.
9. Ruben Vega Garcia and Carlos Perez, "Radical unionism and the workers' struggle in Spain," *Latin American Perspectives*, 27(5), September 2000: 111–33.
10. CIA, "The Spanish succession: Strains in the post-Franco authoritarian system," in: *U.S. Intelligence on Europe*, Leiden and Boston, MA: Brill, 2015: http://primarysources.brillonline.com/browse/us-intelligence-on-europe.
11. CIA, "Key judgements of National Intelligence Analytical Memorandum," May 15, 1975 in *U.S. Intelligence on Europe*, Leiden and Boston, MA: Brill, 2015: http://primarysources.brillonline.com/browse/us-intelligence-on-europe.
12. Raquel Varela and Joana Alcântara, "Social conflicts in the Portugese revolution, 1974–1975," *Labour/Le Travail*, 74, Fall 2014: 153–4.
13. Giulia Strippoli, "Colonial war, anti-colonialism and desertions during the *Estado Novo*: Portugal and abroad," Paper presented to 3rd International Conference, *International Associations Strikes and Social Conflicts*, Barcelona, –June 16–19, 2015.

14. CIA, "The outlook for retention of US Azores base rights in the event of certain courses of action," June 27, 1961 in *U.S. Intelligence on Europe*, Leiden and Boston, MA: Brill, 2015: http://primarysources.brillonline.com/browse/us-intelligence-on-europe.

15. CIA, "Proposed covert action in Portugal," October 16, 1974 in *U.S. Intelligence on Europe*, Leiden and Boston, MA: Brill, 2015: http://primarysources.brillonline.com/browse/us-intelligence-on-europe.

16. White House, Memorandum of Conversation, March 5, 1975 in *U.S. Intelligence on Europe*, Leiden and Boston, MA: Brill, 2015: http://primarysources.brillonline.com/browse/us-intelligence-on-europe.

17. Varela and Alcântara, "Social conflicts," 169–71.

18. White House, Memorandum of Conversation, August 12, 1975 in *U.S. Intelligence on Europe*, Leiden and Boston, MA: Brill, 2015: http://primarysources.brillonline.com/browse/us-intelligence-on-europe.

19. Günter Wallraff, *The Undesirable Journalist*, London: Pluto Press, 1978: 17.

20. Ibid., 39.

21. Varela and Alcântara, "Social conflicts," 177.

22. "Presidential hopeful condemns 'sexist'" article," *Irish Times*, April 5, 2002.

23. CIA, "Student activity in Western Europe," June 29, 1970 in *U.S. Intelligence on Europe*, Leiden and Boston, MA: Brill, 2015: http://primarysources.brillonline.com/browse/us-intelligence-on-europe.

24. Sheila Rowbotham, *Women, Resistance and Revolution: A History of Women and Revolution in the Modern World*, New York: Vintage Books, 1974: 11.

25. Sheila Rowbotham, *Promise of a Dream: Remembering the Sixties*, London: Verso, 2001: 210.

26. Tariq Ali, *Street Fighting Years: An Autobiography of the Sixties*, London: Verso, 2005: 313.

27. Marcus Collins, *Modern Love: An Intimate History of Men and Women in Twentieth-Century Britain*, London: Atlantic Books, 2003: 134.

28. Dagmar Herzog, "Syncopated sex: Transforming European sexual cultures," *The American Historical Review*, 114(5), December 2009: 1295.

29. Pamela Paxton et. al., "The international women's movement and women's political representation, 1893–2003," *American Sociological Review*, 71(6), December 2006: 898–920.

30. Danièle Stewart, "The women's movement in France," *Signs*, 6(2), Winter 1980: 350.

31. Ibid., 354.

32. Lucia Chiavola Birnbaum, *Liberazione delia donna: Feminism in Italy*, Middleton, CT: Wesleyan University Press, 1986.

33. Edith Hoshino Altbach, "The new German women's movement," *Signs*, 9(3), Spring 1984: 455.

34. Atina Groddmann, *Reforming Sex: The German Movement for Birth Control and Abortion Reform, 1920–1950*, Oxford: Oxford University Press, 1997.

35. Myra Marx Ferree, *Varieties of Feminism: German Gender Politics in Global Perspective*, Stanford, ca: Stanford University Press, 2012.

36. Jennifer V. Evans, "The moral state: Men, mining and masculinity in the early GDR," *German History*, 23(3), 2005: 357.
37. Heidi Minning, "Who is the 'I' in 'I love you'? The negotiation of gay and lesbian identities in former East Berlin, Germany," *Anthropology of East Europe Review*, 18(2), Autumn 2000: 103.
38. Jeffrey M. Peck and Jürgen Lemke, "Being gay in Germany: An interview with Jürgen Lemke," *New German Critique*, 52, Winter 1991: 149.
39. National Security Council, Memorandum, May 12, 1979 in *U.S. Intelligence on Europe*, Leiden and Boston, MA: Brill, 2015: http://primarysources.brillonline.com/browse/us-intelligence-on-europe.
40. CIA," "U.K. election prospects—What if Thatcher loses?" May 16, 1983 in *U.S. Intelligence on Europe*, Leiden and Boston, MA: Brill, 2015: http://primarysources.brillonline.com/browse/us-intelligence-on-europe.
41. CIA, "British arms sales: Trends and implications," November 8, 1985 in *U.S. Intelligence on Europe*, Leiden and Boston, MA: Brill, 2015: http://primarysources.brillonline.com/browse/us-intelligence-on-europe.
42. Roy A. Church et al., "The militancy of British miners, 1893–1986: Interdisciplinary problems and perspectives," *The Journal of Interdisciplinary History*, 22(1), Summer 1991: 49.
43. Andrew Taylor, *The NUM and British Politics*, vol. 2, 1969–95, Aldershot: Ashgate, 2005.
44. Ibid., 186.
45. Jim Phillips, "Material and moral resources: The 1984–85 miners' strike in Scotland," *The Economic History Review*, 65(1), February 2012: 256–76.
46. Seumas Milne, *The Enemy Within*, London: Verso, 2014.
47. Karen Beckwith, "Lancashire Women Against Pit Closures: Women's standing in a men's movement, *Signs*, 21(4), Summer 1996: 1037, 1061.
48. Grover C. Furr, "The AFT, the CIA and Solidarnosc," *Comment*, 1(2), Spring 1982: 31–2.
49. Ibid., 33–4.
50. Carl Bernstein, "Cover story: The Holy Alliance," *Time*, June 24, 2001.
51. Ibid.
52. Serge Schmemann, "End of the Soviet Union; Soviet state, born of a dream, dies," *The New York Times*, December 26, 1991.
53. Boris Kagarlitsky, "The unfinished revolution," *Green Left Weekly*, No. 296, November 5, 1997: 4.
54. Ronald Grigor Suny, *The Revenge of the Past: Nationalism, Revolution and the Collapse of the Soviet Union*, Stanford, CA: Stanford University Press, 1994: 101.
55. Boris Kagarlitsky, *The Disintegration of the Monolith*, London: Verso, 1993.
56. Boris Kagarlitsky, *Restoration in Russia: Why Capitalism Failed*, London: Verso, 1995.
57. Mark Griffiths, "Moscow after the apocalypse," *Slavic Review*, 72(3), Fall 2013: 481.
58. Michael A. Lebowitz, *The Contradictions of "Real Socialism": The Conductor and the Conducted*, New York: Monthly Review Press, 2012.

59. Tom Mayer, "The collapse of Soviet Communism: A class dynamics interpretation," *Social Forces*, 80(3), March 2002: 759–811.
60. Stephen F. Cohen, "Was the Soviet system reformable?", *Slavic Review*, 63(3), Autumn 2004: 459–88.

Chapter Sixteen
Europe Falls into the Twenty-First Century

1. Tariq Ali, "The new world disorder," *London Review of Books*, April 9, 2015: 22.
2. In 2013, Edward Snowden, a former CIA contractor, leaked classified information from the National Security Agency that reveals massive global surveillance programs run by the NSA with the help of various European governments and multinational telecommunication companies. It turned out that the Americans had even hacked into the leaders of Germany and France and other European notables' private cell phones.
3. Etienne Balmer, "Women's love lives were better in East Germany before the Berlin Wall fell," *Daily Telegraph*, October 19, 2009.
4. *"Do Communists Have Better Sex?"*, a film by André Meier, New York: Icarus Films at http://icarusfilms.com/new/2007/do.html.
5. Slavoj Žižek, *Trouble in Paradise: From the End of History to the End of Capitalism*, London: Penguin Books, 2014: 38.
6. Milica Z. Bookman, "War and peace: The divergent breakups of Yugoslavia and Czechoslovakia," *Journal of Peace Research*, 31(2), May 1994: 175–87.
7. Richard West, *Tito and the Rise and Fall of Yugoslavia*, New York: Carroll & Graf Publishers, Inc. 1994: 392.
8. Kris Ghodsee, *The Left Side of History: World War II and the Unfulfilled Promise of Communism in Eastern Europe*, Durham, NC and London: Duke University Press, 2015: 130.
9. Ibid., 150.
10. Sabine Kergel, "A harder life after the Wall fell," *Le Monde diplomatique*, June 2015: 15.
11. Katrin Bennhold, "20 years after fall of Wall, women of former East Germany thrive," *New York Times*, October 5, 2010.
12. Kergel, "A harder life," 15.
13. Bennhold, "20 years After fall of Wall."
14. Kergel, "A harder life," 15.
15 Agata Pyzik, *Poor but Sexy: Cultural Clashes in Europe East and West*, Winchester: Zero Books, 2014: 51.
16. Ibid., 286.
17. Amitabh Pal, "Russian dissident slams U.S. media and the left," *The Progressive*, February 23, 2015.
18. Pyzik, *Poor but Sexy*, 13.
19. Žižek, *Trouble in Paradise*, 141.

20. Andrei S. Markovits and Stephen J. Silvia, "The identity crisis of Alliance ''90/ The Greens: The New Left at a crossroads," *New German Critique*, 72, Autumn 1997: 123.

21. Paul Hockenos, *Joschka Fischer and the Making of the Berlin Republic: An Alternative History of Postwar Germany*, New York: Oxford University Press, 2007.

22. Markovits and Silvia, "The identity crisis", 124.

23. Janet Biehl and Peter Staudenmaier, *Ecofascism Revisited: Lessons from the German Experience*, Porsgrunn, Norway: New Compass Press, 2011: 95–6.

24. Ibid., 13–42.

25. James Palmer, "Dutch sex workers form trade union," *The Independent*, October 3, 2001.

26. Günter Wallraff, *Lowest of the Low*, London: Methuen, 1988: 67.

27. Ibid., 70.

28. Ibid., 72–3.

29. Ibid., 178–84.

30. International Monetary Fund, "World economic outlook: Tensions from the two-speed recovery," April 2011.

31. OECD, 2015. StatExtracts. Trade union density: https://stats.oecd.org/Index.aspx?DataSetCode=UN_DEN.

32. Marcel van der Linden, "The crisis of world labor: Decline of the old movements," *Against the Current*, May–June 2015: 32.

33. "Quality of life in Europe – facts and views – material living conditions," http://ec.europa.eu/eurostat/statistics-explained/index.php/Quality_of_life_in_Europe_-_facts_and_views_-_material_living_conditions.

35. Ibid.

36. Florence Aubenas, *The Night Cleaner*, Cambridge: Polity, 2010.

37. Ibid., 79.

38. Ibid., 157.

39. Ibid., 166.

Index

Charts and diagrams are indicated by *"fig"* following the page number.
An "n" following the page number indicates a note; the note number follows.